钱伯林
近代中国考察档案文献汇编

The Compilation of Oriental Educational Investigation
Commission's Archives by Chamberlin,1909

上册

张 雷 主编

学苑出版社

图书在版编目（CIP）数据

钱伯林近代中国考察档案文献汇编 / 张雷主编．—北京：学苑出版社，2016.6
ISBN 978-7-5077-5014-0

Ⅰ．①钱… Ⅱ．①张… Ⅲ．①地理－文献资料－中国－近代 Ⅳ．①K92

中国版本图书馆CIP数据核字（2016）第101073号

出 版 人：孟 白
责任编辑：杨 雷
装帧设计：徐道会
出版发行：学苑出版社
社　　址：北京市丰台区南方庄2号院1号楼
邮政编码：100079
网　　址：www.book001.com
电子信箱：xueyuanpress@163.com
销售电话：010-67675512　67678944　67601101（邮购）
经　　销：新华书店
印 刷 厂：北京中献拓方科技发展有限公司
开本尺寸：889×1194　1/16
印　　张：37.5
字　　数：650千字
版　　次：2016年7月第1版
印　　次：2016年7月第1次印刷
定　　价：980.00元（上下册）

罗林·钱伯林（Rolling Thomas Chamberlin.1881–1948）1908 年照

考察团在四川观音桥客栈,从左到右:伯顿(Ernest D.Burton,1856—1925)、托马斯·钱伯林(Thomas Chrowder Chamberlin.1843—1928)、罗林·钱伯林、王翻译、里德(Horate G.Reed)

罗林·钱伯林在四川

托马斯·钱伯林在四川

罗林·钱伯林在四川归途

罗林·钱伯林在四川罂粟田

考察团在四川归途

王翻译拍摄河南卫辉的小村

考察团随从张、王、段和李三(从左至右)

身着旅行装的王翻译在宜昌

托马斯·钱伯林在太原府客栈

王翻译在四川乘坐独轮车

身着大衣的李三在张家口

考察团在四川的卫队

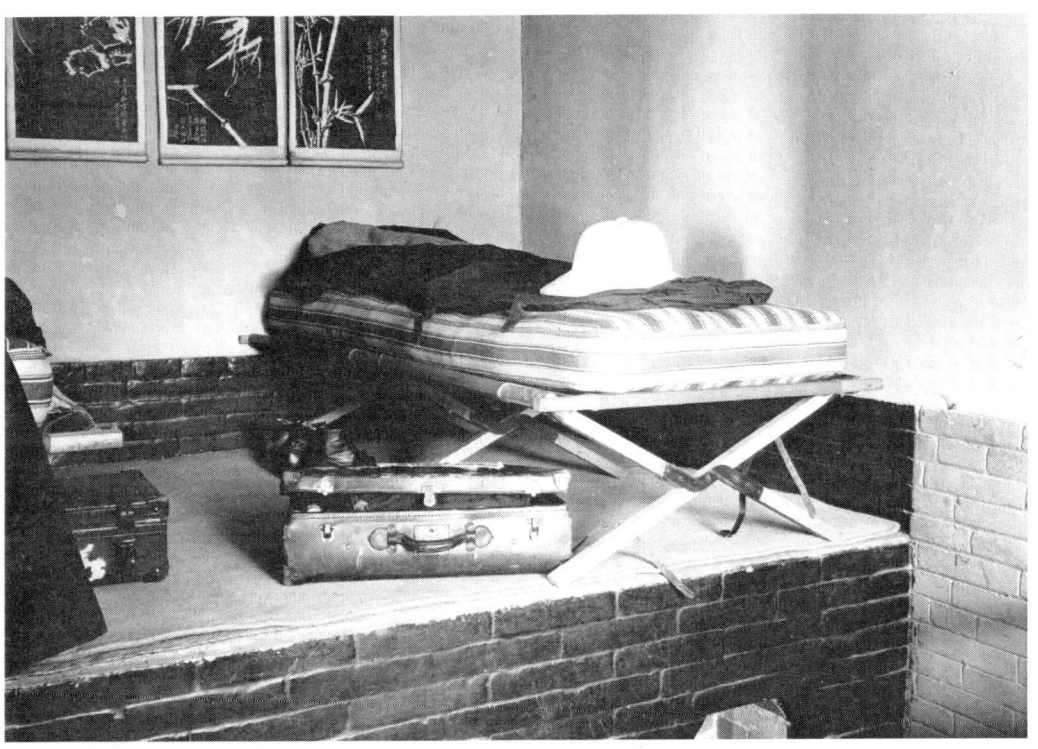

考察团在太原客栈的睡具

20世纪40年代,罗林·钱伯林在芝加哥大学办公室,案头为其父托马斯·钱伯林照片

考察日记手稿

考察笔记手稿

前 言

一次被遗忘的中国考察

一、考察缘起

20世纪伊始，崛起的美国开始重视在中国的影响，而美国芝加哥大学也希望以教育沟通中西，发挥大学在中国教育的意义。与此同时，美国著名的洛克菲勒财团不断接到在华传教士的请求，请求帮助他们在中国的工作。洛克菲勒最终决定考察中国，以便决定最佳资助方式。而这项任务便委托给了与洛克菲勒家族渊源深厚的芝加哥大学。

1908年，芝加哥大学在洛克菲勒基金支持下，为了探索教育在中国的意义，决定派出东方教育考察团（Oriental Educational Investigation Commission）考察中国教育，寻求最佳合作方式。芝加哥大学选定神学院的伯顿（Ernest DeWitt Burton, 1856-1925）和地质系的钱伯林（Thomas Chrowder Chamberlin, 1843-1928）两位教授担此重任，两人搭配是基于人文和自然科学的综合权衡。伯顿教授伯顿为著名圣经学者，代表人文社会方面；而钱伯林则为著名地质学家，代表自然科学方面考察。同时任命两位助理，辅助调查中国的教育、社会以及宗教情况。

托马斯·钱伯林为美国著名地质学家，生于威斯康星州东部的小镇比洛特（Beloit），1866年毕业于比洛特学院，并留校执教数年，后任美国威斯康星大学校长。1893年，钱伯林应邀组建芝加哥大学地质系，并任系主任。钱伯林对于中国的兴趣至少不晚于1901年。是年，他致函芝加哥大学校长哈珀（William Harper），建议芝加哥大学加强与中国合作，以地质帮助中国，招收中国留学生，培育地学人才，助其开发自然资源，造福国家与人民。

1909年钱伯林前往中国的愿望终于实现。1月4日，钱伯林在其儿子兼助理罗林·钱伯林（Rolling Thomas Chamberlin，1881-1948）的陪同下动身前往中国【编者注：为行文方便，以下分以老钱伯林和小钱伯林代指父子二人】。小钱伯林是老钱伯林唯一的儿子，1907年从芝加哥大学地质系获得博士，随后留校执教终生。钱伯林父子此次中国考察的主要任务是考察地形，气候以及自然资源特别是土地利用，研究他们对于教育的意义，以及教育机构的合适选址，同时探索中国引入自然科学方法的可能性。

二、考察网络

芝加哥大学东方教育考察团的中国考察，除洛克菲勒基金资助外，背后还有强大的支撑网络，分别为教会与传教士、中国官员以及地质学者。

1．教会

东方教育考察团的主要任务就是考察中国的教育状况，特别是教会教育，即教会在华兴办的学校，因此教会与传教士是考察团的重要联系对象。这也是考察团选择伯顿教授的重要原因之一。伯顿为著名的圣经学者，在基督教有重要影响和广泛人脉。

在启程来华之前，考察团就积极联络各地传教士，安排考察行程。1908年，伯顿联系在美国加州大学任教的傅兰雅（John Fryer，1839-1928）商谈考察之事。傅兰雅为著名传教士，翻译家，一生在华三十余年，熟悉中国的教育。在华期间，考察团在上海拜会了另一位著名来华传教士李提摩太（Timothy Richard，1845-1919）。李提摩太在华从事慈善和教育四十余年，在朝野均有影响。

在中国期间，欧美教会成为其重要的支撑力量。例如在汉口，考察团入住伦敦会（London Mission Society）汉口驻地。不过教会有时成为羁绊。在张家口，传教士因经常给住店的房钱不足，因此当地所有旅店拒绝外国传教士入住。而考察团也因被误作为传教士无店可住，颇费周折。

前 言

2. 中国官员

中国官员是考察团重点结交的对象。在出发之前，考察团就通过清朝驻美使官，结交中国大员，以求获取庇护，其中最重要的人物是端方。时任两江总督的端方是当时颇开明的满族要员之一。考察团通过美国驻上海领事介绍得以拜会端方，在尚未从太平天国战争中恢复过来的南京，一行人拜访端方，受到殷勤接待，并获得端方的理解和支持，从而打入中国官方的上层网络，为考察铺平了道路。

考察团希望结交的另一位大员是袁世凯。在启程之前，考察团在华盛顿请清朝驻华公使唐绍仪开具给当时如势中天袁世凯的介绍信。可是当考察团抵达中国的时候，袁世凯已经被慈禧解除所有职务，落魄还乡。考察团审时度势，将介绍信秘不示人。当考察团路经河南袁世凯归养的村庄时候，也选择避而远之。

3. 美国地质学者

截至 1909 年，美国地质学者对中国已经进行了两次系统考察。其中第一次是 1860 年代，美国地质学家和探险家庞培里（Raphael Pumpelly，1837–1923）对华北的考察。第二次是 1903 至 1904 年，美国著名地质学家维里士（Bailey Willis，1857–1949）考察中国。

在美国地质学界，钱伯林与维里士私交甚好。1908 年，维里士出版三卷本《中国研究》。钱伯林在《地质学报》(Journal of Geology) 评论此书。同时为了准备中国行程，钱伯林在通信中询问维里士诸多问题。有趣的是，维里士当年在中国考察时曾经雇佣一位名叫李三的向导。李三为人练达，甚有帮助，因此他与李三的联系一直未断。20 世纪 20 年代，李三病逝，穷困的李氏之妻还向远在美国的维里士求助。

维里士将李三推荐给钱伯林。1909 年 3 月 3 日，李三率领一个由一位厨师和两位帮手组成的团队，从天津抵达汉口，加入钱伯林父子的考察团。事后证明李三不负众望，在考察中发挥了重要作用。例如当钱伯林在张家口因被误认为传教士而找不到旅店时，幸亏李三在当地有多年的贩马经验，最终找到一家安身之所。

3

三、考察行程

1908年夏季，东方教育考察团兵分两路。伯顿一行先行往东，前往埃及与印度等考察半年，然后前往中国与钱伯林父子会合。1909年1月4日，钱伯林父子从芝加哥启程，在旧金山搭乘西伯利亚号邮轮，经行夏威夷和日本。1909年2月2日，钱伯林父子抵达中国上海。

考察团在上海会合休整之后，前往南京拜会两江总督端方，获得中国通行证，随后返回上海。2月11日，钱伯林父子从上海搭乘邮轮前往香港。从香港沿西江而上至广西梧州，然后返回考察广州。之后，从香港原路返回上海。

1909年2月28日，考察团从上海溯长江而上，考察武汉三镇，宜昌，穿越三峡，至万县（今万州）登陆，行程四百英里，陆路横穿四川盆地至成都，然后再顺岷江至宜宾。从宜宾顺江而下，再次至武汉。

1909年5月10日，考察团从武汉搭乘火车沿京汉线北上，横穿河南，沿途考察乡村。至郑州转车前往河南省会开封，然后再返回郑州，继续前往石家庄。从石家庄转正太线至太原，之后原路返回石家庄，再利用京汉线前往北京。

1909年5月22日，在北京稍事休息后，考察团乘坐火车沿京张线至张家口，因为此线路尚未完工，只能到宣化附近，考察团改坐骡车前往张家口，考察张家口以及蒙古高原边境，随后返回北京。在京停留一周之后，考察团经山海关前往沈阳考察东北地区，路经长春、哈尔滨。1909年6月10日，考察团搭乘俄国西伯利亚铁路的火车离开中国，经行欧洲返回美国。

钱伯林父子组成的考察团，与伯顿一行时分时合，在中国前后共计四个余月。期间通过轮船、火车、马车、轿子、步行等方式，先后考察当时江苏、广东、广西、湖北、四川、河南、直隶、山西等十三省。

中国考察行程万里，取得丰厚的成果，此次中国考察标志老钱伯林一生野外考察的终结。但也损耗了他的健康，因为老钱伯林此时已经65岁，而且时常坚持徒步考察。他来中国之前体重215磅，考察结束之后只剩180磅。同时，数月的艰苦旅行和粗糙的食物诱发了他严重的胃病旧疾，并折磨其余生。对于小钱伯林而言，中国考察是他职业上的一个转折点，使他体会到野外考察和旅行的乐趣。此前他的学术兴趣曾徘徊于化学和地质之间，中国考察之后尘埃落定，他将地质学作为一生的追求。

四、考察述评

科学的地质学训练使钱伯林父子具有敏锐的野外观察力。在考察途中，老钱伯林不停地思考和规划中国，如铁路、自然资源、农业问题以及西方医学，教育如何适应中国等问题，他甚至为中国规划出完整的铁路网络。更多的时候，老钱伯林不顾旅程劳顿，在中国乡村逆旅如豆的油灯下奋笔疾书，撰写中国考察笔记。而小钱伯林，则将每天所见所闻写成日记，同时利用携带摄影器材，沿途拍摄冲洗了七百余张照片，图文并茂地记录了晚清中国的城市乡村，山川河流，是研究晚清教育，地质与地理的第一手资料。

1. 教育

钱伯林父子以科学角度观察记录中国，因为名为教育，所以教育着墨很多。钱伯林父子每逢一地，遍访教育机关，学校与学堂等，了解办学现状，探索朝野对教育的态度。例如在 3 月 5 日在汉口参观男女学校。男校的学生反应迅速，优于一般美国同龄的孩子。而女校的校园甚至比汉口城内的官衙更有吸引力。

但是对于中国的教育弊病也是一针见血。钱伯林认为学校专业师资很有限，大多数资源都是为了维持冗杂的教育官员，通常官员人数与老师之比是 15∶6。而官员朝令夕改的政策，对科学工作欣赏的缺乏以及大量冗员坐食经费，是中国教育的首要危害。

关于教会教育，钱伯林父子也有不同他人的见解。他们访问了中国许多教会学校，接触传教士和在华外国人，但是发现教会和传教士对科学仍持有怀疑态度。所以，他们最终建议独立于教会，以大学为主体，在中国开办教育事业，这是美国对华教育的一个重要转变。考察团最终的结论是西方对中国最大的帮助应该是医学教育，即通过建立设备精良的医学院，训练中国人解决自己的卫生和健康问题。这为洛克菲勒基金在北京建立协和医学院奠定了基础。

2．地质

钱伯林父子均为地质出身，对沿途地形地貌用功最多，观察精到细致。而他们的考察任务就是通过考察中国的地质地理，服务教育。例如在结束华南考察之后，钱伯林认为广州不适合建设大学，因为气候太酷热，而且可利用的土地太少。

钱伯林父子中国考察用功最深的地方是四川。他们的四川旅行始于1909年3月，沿长江过巫峡、奉节、云阳、至万州上岸从陆地穿越四川。经分水、梁平、大竹、渠县、南充、蓬溪、射洪、中江、到达灌县，后沿岷江经成都、郫县，彭山、乐山到宜宾，再顺长江而下，经重庆、丰都、忠县，回到万州，然后东出三峡于5月返回武汉。四川之行，从三峡峡谷中的古生代的地层剖面，到寒武纪底部的冰川遗迹，地质的多样性令钱伯林父子赞叹不已。例如钱氏父子在蓬溪县参观四川特色的盐井及生产过程，而大竹县煤窑工人的工作条件令其心寒。在四川考察中，小钱伯林还手绘十余张当地地质图。他们戏称四川地质可以作为对"强征"来做教育考察的地质学者的补偿。

对于黄土地区和蒙古高原，钱伯林父子也是兴趣盎然，时有高见。例如在河南，钱伯林父子沿京汉铁路北上，沿途沙丘逐渐增多。他们发现沙丘之上并非普通树木，而是硕果累累的果树，便推断这种沙丘是沉积的黄土而非普通沙子。考察团抵达北京之后，张伯林父子又忙中偷闲从张家口上至蒙古高原边境，考察是否有古代冰期的证据。因为本地区的地图显示有无数的小湖，这可能正是在冰川遗存的证据。可是考察之后发现，小湖仅仅是火山岩地区的凹陷盆地，而非冰川证据。

3．地理

在考察途中，中国沿途变换的地理景观如乡村、城镇、稻田、水车、牌坊、石桥、古塔、庙宇等令钱氏父子叹为观止，屡屡驻足参观。例如在四川云阳县参观张飞庙，在成都灌县的拜访李冰祠，在河南走访寻常村落。

在所有地理景观中，钱伯林最注重的是农业，因为它直接反映当地人与自然的关系。成都平原的麦豆同作，成熟的轮作制度，娴熟的肥料运用都令钱伯林击节赞赏。而河南以梯田形式开发利用山坡，其富有的创造性和建设性，可为美国山区开垦所借鉴。

钱伯林为中国古老农业文明所折服之时，并未忘记以科学家的身份点出问题。例如在两广的西江流域，他指出当地砍伐森林以及运用科技方面有巨大错误。同时钱伯林也就中国农业发展提出自己的见解。例如他认为直隶平原的未来取决稳定高效的农业以及煤铁工业的发展，他为此建议直隶平原发展风车磨坊，充分利用风能，同时建设水坝，控制雨水和河流。

在中国考察的四个月中，钱伯林父子醉心重峦叠嶂的地质景观，而高度发达的农业也展示了古老文明的内在力量。可是在此背后却是顽固的疾病和仍处于中世纪的医疗卫生条件，而这正是考察团可以努力之处。

4．王朝的新与旧

钱伯林父子在大清王朝末年，见证了王朝的新与旧，开放与保守。例如汉口张之洞主持的汉阳钢铁厂，上海与汉口等开放口岸的现代学校，东北地区训练有素的新式警察，无不展示了清王朝的改革与发展。

不过在欣欣向荣的背后，实则危机四伏。例如汉口铁厂将最好的铁矿石出口卖给日本，自己只用二等矿石，如此尚资不抵债，而且坐吃山空，缺少对未来所需铁矿的勘探和研究。在澳门附近，钱伯林父子亲眼目睹一艘悬挂英国国旗的货船堂而皇之地在一艘军舰护卫下，卸载鸦片，销往澳门。

清王朝的式微最能体现在北京鼓楼。晨钟暮鼓曾经是帝国的象征之一。而钱伯林在北京见到的鼓楼几近荒废，无人过问，以至于初来乍到的小钱伯林甚至将这种对公共建筑的漠视归结为中国人的某种特质。

五、整理说明

钱伯林父子中国考察档案部分藏于美国芝加哥大学档案馆，因为父子二人都执教芝加哥大学，而且1909年的中国考察是由芝加哥大学派出的，所以芝加哥大学藏有部分档案是情理之中的。不过，芝加哥大学的所藏档案多为正式官方报告。

中国考察的日记和照片等私人档案仍被小钱伯林个人保存。1948年小钱伯林去世后，由亲属代为保管。直至1997年，这批档案才转交给比洛特学院地质系一位叫做Hank Woodard的荣退教授，由他捐给了比洛特学院档案馆。因为老钱伯林生于比洛特，长于比洛特，而且毕业于比洛特学院地质系，是该院的杰出校友，所以捐给比洛特学院也是实至名归。

1909年返回美国之后，钱伯林父子曾各写了两篇有关中国的文章。除此之外，钱伯林中国考察档案便罕为人知了。编者近年致力于在美国发掘中国档案，利用美国所藏档案研究中国是当今研究中国历史的一种重要手段。2013年，我综合比洛特学院和芝加哥大学所藏的六册日记、一套笔记以及七百张照片，开始整理钱伯林父子的中国考察档案。寒暑两载，在征得档案馆授权下，现在以一套两册形式出版（上册为日记/笔记，下册为图像）。

有关日记部分，原文为英文手写，字迹不易辨认。比洛特学院档案馆自21世纪初开始整理并将其数字化，编者依照其整理成果，编排成书，并由编者加以适当校正断句，删除其日记中的照片目录部分、繁杂的账目记录以及不清晰的手绘地质图样，以求增加文字的可读性。同时，增补笔记部分，与日记合为一册，以示对照。编后附有老钱伯林中国考察信函一封以及小钱伯林的中国考察回忆录一份，以供参考。

有关图像部分，原图有七百余张，编者依据照片清晰度、地点明确性以及代表性等标准，选取其中约五百张，依照考察路线，分省区编著，每区由编者撰写简短说明，介绍考察内容与意义。图像名称（图注）均以作者档案图片原文名称直接翻译为准，个别有错讹之处做了校勘及注解，括号中的字为编者所加。

目 录

I 钱伯林中国考察日记 / 1

    1. Notebook No. 1 / 3

    2. Notebook No. 2 / 35

    3. Notebook No. 3 / 75

    4. Notebook No. 4 / 115

    5. Notebook No. 5 / 155

II 钱伯林中国考察笔记 / 165

    1. Oriental Educational Investigation Synopsis of Notes on South China
    By T. C. Chamberlin and R. T. Chamberlin / 165

    2. Oriental Educational Investigation Synopsis of Studies in Central China
    February 27th to May 3rd, 1909
    By T. C. Chamberlin and R. T. Chamberlin / 171

    3. Oriental Educational Investigation Synopsis of the Observations of the Messrs. Chamberlin North of the Yangtze River
    May 10th. 1909 / 185

    4. Oriental Educational Investigation Synopsis of the Observations of the Messrs. Chamberlin in the Province of Honan
    May 11th to 15th, 1909 / 191

    5. Oriental Educational investigation Synopsis of the Observations of the Messrs. Chamberlin in the Province of Shanxi
    May 16th to 18th, 1909 / 199

6. Oriental Educational Investigation Synopsis of the Observations of the Messrs. Chamberlin in the Province of Chili
May 15th to June 5th, 1909 / 205

7. Oriental Educational Investigation Synopsis of the Observations of the Messrs. Chamberlin on the Borderland of the Gulf of Chili Between Peking and Mukden
June 5th and 6th, 1909 / 211

8. Oriental Educational Investigation Synopsis of the Observations of the Messrs. Chamberlin on Manchuria
June 6th-10th, 1909 / 219

Ⅲ 附录 / 227

1. Thomas C. Chamberlin's letter to the President of the University of Chicago regading Chinese Expedition,1901 / 229

2. The Chinese Expedition of 1909. Recollections by Rolling T.Chamerlin,1929 / 235

I 钱伯林中国考察日记

Oriental Educational Investigation Commission, University of Chicago, Chicago, U.S.A.

R.T. Chamberlin
Jan – June 1909.

Notebook
No. 1

Monday Jan 4th. 1909

Left Chicago at 6.P.M on the Overland Limited leaving from the C & N.W. Station.

Tuesday Jan 5th. 1909

Reached Omaha Neb at 8.20 A.M. All day in following the valley of the North Platte. Very cold. Temperature at Grand Island -8°.

Wednesday Jan 6th. 1909

Woke up in Southern Wyoming. Raining. Green River. Point from which Major Powell set out for trip through the Grand Canyon. The great plains extend for a surprising distance to the west in Southern Wyoming. Most of the day spent in dissected upland country until the descent down the long valley and canyon to Odgen. Very steeply inclined beds in the Wasatch. Evidently repetition of the series. Reached Ogden at 4.50 P.M. and soon after started across Great Salt Lake on the Lucin cut off. Crossed the first arm of the lake before dark.

Thursday Jan 7th. 1909

Woke up in Western Nevada. Typical basin topography. A beautifully clear morning at first but later became clouded. The temperature, like yesterday, was above the freezing point. West of Reno the ascent of the Sierras begins. Snow soon appears on the ground.

The scenery is moderately attractive. Soon in a snow storm which continues to increase in intensity to the summit of the Pass at 7000 ft. The ascent is not very abrupt for a faulted range. The upper part of the trip (some 45 miles) is almost entirely in snow sheds. Trees and ground heavily covered with fresh snow making the glimpses through the snow sheds very picturesque. The snow extended down to about 5000 ft on the Pacific slope of the Sierras. Long gradual foothill slopes for the most part heavily wooded. Sacramento reached on time at 4.50 P.M. Sacramento lies on a nearly flat plain about 30 ft. above tide level. Sacramento River is broad and little more than back water from the sea. Got off at 16st Oakland at 7.48 P.M. and were conducted to Berkeley.

Friday Jan 8th.1909

In morning went across on ferry to San Francisco and visited our steamer, the Siberia. Attended to various matters and returned to Berkeley. In afternoon visited the campus of the University of California and saw the sights of Berkeley. A rainy day.

Saturday Jan 9th.1909

A beautiful day. Crossed the bay to San Francisco and proceeded to the S.S. Siberia. Saw baggage put aboard and said farewells. Steamer sailed at 1. P.M. Passage of the famous Golden Gate very picturesque. Followed the north channel after passing the gate and then swung to the S.W. The Pacific cliffs were abrupt in places but we came to the conclusion that perhaps too much has been made of erosion by the sea waves compared with that by rivers. Sharp granitic islands some ten miles off shore. Older remnants.

Sunday Jan 10th. 1909

Sea much calmer. Wind has changed from the N.W to the south. Intermittent rain and fog. Day's run 346 miles. Temperatue at 4. P.M was 59º F. Latitude 35º 46'. Weather at time cloudy.

Monday Jan 11th. 1909

Quite rough this morning Wind nearly due west. Much warmer. No overcoats necessary. Temperature at 9 A.M. was 64º F. Moderately foggy. Day's run 351 miles. Noon latitude was 33º 26'. Temperature at 5.30 P.M was 65º

It is to be noted that no evidence of any life outside the ship was seen today. No fish, porpoises, birds nor any fragment of floating vegetation. Yesterday several large sea gulls or sea tern were seen but no fish or vegetation. I think this should have some bearing upon the liklihood of life having originated in the open ocean. Life must be largely confined to the upper 100 ft of the ocean on account of the light being cut off. At this latitude and warm climate it would seem as if there were a great abundance of life in the open ocean we should see evidence of it. It therefore seems likely that it is chiefly in the neighborhood of land that the ocean abounds in life. In this clear water of uniform composition and uniform salt concentration there should seem little activity going on which could inaugurate life. Nothing doing.

I should notes here that under last Saturday's notes should have been one upon the apparent absence of terraces or high beach lines upon the hillsides and cliffs along the coast in the neighborhood of the Golden Gate. We saw no evidence that the sea had been for any prolonged period at a notably higher elevation than at the present.

Tuesday Jan 12th. 1909

A bright, balmy morning. Temperature at 9 AM was 67° F. Wind S.W. Day's run 366 miles. Latitude at noon 30° 26' Longitude 142° 05' W. Temperature at 4.30 P.M. was 68° F. Cloudy. Some of the men have been playing shuffle board in their shirt sleeves. I got a little too warm playing shuffle board and got uncomfortably warm punching the bag. I have gone most of the day without my cap.

Wednesday Jan 13th. 1909

A bright clear day. Temperature at 9. AM. was 70°; at noon 71° F; at 4 P.M 72°. The temperature has thus been steadily rising throughout the voyage. The time of day apparently makes but little difference. Days run 352 miles Latitude at noon 27° 14' Longitude " " 147° 42' Temperature at 9.30 P.M was 71° F

Notes on what ought to be taught and what ought not to be taught under each of the sciences. Geography & Physiography Teach here the processes ie. the way in which geographic features come to be. Teach how these affect human affairs. How the burial of or sinking of river mouths or valley months gives rise to harbors and so promotes commerce. Teach how rivers afford transportation and so develop commerce. How they afford water power and hence locate industry and cities. How the head of navigation forces shifting of carriage means and so locates cities. And thus proceed through the list of agencies that affect the distribution and concentration of inhabitants. Agriculture, forestry, mining, manufactures would be among the topics to be treated.

Physiography. Use essentially the substance and matter of Salisbury's Physiography. Geology Develop in this processes and history reducing the technical divisions to the minimum and substituting oriental divisions as far as practicable for occidental.

Botany. Teach the vital things about the life and the development of the plant. Teach the great classes of plants not as classes but as plants of a kind doing their life work and accomplishing their results in their own individual ways. Reduce to a minimum the minor classifications and put these in the form of tables of reference or appendices, or in some similar form which shall make them merely sources of reference as need may arise. Introduce the vital features of the youthful plants and connect them as far as practicable with the conditions suitable for their development. In other words introduce in essence agricultural botany in as stimulating a way as practicable.

Zoology. Follow the same principles and select those animals which abound in the country and minimize the rest except as they illustrate important features of the animal kingdom or of the animal development.

In the matter of morphology a carefully guarded position should be assumed drawing the lives justly between structure as a vital element in the development of animals and that were laboratory practice in dissection which has been made a fad under of discipline etc and which has too often killed out the vitality of the subject. It seems to me possible to treat the morphology as a vital factor in making the animal what it is as a living organism without entering into the details of form variation which have little or no meaning in the animal economy or, if they have, it is too obscure & remote to be effective with most students.

Chemistry. Begin essentially with the actual chemicals & work up the facts, & the laws and the necessary parts of the nomenclature from concrete practise. In the selection of matter choose those elements that most concern the people.

Physics. Develop on the same principles starting with the concrete and developing facts, laws, principles & generalizations from them. Make the selection adaptive as in the other cases.

Mechanics. It would seem to be best to develop mechanics by itself taking such subjects as the levers wheels, pulleys etc to start with and proceeding thence to machinery. The principles of common industrial mechanics should be well brought out. Test problems to develop original thinking should be freely introduced in this subject and so far as practicable in the proceeding.

Physiology. The animal structure should be taught as the basis of animal function and animal function should be the basis of hygienic inferences. The effort should be to give the essential basis for sound thinking and intelligent appreciation rather than dicta as to hygiene. A difficulty arises from the fact that chemistry seems to be needed as a precedent to digestion, assimilation and rebuilding up of structure. There are two ways of meeting this. The one to teach what chemistry is needed when the need is reached in the study of physiology; the other is to defer physiology until after chemistry has been learned. But if we wait until the chemistry of the organic processes and structures are mastered as a part of systemic chemistry it will defer physiology for the lifetime of the great majority of students and so practically the former method is the better.

Astronomy. It would seem that the main fact of astronomy ought to be made accessible to the students of high schools and academy grades. If so the selection and treatment should follow the same principles as the preceeding.

Mineralogy & Petrography. The first courses in mineralogy & petrology should seek to give students a clear vital idea as to how chemical substances organize themselves into crystalline, concretionary & other masses & how these aggregate themselves into rocks, and how rocks disintegrate, or become liquids on the one side, and how they grow up on the other. The general treatment should follow somewhat the lines of my origin and descent of rocks. Probably that chapter might be developed into a serviceable work by starting with the chemical elements & building then up into minerals. Then deploy the minerals through the requisite extent. Then build the minerals up into rocks. Then treat the disintegration and the metamorphism of rocks.

Thursday Jan 14th. 1909

A perfect day. Temp. at 9 A.M 72° " " noon 72° " " 4 P.M 72° Day's run 367 miles. Wind S.W. Noon latitude 23° 57' N " longitude 153° 25' W Most of the ladies are wearing white summer dresses and judge Ballow in the afternoon. In the evening flashes of phosphorescence were abundant in the water. The general effect was similar to that produced by fire flies on land. The flashes were connected with distinct individual organisms and not a general phosphorescence. They were slightly below the surface of the water.

Friday Jan 15th. 1909

Got up at 6.30 A.M. Were just reaching the island of Oahu. Attractive views of the Southern coast. Passed the Diamond head – an extinct broken down crater and entered Honolulu harbor left the steamer a few minutes before 9 o'clock.

Were met by Mr. Frank Atherton and Rev. F.W. Damon. Picked up Dr D. Scudder at his church. We commenced the automobile sight seeing journey by passing the former royal palace (now the government building) and several other public buildings. On the way to the aquarium passed by Mrs. J.B. Atherton's home, which was notable for its yard filled with almost every variety of tropical plant.

Stopped at a public school where the scholars were saluting the flag in the school yard before commencing the day's studies. Visited a few of the rooms and saw the 8th grade salute the flag by an appropriate recitation in concert given with gestures toward the flag and ending with a pledge of loyalty to it. We were told that 17 nationalities were represented in the school. It was very suggestive of one of the race problems being worked out by education with apparent success.

We passed what had been a marshy unserviceable tract that had been reclaimed by the Chinese by digging trenches perhaps 6-8 ft. wide and raising the ground adjacent perhaps a ft. above water level, for a width of four to six ft. and this was planted to bananas of the Chinese variety which appeared to be reasonably flourishing.

We spent some time in the aquarium with the greatest pleasure and instruction. With rare exceptions the fish are those of the islands or similar situations in the Pacific. They are notable for their extraordinary coloring as well as for variety and attractiveness of form. While much of the coloring was strong and deep it was yet singularly blended so as to produce exceedingly harmonious effects. The general effect was softness. In this respect they are rather to be contrasted than compared with Atlantic fishes so far as we have seen them. Some octopi, see eels, and sea urchins and other forms gave variety to the collection.

On the return we passed by rice fields in an early state, cultivated in part by hand, by the water buffalo and by horses. See photos. On the route we passed many examples of an acacia of the musquite variety, locally known as which is said to grow rapidly in arid tracts and on rocky ground, to produce an excellent fire wood and most notably a pod like fruit which carries an unusually large percentage of nutrient. When fed to cattle & horses in the raw pod form it sometimes produces injurious effects from its gummy consistency and concentrated form but when dried and ground it is serviceable food, particularly when mixed with less nutritious material as rice straw. It suggests the possibility of extending its use to warm arid tracts where it would assist in reducing rocky tracts to an arable condition while clothing the surface with vegetation and preventing wash, meanwhile being itself serviccable for food & fuel. Most of the statements regarding this were made by Rev. Dr Scudder, but similar statements were made by Mr J.B. Castle and others. Literature on this subject asked & promised. On the route saw banyan trees, coca, date royal & other palms, bread fruit tree, and many other tropical plants. With great luxuriance of flower.

Visited Oahu College (agriculture school?) and met Prof. W.A. Griffiths who is also secretary of the Pacific Scientific association. Were shown some of the excellent appointments of the institution. At present the grades of the college are essentially those of a preparatory school in which various nationalities are represented. Later visited the missionary school founded by Rev. Damon where we saw classes chiefly of Chinese boys at work. The superintendent reported that they were excellent pupils, faithful, more easily controlled than white pupils.

He answered in a rather emphatic negative the question whether the Chinese pupils studied merely by rote & imitation. The new students still wore their quxeues but the older ones had the hair cut. This is left to the pupil but he soon follows the fashion.

We visited the Bishop museum famous for its exhibit of Polynesian implements & manufactures. Perhaps the most notable feature is the manufacture of a kind of paper cloth by pounding fiber. A notable feature is an excellent relief of the volcano Kilauea.

Visited the girl's school founded by the Athertons as a memorial to their father. The building is built of lava blocks in rough artistic form and is finished attractively in native woods. All the appointments were not only excellent but distinctly attractive. Visited briefly the location of the companion boys school whose foundations were being laid. Both of these are located in attractive positions with beautiful outlooks upon the mountains and the sea.

Visited the Pali, a notable pass, or col, at the head of the valley. From the Pali there is a precipitous descent of several hundred feet followed a rapid slope down to a rough plain not greatly above the sea level. Coral reefs abound on the coast opposite and are said to be exceedingly rich biological fields. The valley leading up to the Pali is unique in form so far as our observation goes. The mountain slopes on either side are exceptionally steep, ranging up to 60° in some places and perhaps even more although generally clothed with vegetation. There seemed to be little or no talus at the bottom of the slope but instead a rather shape curve into the plain of the valley. The valley bottoms had a general planeness but were rough in detail and usually quite rocky. A stream flows along either side in portions of the valley at least, and this perhaps aids in giving it its peculiar cross section which is much more nearly that of a U-shaped glacial valley than a typical V-shaped valley but it obviously had no connection with a glacial valley so far as origin is concerned. It may be merely an exceptional case. The sides of the valley were well creased by erosion trenches. Soil was not abundant, except locally, in the upper part of the valley. Many features of the valley correspond with those seen east of Orizaba in Mexico, particularly in the absence of talus and foot slope accumulation. The flat portion near the seashore on which a part of Honolulu is built has a coral reef bottom. Apparently a part is also alluvial. A portion of the soil is dark and a portion deep red. The latter was spoken of as exceptionally fertile. The absence of the quartzose element is very notable. Many of the roadways are constructed of basaltic macadam and are very excellent. Oil is said to have been used on some of them with excellent results. In particular it is said to protect them from the wash of the heavy rains.

A very suggestive feature of the day's acquisitions is the part which Honolulu is playing in the relations of Americans to Asiatics. Both Ms. Damon and Mr. Scudder seemed to feel that there were great advantages in introducing the Asiatics to American life and methods under conditions intermediate between those of America and those of Asia and also under conditions comparatively free from the race prejudices that prevail on the Pacific coast. They said that there is no Chinese problem in Hawaii. The races live together here in a genial way with mutual respect.

I think the point is well taken and that it is one of radical importance. There were many little signs all through the day that very cordial relations prevailed between those who guided us and natives of various classes. Salutations were very common and seemed very cordial and genuine. The suggestion arose that the genial climate and the soft luxuriance of vegetation and all life conditions may be an important element thus, but whether this is so or not the fact that here the problem of the races is being solved in a degree with peculiar success appears to be a genuine reality and not a superficial appearance. Our friends made some very radical suggestions regarding possible solutions of a far reaching nature as the result of the intermarriage of the races. The suggestions were discreet and reserved but the authors appeared to have good grounds in observations for the conclusions reached. All that was said during the day of the Chinese was of the favorable kind both as to their ability and general attitude. The manifestations of missionary effort, especially those of later date, were full of thoughtfulness for the general well being of the Asiatic peoples and nothing was conspicuous that could be regarded as a religious propagandum as such. The work appeared to be thoroughly humanitarian rather than doctrinal though doubtless that had its place and was no doubt all the more affective because accompanied and preceded by the humanitarian element. Suggestion as to Recommendation. Is not Hawaii choice ground for establishing an intermediate college to which Chinese and other Oriental students shall go preparatory to taking advanced courses in the universities of the States?

Definitely might not Oahu College be extended say through the junior College courses and made strong in Science and then serve thus purpose effectively? The temperature at 10 P.M on the deck below the bridge was 74°. Wind S.W.

Saturday Jan 16th. 1909

Fine weather. Temp at 9 AM 74° Wind S.W. Noon latitude 22° 00' " longitude 162° 54' Day's run 288 miles. Temp at 4 P.M 75°. Spent the morning whipping my briefer papers on "The Gases in Rock" for the journal of Geology into shape. In the afternoon I developed the two rolls of film which I exposed at Honolulu. The 7 inch developing tank proved inadequate to the task of developing the long rolls of 12 exposures of 3 ¼ X 4 ¼ film. The apron is too short; the result was the first three pictures flogged. Temp of air 75°. Temp of solutions 80°.

Sunday Jan 17th. 1909

Strong head winds and rough seas. Temp 9 AM was 76°, " Noon " 76.5° . Days run 357 miles. This seemed an unusually long day for the decks were wet driving the people inside. In addition being Sunday there was little going on indoors.

Monday Jan 18th. 1909

Temp at 9 AM 76.5° . Day's run 330 miles. Latitude at noon 24° 17' N., Longitude 175° 6' W. Temp. at 4 P.M 76°. Rough weather all day strong head winds reduced the day's run. Decks were wet with spray and fine rain most of the day. Played a good deal of chess but still found the day a long one. Wind WSW.

Interview with Dr Samuel Cochran, missionary physician located about 150 miles NNW. of Nanking. Had a long talk about a variety of subjects connected with the Chinese situation. In the medical line it appears that there is an association of physicians the number he could not state accurately but thought there might be 400-500 who are endeavoring to organize and put into Chinese the essence of modern medical and surgical science. He stated at some length & with much detail the difficulties of nomenclature which they are encouraging. At fist the nomenclature was so heterogeneous that students under one physician could scarcely use the matter produced by another physician, but through a committee of the association they have now developed what he thinks is a fair system. They make no attempt to introduce the technical European or Latin nomenclature but have made up a Chinese system.

In explaining this Dr. Cochran at the same time explained one feature of the Chinese language. There are, he says, a series of radial ideographs to the number of 414 from which other ideographs are manufactured by additions. For example: there is an ideograph which signifies "bone" and all the bones of the body theoretically contain this radical with modification, as for example, the radius has the ideograph for turn prefixed to that for bone, so that it means "turn bone." Sometimes to this is added the ideograph for forearm or arm, so that the complex ideograph means the turn bone of the arm. This in turn is simplified by dropping out the radical ideograph and calling this bone simply the turn. So if they wish to designate the radical artery they use the ideograph for artery with the ideograph for turn, and so on. This gives the essence of the method of building up a Chinese nomenclature on a Chinese basis. Some earlier attempts were made by representing Chinese sounds as nearly corresponding to German sounds for example as practicable. For example he cited Harnsaure = uric acid. The Chinese were then required to learn the strange phase Harnsaure which had no meaning to them. This Dr. Cochran thought a very bad system involving very great wastage of labor and trammeling the acquisition of the ideas sought.

In connection with this the conversation ran on to the radical subject of language in general. I sounded him on the tentative idea I have entertained of printing the language phonetically to avoid the great labor involved in the ideographic system. He thought that there might be some notable advantage in this but that there is a rather formidable difficulty growing out of the fact that the same sound has many meanings. This he illustrated by the simple word "fu" which had a long list, say 20-30, quite different ideographs with very different meanings. In other words the spoken language is much less complete in its discriminations than the written language. A part of this difficulty is met by what are called "tones", ie different pitches as we would say in music. To this extent of course it would be easy to indicate the tones in a phonetic system. There are, Dr. Cochran says, 5 such tones recognized & so it would be easy to add an exponential numeral or some similar device to discriminate between these.

This, however, would apparently meet only a part of the difficulty, but I suppose the residue of the difficulty would not be very different from that which we have in English and other languages where the same word has several meanings. At any rate it would seem that a phonetic system might be made as satisfactory as the phonetic representation of the language. It would seem further that it is desirable to develop the phonetic competency of the language so that it shall be adequate to the real needs of expression. Dr Cochran cited a device made use of in speech by which the class to which the meaning belongs is indicated. I do not recall the precise illustration but the following will perhaps answer. If the sound for turn has several meanings not discriminated by the sound the addition of the sound for bone would indicate the class to which it belonged and the phrase "turn bone" would not be equivocal.

Dr. Cochran suggested another line of improvement in the simplification of the ideographs themselves. He thought that many of them were much more complicated than they need be. While he did not use any reference to stenographic characters, it occurred to me that perhaps the general method used in developing a stenographic system might be made applicable to the ideographic system. It is worth while to enquire further how far there is anything in common between the ideographic method and the stenographic method. It is worth while also to enquire into the fundamental utility of an ideographic system as compared with a phonetic system.

In the line of education Dr. Cochran was profoundly impressed with the difficulty of securing adequate teachers. This difficulty has been greatly intensified by the recent edicts of the Dowager Empress (2 years? ago) by which the old system of literary examination was abolished and instruction in foreign lines imposed. There are, he says, 1700 districts governed by district magistrates corresponding to our county and each of these under the edict is directed to establish a school of the occidental type. It is practically impossible to do this because there are not so many teachers of adequate preparation in China.

Dr. Cochran went into some detail regarding the effort to secure western education through the Japanese schools. His comments were decidedly adverse. The individual morality of the Chinese students in Japan suffered and to a considerable extent they became impregnated with revolutionary sentiments. He had individual knowledge of their having imbibed sentiments akin to those which promoted the French Revolution, and there was an open laudation of such characters as Robespierre etc. There was also a seditious attitude toward the Manchu dynasty coupled with the notion that the overthrow of the dynasty was one of the things to be sought, etc. There was also developed a spirit of antagonism and hostility to Buddism and Taoism. This if I remember was not confined to students in Japanese institutions but was general among students of western ideas. Dr Cochran thought that the introduction of western education would do away with both of these religions inevitably. Confucianism he did not regard as a religion in the strict sense, but rather as a system of philosophy & morals & that much of it – perhaps most of it - might remain consistently with Christian enlightenment. He spoke candidly regarding the differences of western view as to the necessity of any at all in an advanced system of education & civilization, and did not seem to entertain strongly biased feelings in the matter though he stated frankly that from the standpoint of the missionaries the Christian religion was deemed vital. In this connection he clearly indicated a belief in considerable transformation of the western form which Christianity assumes and an expectation that Christianity in China would take a form adapted to the Chinese eliminating any of the incidental features which it assumes among western nations. Many other points were touched upon but as further conversation will probably develop them into more definite and accurate form they may be noted to better advantage later.

Tuesday Jan 19th. 1909

Wind less but swells still heavy. Temp 9 AM 72°. The wind is now nearly due west. Ever since the day we left San Francisco the wind has been S.W. until today. 4° drop in temperature since yesterday. Days run 337 miles. Latitude at noon 25° N Longitude 178° E. We have now crossed the 180° meridian so that it is really tomorrow the 20th. But for convience we skip tomorrow (Wed. the 20th) and jump at midnight with the day after tomorrow (Thursday jan 21st). Temp. at 4 P.M 70°.

Wednesday Jan 20th. 1909

This day was omitted together. We passed from the 19th to the 21st directly. No work but full days pay.

Thursday Jan 21st. 1909

Boat sill pitches. Wind is now N. W. Clear weather Temp. at 9 am is 68. Day's run 332 miles latitude at noon.

Friday Jan 22nd. 1909

Temp at 9 am was 66. Clear weather with wind due to North and much reduce in force. Sea calmer. Boat rolls now instead of pitching because of cross seas.

This is the Chinese New years. The Chinese in the steerage celebrate the day by shooting off bunches of firecrackers which explode with much sharper reports than those used in the states on the 4th of July.

Apparently we get an inferior grade of firecracker. The bunches exploded very quickly – the whole bunch of 10 – 12 going off while in the air. The Chinese were dressed up and games of chance were more numerous than ordinarily. A form of dominoes was the favorite. Sometimes they played for black and white beads which were afterwards cashed and sometimes for money. In one game money of all kinds (Chinese, Japanese, U.S. Mexican and English) changed hands rapidly. Silver coins (about 20cts?) were the most common stake. Many of the Chinese were frozen out & had to leave the game broke. All luck; no skill or cheating.

Saturday Jan 23rd. 1909

Cloudy. Wind W.S.W., Temp at 9 AM 68°. Warmer due to change in the wind.

Day's run 377 miles. Best yet because of little adverse wind.

Temp at 4 P.M 67°.

Sunday Jan 24th. 1909

Clear weather Temp at 9 am 61. The wind has changed to nearly due north. The sea is choppy but does not rock the ship badly.

Monday Jan 25th. 1909

Cloudy. Sea very quiet, Temp at 9am 61. During the night we experienced a very hard wind storm accompanied by same lightening. The steamer rolled a bit but by morning the storm had passed by.

Tuesday Jan 26th. 1909

Awoke during clear weather. Later it clouded & rained. Temp at 9 am 52. Land in sight on starboard. Wind off the land. Later the weather cleared affording very picturesque views of approaches to Yoho Hama Bay. Hillsides terraced for cultivation. As we were entering the Bay proper Fujiyama the scared mountain of Japan at last emerged from the clouds. It is a very fine volcano. The coast line hillsides have a knobby appearance on their crests. This peculiar erosion profile suggests igneous rocks. The soil has a somewhat reddish appearance.

Passed several forts built in the shallow waters of the Bay. Attempted to anchor to buoys but pulled them up. Long delay. Reached Yokohama harbor before 2 P.M but did not get ashore until 4 P.M. Landed in Hotel launch. Went to Wright's Hotel. Missed Mr Wang. Went to Pacific Mail Office, Cooks, Post & Telegraph offices and attended to necessary business. Then took 40 minute jiurikisha ride about the streets to see the city. The shops are mostly open without glass windows in front or other means of keeping out the cold. The buildings are low – one or two stories – and picturesque. A great many English signs are in evidence. English is easily the second language of the city. Noticed that the windows of the buildings were mostly after the American style rather than the European.

Wednesday Jan 27th. 1909

Transacted business in Yokohama. Bought Murray's Guide to Japan; Cabled Prof. Burton; bought tickets at Cook's to Kobe; extended passage to Hong Kong on Siberia. Left for Tokyo at 11.00 AM. Surface traversed flat adjoining sea but few feet above tide level occupied largely by rice flats interspersed with truck garden flats, small orchards & vineyards. General aspect of prosperity. Homes mostly neat many picturesque. Forms much more agreeable than similar classes of houses in America, chiefly due to tile roofs of the typical Japano Chinese type. A little to the west of the R.R. line the surface rises 70-80 ft into an upland of which little was seen – apparently a plateau. The material of this plateau was yellowish & reddish and slightly consolidated – probably Tertiary or Quaternary. No high elevations near the land.

On reaching Tokyo took carriage (2 yen per hour) and called first on the Hon. Thomas J. O'Brian American Ambassador. We were accompanied by Y. T. Wang and his Chinese friend, Hsiao, who acted as Japanese interpreter. Were cordially received by Ambassador O'Brien who gave various suggestions and some facts regarding Japanese education chiefly relating to external matters of form, appointments and personal. He permitted us to take for the purpose of abstract, a report from the American consul at Kobe relative to the Kobe Higher Commercial School which is one of a class of schools recently instituted. For abstract see below. Also gave a letter of introduction to Prof. Rikizo Nakashima, a graduate of Yale specially interested in the ethical development of Japanese education. Letter through R. S. Miller. Called at the department of Public Instruction but found the Hon. R. Okado, Vince minister of State for Education, absent.

Called at the Imperial University of Tokyo& were cordially received by Baron Hamao, president, and by Prof. Bundjiro Koto of the Department of Geology, by Dr. Shozaburo Watase and by Prof. Joji Sakurai of the Department of Chemistry and director of the college of Science. After the conference at the President's we visited the seismological station conducted by Prof Omori who was however absent. His associate showed us to the extent of time at our command the very unusual installment of seismographs which are there assembled, a considerable portion of which are the invention of Omori & his associates. The station has a fine collection of photographs of seismologic subjects & models of buildings constructed to resist earthquakes. Visited the Geological museum & laboratories. The appointments and work in progress are fairly comparable to those of the better American Universities. Our time was altogether too short to adequately inspect this large university whose students number above 5,000. We were given a calendar of the university, 330 pages illustrated by photographs of the buildings & containing much valuable information concerning the organization of the institution.

Returned to Yokohama. Tokyo is far as seen, is as attractive city rendered picturesque by the Japanese style of architecture. It is not however impressive, as the buildings are small, chiefly wooden. The uniformity which characterizes most American cities, is replaced by notable variation due to the breaking of skylines & frontage lines by variations of height & projection as well as of form. There are however not a few buildings of American & European modern styles which do not on the whole add to the beauty of the place, though they constitute the larger & more expensive buildings. The University buildings belong to this class, being constructed of red brick trimmed with light gray stone and this combination is the prevailing one with the occidental structures. The city is well supplied with street cars of modern type (trolley) but otherwise transportation is chiefly by jiurikishas. The people were stouter, heavier and more rugged than I had pictured them. There was considerable variation in the apparent state of health but the majority, perhaps two thirds, seemed lusty and vigorous. The children seemed in the main hearty & full of good spirits. A minority showed obvious signs of decrepitude which suggested lack of nourishment & care in a portion of the cases & physiological abuse in another however seemed to constitute a decided minority of the whole. The people moved briskly in the main and evidences of muscular strength were abundant in the handling of jiurikishas and of freightage carts which were rather numerous. Draywagons with one horse being formally led rather than driven were common. The women seemed healthy in the main, glowing cheeks being abundant. However it was a bright coldish day and this doubtless had something to do with the glowing cheeks & the general sprightliness of the people seen on the streets. The general effect of the bearing & behavior of the people on the streets & on the cars was pleasant. Nothing boisterous or rude was observed.

Thursday Jan 28th. 1909

Left Hiranuma station (suburb of Yokohama) at 8.36 AM on express train for Kyoto. Between Hiranuma and the head of the Sajami Bay the hillslopes are to a considerable extent covered with shrubs & grasses that do not seem to be specially cultivated, nor is any notable serviceability obvious. Doubtless the material is used for fuel etc. Some of the hills are clothed with pines of rather small size on the average. The point of chief note here is that the problem of steep slopes is not solved. Apparently the slopes are covered with appreciable soil. Bare slopes were rare. The valleys & lower slopes are terraced & generally made for rice & coordinate crops.

Friday Jan 29th. 1909

Spent at Kyoto under the guidance of Rev J. D. Davis my college classmate who has been connected with the Doshisha for 38 years and who is intimately familiar with the history of accidental education in Japan.

Saturday Jan 30th. 1909

Journey through the Inland sea. Steamer sailed from Kobe about 1 am.

Sunday Jan 31st. 1909

Woke up as we were slowly entering the harbor of Nagasaki. Went ashore on 9.30 launch and strolled about the streets until 12.30 observing the habits, customs and general appearance of the people. The inhabitants impressed us as active and industrious and fairly clean as a general rule. The children which were very numerous and everywhere in evidence were bright and full of life. They were very generally engaged in some sort of games or athletic sports. At one of the temples several young priests were playing catch in the yard. Mr. Wang accompanied them from US to China.

Monday Feb 1st. 1909

Awoke in the midst of China Sea. The water instead of being the pure blue of pacific has now assumed a distinct greenish tint. Temperature at 1 P.M. was 52°. By this time the color of the water had become yellow green. Temp at 4.30 P.M 50°. Wind N.W. The water at the time of this observation was decidedly roily. By 5.30 P.M it had become a true yellow brown color. This is indeed the Yellow Sea or Hwang Hai. The rivers must carry an extraordinary quality of sediment with this sea for the effect of the sediment held in suspension upon the color of the water is felt practically across to the Japanese coast.

Tuesday Feb 2nd. 1909

At day break steamer was lying quietly near the mouth of the Wu Sung river. Left the Siberia on the launch shortly after 8.30 AM. Stopped and took off passengers & baggage from the SS. Korea (our sister ship) which arrived from Hong Kong shortly after us. Met Mr Thoman Hills & wife who came from Hong Kong & are on their way through East China & Japan. We were met at the wharf in Shanghai by Prof. Burton & Dr. Reed and were conducted to the Astor House.

Jointly with Consul Denby and Prof. Burton called upon His Excellency Viceroy Tuan Fang who is spending 2-3 days in Shanghai in connection with the Opium Commission. It is perhaps mostly of note that although the Viceroy's appointments for the day covered his time he made a place for our reception. He met us with great cordiality and said that on account of the pressure upon his time he could not talk with us as he wished but wanted to sit down with us quietly and to lay before us some of his over plans for education. To do this he invited us to come to Nanking and in response to Prof Burton's inquiry regarding a convenient time named the first 4 days of next week. He kindly left it optional with us to name the date within these limits but requested that we notify him by telegraph so that he could send down two deputies to escort us to Nanking. At Prof. Burton's request he permitted us to take time for counsel regarding the date and to notify him through consul Denby. The manner & expressions of his interpreters were such as to give the impression that behind their marked politeness there was a genuine cordiality. They particularly referred to their warm feelings toward Americans. Consul Denby is evidently held in cordial regard & he was very hearty in all that he did for us. In the course of the interview after it had passed the formal stages & we were saying pleasant things preparatory to withdrawing that the Viceroy had accepted the dinner given by Mr. Rockefeller at which Consul Denby was present. It seemed a pleasant memory on both sides and served very happily its place in the closing of the interview. The interpreters have both traveled in America & had American education in part & his Excellency has also traveled in America. On the whole our reception could not well have been more felicitous under the circumstances. Time of interview 1 P.M.

At 4 P.M by invitation we attended the unveiling of a memorial tablet in honor of Yen Shao-Fang at the International Institute. I have not yet gained a perfectly clear idea of this institute but it appears that its central purpose is to bring together the various nationalities that they may become mutually acquainted & through this come into cordial working relations. The fundamental proposition is that an intelligent acquaintance with one another's ideas & motives will obviate most of the difficulties that arise among diverse people. There is an instructional feature, the extent & nature of which I do not yet know. The institute has some excellent buildings and considerable ground. The ground was largely given by Yen Shao-Fang and by his son. The speakers embraced Chinese Americans, English & a German, the Chinese predominating. Chinese and English were employed, the essence of all remarks being translated into the alternate language. Prof. Burton was asked to take part in the exercise & acquitted himself very felicitously expressing the interest of the University he represents & the American people. Met Dr Gilbert Reid, Mr. Richards, Prof Frier of the Univ. of California and several others. Consul Denby was present.

I found awaiting me an invitation to dinner in connection with the opium Commission for last evening (Mon. Feb 1) Also a note of invitation to tiffin from Mr Richards on Thursday and an invitation from Messrs Y.C. Tong and K.S. Tong to dinner at the Chao Gardens on Thursday evening. This is an exclusive Chinese dinner. Also an invitation from the Chinese Y.M.C.A. to a reception given the members of the International Opium Commission on Wednesday Feb. 3rd. Prof. Burton has also made engagements that will facilitate our work. It appears that our coming has been made much of in the Shanghai press and opportunities of unexpected kind are opened to us.

Notes upon letter sent by John H. Snodgrass, Am. Consul at Kobe to Hon. Thomas J. O'Brien Am. Ambassador at Tokyo. Kindly loaned to us by Mr. O'Brien. Subject: Kobe Higher Commercial Salad: Is a Government Institution of which there are four, viz: one each at Tokyo, Yamaguchi, Nagasaki and Kobe, the Tokyo and Kobe schools being on the same level while the Yamaguchi and Nagasaki schools come next. There is a Higher Commercial School at Osaka which is under the control of the municipality. The ordinary commercial School in Japan is similar to the average Higher Commercial School of America, the Middle school being like a foreign Grammar School. Two courses in the Kobe institution, the preparatory and the principal course. Preparatory course consists of two classes, the average age of students being 19 yrs 8 months. The highest is known as the graduating class, the average age of students being 23 yrs. School has accommodations for 500 students; there are now 526 scholars. 92 were graduated in 1907; 142,1908; 102 are expected to graduate in March 1909. Curriculum of school includes: Book-keeping, Geography, Economics, Finance, Civil, Commercial & International Law and Languages. Of the latter each pupil takes English and one other language, either French German, Russian, Spanish or Chinese. Students take one year in preparatory course and three in the higher grade. Graduation ceremony in March of every year. Library consists of 5,000 vols. In Japanese & 3,500 in foreign languages. Chemical & electrical laboratories are filled with latest instruments for examination & experiments, including wireless telegraphy and X ray apparatus & a specimen of radium. The commercial museum contains collection of nature & foreign manufactures of great variety. Collection is under the immediate attention of an Am. Prof. of chemistry who examines specimens from time to time & lectures upon the subject. Teaching staff consists of 30 members; the applicants for admission in 1907 numbered 709.

Wednesday Feb 3rd. 1909

The essential features of Wednesday's work were a visit to consul Denby in the forenoon to advise respecting the visit to his Excellency, Viceroy Tuan Fang in accordance with his invitation of yesterday. A tiffin at Dr. Timothy Richards followed by a long conference in which Mr Richards set forth the essential points of his views. The attendance of a reception in the evening given by the Y.M.C.A. to the Opium Commission and between these events such conferences with Prof Burton as were possible.

The general attitude of Mr. Richards gained from this interview and subsequent conversations is this: China is to be advanced by finding the best in all fields of thought and bringing them in translating and disseminating them where possible and giving them personal propagation where this is possible. Mr. Richards appears to embody in these general propositions very much what is in our own minds save that the investigative factor does not appear to have so large and concrete a place in it as is natural from his personal history. Mr. Richards is not in sympathy, perhaps it might be said is pronouncedly opposed to sectarian propagation but this does not appear to be associated with bitterness that interferes with hearty cooperation with all good efforts. He seems genuinely broad minded and is a hearty whole souled, jovial, witty, keen, forceful workers: He belongs in the class of great men.

The Y.M.C.A reception afforded an opportunity to meet a large number of Chinese and American gentlemen and to observe their relations to one another. These seem to be most cordial and unrestrained. Of course it is to be observed that the assemblage was a selected one in the nature of the case, but there were not a few from distant points, both Chinese and foreigners. Some of the former were the imperial delegates to the Commission. There were brief address by the president of the association, Mr Wong, Bishop Brent and Pres. of the Opium Commission. Following this there was an exhibit of athletes and gymnastics under a new director who has been in charge about 2 months. The exhibit gave an opportunity to see something of the athletic capabilities of the young Chinese with very favorable results. It is fair to say that this is fully up to what might be expected from American boys under similar tutelage. It was heartly appreciated by both Chinese & foreign spectators & discriminatingly applauded. The Chinese appeared to be quite as keen & discriminating in the points appreciated as the Europeans. From several sources we gained the impression that this feature of the Y.M.C.A. movement is very important not alone in its direct physical effects but also in bringing together in an effective way the two peoples on a common ground of sympathy & interest. The appointments of the building are excellent and would be creditable in any American or European City.

Thursday Feb 4th. 1909

The forenoon was spent with Prof. Burton in conference. At midday a tiffin was given us in one of the private dining rooms of the Astor House by Dr. Gilbert Reid and members of the International Institute. At this Dr. Reid set forth at some length the nature and purposes of the Institute. Some notes on which appear in Tuesday's memoranda. Prof. Burton responded in part to the friendly words of appreciation of Dr. Reid and called upon me to say something also. Further remarks were made by an English and a Chinese gentleman. There were perhaps 35 persons present about equally divided between Chinese & foreigners. Cooperation was the central sentiment of the hour and was expressed in the social features of the gathering.

In the evening a special banquet was tendered the Commission by Messrs Y.C. and K.S.

Tong. The following were present: Tong Kai – Sou Yale '84, Lew Yuk Lin Chinese com to Opium Commission, F.L. Hawks Pott Columbia '83, Pres pf St. Johns College, Wong Chung Liang, Lehigh '83, H.B. Hawkins Wisconsin '05, John C. Ferguson Boston Univ. '86, Horace G. Reed Chicago '06, Taotai & interpreter to Viceroy was present at first interview. S.T. Tseng Yale '80, K.E. Charles D. Teuney Hamilton Wright Am member Opium Comm. Admiral C. Sah. Senior admiral of Chinese fleet Bishop C.H. Brent Trinity Col. Toronto '84. Philippines: Opium com. W.T. Hsii T.H. Lee Yale Pres of world's Chinese students' Federation R.T.C. Dr. Gilbert Reid Pres International Institute, Y.C. Tong. Columbia. Director of Telegraph, Dr. Timothy Richards '69 Director Shansi Univ & Pres Christian Literature Society H. West Wales Y.C. Wong Prof. Ernest D. Burton, T.C.C.

Admiral Sah opened the speaking with a few words of welcome and greeting. Tong Kai-Sou as toastmaster of the evening, made an admirable address in well chosen language, reciting the grounds of friendship between America and China, discretely omitting all references to causes of irritation between these nations and warmly welcoming the representations of Chicago University. At a signal from Mr Burton I responded citing the reasons which should prompt the peoples of the earth to come together in efforts to be mutually helpful and expressing our appreciation of the courtesies & honors shown us. Prof Burtons followed with supplementary remarks of like import. His main point was to urge that the dominant effort should be to get at the exact truth. He said that we do not come with a completed assemblage of truth or of doctrine to offer to the Chinese but rather to join them in an effort to find out what is true & best for both peoples. Prof Burton was followed by Hamilton Wright, Bishop of Brent, Pres. Pott Mr Ferguson, Gilbert Reid Teuney and Timothy Richard. The general purport was harmony and cooperation. The banquet was notable for its self rather than for what was said in that it was visible expression of cooperation and spontaneous interest in our mission since there were no circumstances that made it an obligation.

Friday Feb 5th. 1909

The day was spent under the guidance of Dr. Gilbert Reid who took us in an automobile generously placed at our disposal by Mr Tucker. Prof. Burton unfortunately took additional cold the previous evening and was confined to his bed. We went first to the Y. Ching Chang School which is under British direction and were shown through the essential portions of the quarters. Neither this nor other schools were in session as the Chinese holidays were not yet completed. The appointments were in part fairly good and in part inheritances of more straightened financial conditions. We saw no laboratories and very little apparatus of any kind. (There is pencil writing in between the lines written in different hand of the previous sentence which states as follows: We saw one small chemical laboratory which indicate the were begin in of modern scientific instruction). The work apparently was all subcollegiate. Connected with it was a girl's school which we also inspected and in which the appointments were on the whole superior of those of the boy's school.

After leaving the Y. Ching Chang school we passed near enough to catch an external view of the St. Xavier Catholic school but did not examine it. We next visited the Anglo-Chinese College of which J.W. Kline is principal. This is a Methodist institution associated, I believe with the Soochow College which is regarded as the main branch. The appointments were those of a struggling institution whose work is mainly preparatory and lower collegiate according to our standards. We next visited the Anglo Chinese School of which Mr Mouhle is master whose work lies within the range of our graded schools but of which we learned little. Next came a Chinese Public School under the municipal control. In the absence of school itself as in other cases we could only inspect the physical appointments which gave evidence of larger means and a fairly progressive spirit.

We next visited the Deutsche Medizin schule which we understand to be a semi private enterprise of much the same order as many of the American Medical Schools in the large cities in their incipient stages. The physical appointments so far as building, rooms etc are concerned were cheap & poor, but there was a fair supply of chemical and an atomical appliances with microscopes, testing apparatus etc. Apparently good work was being attempted under conditions of notable limitations. We did not find any of the principal workers present but the Chinese young men who showed us about seemed proud of what they were doing & glad to show it. Chief workers are Prof. Dr. Amman, Prof. du bois-Reymond.

We spent a short time in inspecting the premises of the Polytechniskum which seems, however, to be the name of a past enterprise & of a property than of anything having vital life at present. It was only represented as being a library but it was scarsely worthy of that name. The property is said to be quite valuable, i.e. would perhaps bring several tens of thousands of dollars chiefly on account of location suitable for business. The location is not good, nor the grounds sufficiently extensive to be serviceable for a college. There have been nogoiations looking to its union with the International Institute, but nothing is in progress at present. The enterprise I think was under the charge of Prof. Frier before he went to California and I think he is now endeavoring to resuscitate it. I think Prof Burton is informed on these points.

We called for a short time at the room of the World's Chinese Student's Federation. We were met by Mr Wong, Pres. of Y.M.C.A. and an officer of the Federation and refreshments were served us. We were shown about by Mr Lin, Secretary of the Federation & instructor in Technology in the Nanyang government college. The rooms consisted essentially of the reception room below & a lecture room accommodating 60-80, above. They are well situated on the corner of a block in a well settled district. A fair supply of periodicals are kept for the entertainment of members of the Federation. It is the hope of the Federation that it will be able soon to erect a building which may form a home for resident & transient Chinese students in foreign countries with reading rooms and appliances for laudable entertainment as well as sleeping rooms & cafe for transients. The general scheme is not unlike that of the Cosmos Club in Washington D.C. save that the latter is exclusively scientific. It is represented that students going to & returning from foreign institutions & stopping transiently in Shanghai are now forced by limitation of means into hotels or lodging houses of the inferior class and are subject to temptations, or else waste their means by stopping at hotels of higher order. Without our knowledge it was the purpose of Pres. T.H. Lee of the Federation to meet us as Dr Reid had indicated the previous evening that we would call but we left just before he arrived.

We visited at more length than in most cases the Mc Tyeire school of Chinese Girls under the auspices of the Methodist Church, South, Miss Richardson, Principal. We were shown about by the teacher of natural sciences and were pleased to see evidences of modern methods and spirit in the instruction and that good text books were in use. The appointments were fairly good though limited and the building and grounds excellent & pleasant. The principal was engaged in organizing students preparatory to beginning work on the following Monday. Here was the only place where we saw scholars. Miss Richardson discussed with perfect freedom many of the features of school in the presence of the scholars giving the impression that a spirit of frankness & mutual confidence prevailed. She spoke cordially of the ability & devotion of the scholars who were in the early teens mostly. She said that a part of their work was to teach the girls to play, from which on account of the binding of the feet they had been habitually shut out & hence were more accustomed to study & other sedentary pursuits than to those things that brought their feet into service. She seemed to be a woman of ability & adaptation to her work. Scholars of lower grade were being organized in other rooms which we visited. A notable feature was the rising of the pupils at a signal to salute visitors a courtesy which seems to prevail in the Orient. On the whole the impression made by this institution was decidedly favorable.

Next we took tiffin with Dr. Reid at his quarters at the International Institute where we met Mrs Reid, a former teacher in the Mc Tyeire School. This gave us an opportunity to see the buildings & grounds of the institute under more favorable circumstances than on the occasion of the unveiling of the memorial tablet on Tuesday. The grounds form a block perhaps 300 ft on a side. The buildings occupy the northern border leaving a large and pleasant lawn in front. The plans for future extension contemplate a quadrangle. There are two entirely vacant blocks of similar size lying next east & owned by a party who donated generously to the institute when it purchased its land from him. In 2 or 3 lots separated from these only by streets there are few buildings so that an enlargement to the extent of 4-5 bocks might perhaps be possible without involving land on which buildings have already been erected. The general location relative to the city is fairly good. The present buildings are substantial brick structures; practically all the better buildings in Shanghai are made of a bluish gray brick relieved by a light red brick both of which seem to be of excellent character.

In the afternoon we visited Li Ka Wei a Catholic Institution which embraces schools & an observatory associated With a large Cathedral. We only examined the Observatory and that only in part. The astronomical portion has been moved some distance from the city while the magnetic observatory has been moved to a more suburban point than the main institution which is itself well out in the suburbs. The street car lines are the main reason for removing these elements of the observatory. The meteorological portions only remain at the old center. We were shown not a little to our surprise weather maps of eastern Asia which are made out twice daily though only published in simpler form at longer intervals. The construction of these maps is made possible by the free transmission on the part of the telegraph companies of observations from various points. Some of these were as far away as Chung King on the upper Yang tze, Manchuria, Siberia, Japan, Philippines and South China. The last map showed a well defined high in N. Western China & a low over the China Sea. These imply a similar atmospheric movement to that which prevails in America and Europe and raises questions as to the trustworthiness of the impression which prevails in America that the cyclonic movements chiefly originate in N. Western North America. The work done at this observatory seemed admirable so far as could be judged.

We next visited St. John's College, passing on the way Nanying College a government institution said to rank next to the corresponding institution in Tientsin in size. It has about 400 students. There are several brick buildings pleasantly grouped, and a pleasant aspect. St. John's College is notably the most attractive institution visited, having a group of 5-6 attractive buildings, at the sizes & rear of a well kept, pleasant lawn adorned with a variety of shade trees. We met President Pott, Prof. Walker, Dr Lincoln and two other professors, and took tea with Mrs Pott and these gentlemen. The schoolrooms compare favorably with those of American Colleges and are of about the same order. There is a chemical laboratory with tables for 12 students the appointments of which are excellent. There is a physical laboratory with a supply of good balances and other apparatus for laboratory work in physics. There are also drawing tables of standard type. There was the beginning of a museum but it has not yet reached much development. A notable feature is a large assembly room with furniture which combine the features of opera chairs with movable tablets for lecture notes. There is also a very pleasant chapel in a building by itself, a notable feature of which is the complete supply of kneeling cushions, the physical expression of compulsory religions service.

We visited the woman's school associated with the college whose building stands in the rear of the college buildings separated by a high wall. The appointments here are of the same order as in the men's college, a notable feature being a large attractive assembly hall. Still further in the rear is a home for orphans. The grounds of the combined institution occupy a peninsula in the bend of a river, 5-6 rods wide. The use of this river by boats makes its bridging impracticable and thus the extension of the college grounds on the three sides occupied by the streams is embarrassed by the river while other buildings & occupied ground limit it in front. The question of extension has already become a serious one to the college with its present outlook & would embarrass any larger enterprise. Otherwise than this the ground on the opposite side of the river would be available as it is unoccupied by buildings for considerable distance. Pres. Pott's plan is to transfer the woman's college to some other location but this would only be a limited source of relief. The number of students expected at the term about to open is 400 of which about 80-90 would be in the college department. A catalogue and other documents containing statistical data were obtained.

In the evening, Mrs. Burton entertained Mr. Richard & his two daughters, and Mr. & Mrs. Frier and ourselves at dinner at the Astor House, Prof. Burton being unable to attend. After dinner conservation with Richard & Frier touched on various points which have bearings on the educational problem but no specific discussion was made.

Saturday Feb 6th, 1909

During the forenoon, Dr. Timothy Richard took me to see the several leading publication enterprises, Prof. Burton still being confined to his room. We first visited Dr. Richard's own enterprise, the Institute of Christian Literature and introduced me to the leaders of the several subdivisions. The institution is essentially devoted to the translation, publication and dissemination of such literature as is thought best. It has no printing department. A catalogue and other documents procured show the range & nature of the publications (q.v.). The institute at present has quarters in a rented building but is soon to move to quarters of its own which is now in the plastering stage. These quarters will be very excellent, the building being a substantial structure of brick with all sides free and hence suitably lighted. It is arranged that all the leading departments will have their chief offices on a single floor wheras now they are scattered through three floors. I saw at a little distance the printing establishment of the Presbyterian Press which is a large substantial brick building. I saw also at similar distance the printing establishment of the Commercial Press which is still larger, I believe the largest in China if not in the far Orient.

We called at the offices of the British Bible Society and off the Associated Tract Society and procured catalogues and other literature. We also visited the offices of the Presbyterian Press, the salesroom of the Institute of Religious literature and of the Commercial Press securing catalogues and other documents at each. These will show quite adequately the range and character of the work of these enterprises. At the salesroom of the Commercial Press the show cases showed a large assortment of drawing tools and of some of the more common scientific appliances. They seemed to be of a good order of workmanship. It was said that the Japanese instruments are not as satisfactory in practical service as in appearance, but of this I had no means for personal judgment. Without a more critical examination of the printed matter than I have been able to make as yet I can only record the impression of marked activity without forming an opinion as to the quality and good judgment of the work from the scientific point of view. In the afternoon R.T.C. spent 2-3 hours in inspecting a chemical establishment respecting which he will introduce notes below. During the afternoon I had a long conference with Prof Burton upon various matters connected with our enterprise.

R. T. C. Notes:

I was conducted to and shown about this institution by Dr Livio Silva. It is an analytical laboratory belonging to Brighten, Malcolm & Co who are also in Hong Kong. Mr. Z.D. King, Chinese, is director. Were about 8 Chinese guests invited to share in the inspection. Dr. Silva preformed some of the more showy operations of some of the processes of assaying & several other chemical experiments. Is a commercial analytical & assaying plant surprisingly well equipped. Much complicated and elaborate apparatus was in use at the time of my visit – determination of fats in yolk of egg. etc. Everything extremely neat. Won my admiration as a chemist. Better balances than at U. of C. I would have confidence in the results of any work done in this laboratory.

In the evening we attended by invitation the annual banquet of the World's Chinese Students Federation. Prof. Burton was unable to attend but Mr. Reid & Mr. Wang made up the party of four. The opening address was given in English by Tong Kai-Son, the central though being the great opportunity of the hour for educated Chinese students. A patriotic strain ran through the address. There followed three addresses in different Chinese dialects. Mr. T. H Lee, Pres. Of the Federation followed with an address, the central thought of which was altruism with definite application to the stage in historical development. Upon which we are entering, I was then called upon and spoke at some length upon the new and broader outlook which the present phase of scientific development presents. I took occasion at the close to urge a loyalty as an important factor and pointed out the disastrous effects of a seditious attitude such as that presented by many Russian students on the very objects they were mistakenly seeking though the objects are in themselves desirable and the provocation to disloyalty may be great. A Honolulu gentleman spoke in Cantonese and a Chinese student in Chinese. The speaking was closed by a short address by Dr. Richard summarizing the points of previous speakers and laying special emphasis on the points I had touched. There were perhaps 100 persons present.

Sunday Feb 7th. 1909

We had tiffin at Consul Denby's where we again met Mr Richard & Prof Frier & their families. Later in the day calls on us were made by Pres Procter and Pres. T.H. Lee.

Monday Feb 8th. 1909

The forenoon was chiefly occupied in preparations for visiting Nanking and stocking up provisions for the upper Yang tze trip. We took the noon train to Nanking arriving at 8.11 P.M. where we were met by Taotai U.K. Cheng, secretary of the Viceroy's Yamen and Councillor of the Bureau of Foreign Affairs, who escorted us to the Yamen of the Viceroy Tuan Fang. On the route from Shanghai to Nanking we made such topographic and industrial observations as practicable and these were supplemented by similar observations on the return trip on Wednesday afternoon, Feb 10th.

The country about Shanghai and thence to Soochow is an alluvial flat traversed at frequent intervals by canals and small streams from which a system of secondaries is developed so as to flood the rice fields which cover nearly the whole plain. Just now the waters are low and the winter crops of cereals are growing or being prepared for. Apparently these crops make nearly all their growth later in the season, for they were but slightly developed and in some cases preparation for the crops seemed to be in progress. Beyond Soochow there were hills and even moderate mountains in view on the left for the larger portion of the distance, i.e. until the Yang tze was approached. On the line of the railway and to the right (N.E.) the alluvial plain extended as far as the eye could reach, and was cultivated as above indicated.

To the N.W. as the Yang tze was approached the hills were more numerous and nearer at hand while in the vicinity of Nanking they prevail to the partial exclusion of the alluvial bottoms. In this region the cuts often show a deep deposit of which looks like secondary or aqueous loess and seems to be a deposit of greater age than the present alluvial flat but of similar character.

It was not clear just what this signifies historically. Its erosion features simply late Tertiary or early Quaternary age. The rock of the hill and mountains was rarely seen until the vicinity of Nanking was reached. It appeared to be in part igneous and in part stratified, the latter prevailing. At Nanking where we were permitted to see the formations at hand quartzite and quartzite conglomerate prevailed. The strata stood at high angles implying prevalent folding. The slopes are not generally stripped of soil though they rarely bear trees. Where we were able to examine them at hand in the northern outskirts of Nanking, the surface even where steep is mantled by a strong dull reddish or brownish soil. Tree planting was in progress and the doctrine of forestration seemed to be gaining practical hold. At a few points some miles S.E of Nanking rather serious gullying & wash were seen, but nothing approaching the destructive [actron] in our southern states was observed. The higher slopes do not appear to be cultivated except in the sense of bearing grasses. These did not appear to be cropped so exceptionally closely as reports led me to expect. In some places there were pines and brush on the uplands which bore the same aspect as our uncultivated and unpastured grounds. The terracing does not impress one as being pushed as far here as in Japan, nor on the whole did the population seem to be as dense as in the portions of Japan seen between Yokohama and Kobe but little weight is to be given this statement for the houses were much gathered into clusters (villages) and so there were considerable tracts that bore few houses. I think, however, the impression that this is not an over crowded tract is essentially true if by over crowded one means too dense for this kind of cultivation. Some of the steeper cuts near Nanking (not all) were admirably protected by stone gutters which were thrown into arches sometimes one above another which catch the slope wash and carry it down and laterally into the gutters that form the springing part of the arch as per diagram. The configuration of the mountains is much less knobby than that which prevails in the tract seen in Japan and more nearly corresponds to the American type with which we are familiar. This doubtless means that they are formed of sedimentary strata of fairly uniform hardness or at least of homogeneity of structure instead of igneous with its irregularities. Many of the hills were isolated by the alluvial plain which appears to have been built up about them. This perhaps implies relative depression. It may of course possibly imply a relative building up of the alluvial plain or a combination of the two. Observations on the coast tract lying to the southward should bear upon this point. Even where the ridges adjacent to the hills rise to heights of some tens or scores of feet are cut by the railway, they seldom show stoniness in the loose material but rather loess like alluvium.

The Nanking station is some distance (say ½ mile in a straight line) outside the Nanking wall and the present city is reached by a separate railway said to be the shortest in the Empire. It is perhaps 5 miles from the wall to the borders of the thickly settled portion of the city, a fact which indicates partially the degree of recovery of the modern city. The wall is said to be 35 miles in extent and so far as seen is now in good repair though it was necessary to rebuild it in parts to secure this. The city is said to now have 600 000 inhabitants while the former city had 3,000 000. In rebuilding it provision is being made for carriageways though these are only about half as wide as Chicago streets.

Soon after arrival we were escorted from the residence quarters where we were housed through quadrangles of the viceroys grounds to his reception and dining halls without the formality of change of dress. The viceroy came to meet us in front of the entrance and cordially invited us to enter where we found about 8 gentlemen awaiting us embracing Taotai Wen, Chinese officials & some recently returned students. Hermann F. Eusigner, a German, formerly in the consular service but now under the Viceroy of Hupeh, located at Hankow, was present. It may here be noted that he seemed to watch proceedings with keenness and aroused the suspicion that he might be doing so with special purpose, but this may be quite without foundation. We were invited at once to sit down to a quite elaborate banquet of Chinese order in the main. Bird nest soup, shark's fins, & other characteristic dishes making up the menu, but they were served with knives & forks in western fashion. Several wines were served in western style. The conversation interpreted by Taotai Wen related to a variety of subjects including antiquities, jade, jewels etc. At the close of the banquet he showed us some remarkable specimens of jade of unusual size and later some bronze articles recently excavated in the province of Shansi. The party broke up shortly before midnight. Further details regarding the yamen the viceroy's residence, viceroy etc are added by R.T.C.

R. T. C notes:

The Visit to Nanking. Reached Nanking station outside the city walls at 8.11 P.M. Met by Taotai U.K. Cheng who showed us into the ticket office while the other passengers waited outside. After 20 minutes perhaps the taotai put us in the viceroys private car on the branch line leading to the present city. Soon pierced the great wall and entered the former capital of the Empire but we were still in the open country. Only moorlands, groves of bamboo, and patches of still water where once a busy city flourished, gave a picture of the destructiveness of the terrible Taiping rebellion. Of the 3 000 000 people who lived within the wall of Nanking, only a few thousand survived the rebellion. Since then the city has partially recovered and has now grown to about 600,000.

The moon peering through a thin night mist which dimmed the edge of the lunar disc ever and anon reflected in the sheets of water lighted up the landscape and shed over the ravaged land an uncertain tragic light. We at length reached the living city and were driven through its streets to the Viceroy's yamen where we were lodged in the quarters fitted up for foreign guests. We occupied three very large rooms-the first a reception room where our interview with the Viceroy later was held, the second bedroom with two fine canopied beds, occupied by T.C.C. & R.T.C. and the third a like bedroom occupied by Prof. Burton. Adjoining this was the washroom. These rooms were arranged in a suite and constituted the whole of the left wing of the building. To the right of the main hall was an anteroom which led into a very large dining room where our meals were served with Taotai Wen usually presiding. The kitchen beyond doubtless completed the building. The walls were well covered with a great variety of paintings by foreign artists. Each room had a fire in the grate, and in addition was provided with an elaborate brazier and an excellent oil stove which was both ornamental and furnished a great deal of heat. The temperature even reached 73° the second evening of our visit.

The beds were made in Chinese style, the sleeper rolling up in the quilts which rested on the mattresses. The pillows (2 in no.) were about 8 x 24 inches, stuffed apparently with straw and very hard. Each morning when he visited us the Viceroy personally inspected these beds to see that we had been properly attended to. Before we arose in the morning the various servants swarmed in, attended to the fires & carried out our cloths which they afterwards returned with everything removed from the pockets, money, pocket books, notebooks, knives, pens, pencils, handkerchiefs, cards etc. etc which they piled separately on the table. They did not, however, humiliate me by taking a handful of copper cash (worth altogether $.02) from my overcoat pocket. Coffee and toast were served in our room as soon as we got up. Some time later a hearty breakfast was served in the main dining room.

Notebook
No. 2

Tuesday Feb 9th. 1909

At Nanking, Viceroy's Yamên. After a late breakfast in the dining room of the guests' quarter of the yâmen, prepared especially for foreign visitors we awaited the coming of His Excellency the Viceroy who appeared about noon attended by Taotai Cheng, who acted as interpreter, by the Superintendent of Education of the province, the Treasurer of the province and by the head master of the yamen schools which had previously visited during the morning, by the German H.F. Ensiguer and by other Chinese officials. There were present of our party Prof. Burton, T.C. Chamberlin, R.T. Chamberlin and Y.T. Wang, Mr Reid having remained at Shanghai. There followed a conference of one hour and forty minutes in which his Excellency the Viceroy, Mr Burton & myself chiefly participated but in which the Superintendent & Treasures also participated. Mr Burton and ourselves conferred subsequently in making up a skeleton of the interview which Mr. Burton will elaborate. Rollin took this down also & it is here inserted as a guard against loss.

Interview with His Excellency, the Viceroy Tuan Fang. In opening the interview His Excellency the Viceroy so directed his preliminary remarks to practically call upon T.C.C. for reply and so the earlier part of the interview was between T.C.C and His Excellency until later it was practicable to shift the interview to Prof. Burton. After some preliminary remarks of a general kind T.C.C asked what was the secret of China's stability through such long ages. The Viceroy responded by attributing it to patriotism and filial loyalty. His Excellency then asked whether it was the ancient or modern China in which we were most interested. T.C.C. replied modern and asked for particulars concerning the lines which Chinese schools were taking up. The Viceroy said there lines were mathematics, English etc. He stated that what China was weakest in was science. Then T. C.C stated his relation to the commission as a man of science. T. C. C asked what was most needed. Viceroy said: Industrials, agriculture & engineering. Prof Burton inquired which of the three following plans the Viceroy most favored. 1. Cooperation with the Chinese government in an educational institution, 2. An institution independent of the Government but subject to & conforming to its laws. 3. Cooperation with the mission schools. His Excellency strongly disapproved of the 3rd plan stating that while the mission schools train students so as to make good business men, these students do not make good government officials. To the question: what is the trouble with the Mission schools the Viceroy brought out the following points. (1) Religious training should be elective and not compulsory. (2) The students so not know the Chinese classics and hence are not in touch with Chinese ideas. Viceroy said Chinese students in America do not know Chinese classics. Could we not remedy this by having these students taught Chinese in American Universities. T.C.C. suggested that American students coming to China previously prepare themselves in Chinese before coming to China. The Viceroy did not fully comprehend this point because the interpreter (according to Wang) did not translate fully but abbreviated some of the ideas. The Viceroy said that of all the Chinese students abroad only three were competent to teach Chinese and that they were in Germany. His Excellency said that of the three alternative plans, the first cooperation with the Chinese Government, was the best. He dodged committing himself on the second, independent institutions. But he promised to put his views in writing for us.

Today's interview was to be informal. However he stated his strong preference for the first proposal. America could furnish the foreign professors, and the government the Chinese professors. The government also would be ready to furnish a part of the money also. The Viceroy at length asked: What is your real purpose? And what are Mr. Rockefeller's intentions in this matter? Prefacing his question by the remark that he realized its delicacy. (Note. This is not the exact way in which the question was put for it was a diplomatic question intended to hit anything in sight, but it gives pretty closely the points at which the Viceroy was aiming.). Prof. Burton responded: We shall be glad to answer frankly. We represent the U of C and not Mr. Rockefeller. The General plan has been under consideration 6-7 years. The means originally in sight failed. Now we are engaged in an inquiry only. Must report & nothing may come of it. Where will the money come from? The first means fail; Mr. Rockefeller has contributed tow thirds of the money which has gone with the U. of C.; may get money from Mr. Rockefeller. But Mr. Rockefeller has made no promise. The seriousness of our mission, however, is shown by the fact that the U. of C. has sent out this commission fully aware of the great expense which will be required to carry out any plans formed. We were most uncertain how we would be welcomed in our mission. The Viceroy was very cordial in his welcome of our mission and said that the idea of our being a nuisance was absurd. His Excellency said "You are not only welcome but the government is willing to furnish part of the money. But he added that if it had been Germany instead of America it would have been different. T. C. C pointed out the fact that we have both Government and private schools in the U.S and suggested that the best results are obtained by having both kinds of "institutions. The Viceroy said go and compare the two types of schools in China: U.S. a republic; China a monarchy. The Viceroy asked if we were going to Peking and said that he wished to telegraph ahead. He was confident the Minister of Education would approve of our plan.

Notes by T.C.C. In our visit to the yâmen school we found the boys and girls lunching together i.e. in the opposite ends of the room and were informed that they attended school together. They were however mostly under 12 years. The physical appointments of the school were not essentially different from those of American schools of similar grade. We understood that the children were chiefly those of the Viceroy's court. In the afternoon we visited the military school of the province located not far from the yamen. There are three grades of these (1) a school for officers now in service. It is intended to give them the education which they should have theoretically before entering service. Some of the members are in continuous residence & some come in from their commands for the lectures which constitute a part of the course. (2) a school for cadets, apparently on much the same general plans as that at West Point. We did not however inquire with details. (3) a school for younger boys preparatory to cadetship. We went through the barracks which were plain but comfortable. The cadets in the several rooms came to a standing portion at a sharp command on the appearance of our party in the corridor. Whether this was a salute to the general who showed us through or for us we did not know or inquire.

Later we visited some of the temples on hills in the outskirts of the city near the wall. One of these was Buddhistic; another Taostic; others were not designated. We climbed a pagoda associated with the temple of the north star and obtained an excellent view of the city and the surrounding country. See photographs. We also visited the place known as Hades (usually named in the English form) where there was a large collection of images illustrating the various punishments inflicted upon those who were condemned by the 10 several judges presiding over the several departments of misdomenors. The evening was spent in conference among ourselves and in making memoranda. Mr. Wan had an appointment with the Viceroy late in the evening. He was questioned rather pointedly as to our real mission implying some doubt in the mind of the Viceroy or else a desire for further confirmation. Mr Wang got the impression that the Viceroy did not fully realize the exact position which the commission occupies and the sufficiency of the purposes we assign as a reason for spending so much in sending so large a commission. It was clear from what was said at the banquet immediately after our arrival that the Viceroy supposed that we were commissioners of Mr. Rockefeller and were carrying out his wishes either respecting some educational purpose or some commercial one under educational cover. No doubt he had heard the newspaper reports which had been republished in the Shanghai papers. So far as we could learn the responses of Mr Wang were probably received with confidence for both of the Taotai's spoke of him the next day as a clean, conscientious boy.

Wednesday Feb 10th. 1909

We had made it known the previous day that it was necessary for us to leave on the noon train to catch the steamer China at Woo Sung forts that evening and the program of the forenoon was advanced on account of this. A reception by the educational authorities at the government normal school in the north border of the city was announced for 9.30 A.M. This was much more of an affair than we anticipated. The Viceroy attended by many officers among whom were the Superintendent of Education, the provincial treasurer, Taotais Wen & Cheng, officers of the army and many others came to our quarters in the yamen whence we proceeded in the court carriages to the normal school escorted by a mounted guard and preceded by the Viceroy's standard bearers. The carriages of the procession haltered somewhat more than a block from the entrance to the normal school grounds and proceeded thence between lines of soldiers, cadets and students to the entrance to the grounds where we found a canopy stretching from the building to the street and the pathway carpeted by reed matting.

The canopy was formed of colored cloths and this together with the decorations presented a gala appearance. At the entrance to the building we met the American consul, Judge McNally, Prof. Charles and Mr Carr an American instructor from Virginia together with magistrates and numerous officials. The reception room was decorated and even without this must have been an attractive room. With little delay we passed to a large room in an adjoining room where we were surprised by an elegant banquet with perhaps 125 covers. The tables were decorated at intervals by large bouquets, each of which was adorned with two Chinese and two American flags. When it is understood that this was ordered the day previous it shows enterprise as well as unusual courtesy. The menu consisted of ten courses beginning with swallow nest soup, sharks fins etc. After the third course it was necessary for us (T.C.C & R.T.C) to leave in order to catch our train (though Mr. Burton remained) .The Viceroy at that point read a speech setting forth his appreciation of our mission & our visit and expressed cordial sentiments toward our mission & the endeavors being made to promote mutual good. (I hope Prof. Burton secured the manuscript which was written on a large roll of yellow paper). To these remarks of his Excellency, Prof. Burton replied very felicitously after which the Viceroy escorted me to the door of the banquet hall and bade me good bye, Mr. Wang expressing for me thanks and appreciation. Taotai Cheng and Mr. Wang with attendants took us to the city depot where the Viceroy's special car took us to the Shanghai R.R. Station outside the city's walls. Not content with this we were handed tickets to Shanghai. After cordial farewell to Taotai Cheng & Mr Wang who returned to remain with Prof. Burton and subsequently go with him to Peking, we started for Shanghai. I have given these details at this length because they seem to bear definitely on the attitude of the Viceroy toward our mission after he had listened to a frank and full statement of the precise purposes of the commission though it is possible that he had given orders for the banquet previous to this statement. At any rate it shows his attitude toward the mission after our brief interview at

Shanghai.

The geological and physiographic notes made on the return trip have been microporated with those of the up trip. By the kindness of the officials of the railway, extended rather to other passengers of the Siberia who made the trip to & from Nanking at the same time, that we did, the train at Shanghai for the Woo Sung forts was held a little to insure connection and a special launch met it at the forts so that we reached the steamer China about 9 P.M and thus made good our connection to Hong Kong.

Thursday Feb 11th. 1909

On board Pacific Mails S.S. China en route to Hong Kong. All the water of the China Sea traversed during the day was pronouncedly yellow from the land silt. It seems improbable that all of this came from the Yangtze. Indeed a little before we were opposite the mouth of the Wu Kiang we encountered a sharply defined reddish roily water which undoubtedly had a local origin in the adjacent land, perhaps from the river named. This was 6-10 miles from the head lands which were themselves some miles from the mainland. The configuration of the coast islands wherever seen during the day was of the familiar mountain type rather than the pronouncedly knobby Japan type. The basal horizon could not be seen but the lower slopes favored the view that they entered the sea abruptly. This seemed to favor relative depression of the coast in recent geologic times if not in progress at present. At one point the island seemed to be formed of highly inclined strata.

Impressions concerning the attitude of Viceroy Tuan Fang. Reflecting on all the incidents of our interviews with the Viceroy and his unusual courtesies to us I am convinced that he is really deeply interested in the outcome of our mission. It is evident that he strongly favors cooperation with the government. His silence on the proposition to establish independent institutions is probably significant but perhaps does not mean opposition if they are established on a basis which looks primarily to the benefit of China and does not introduce an objectionable foreign element. He appears to be declaredly opposed to the mission schools with compulsory religious attendance but is perhaps not really hostile to their existence. He did not seem cordial toward the proposition to improve them, though he gave no evidence of hostility toward them. The point which he made that they are un-Chinese (not necessarily anti-Chinese) in influence is one that was very strongly taken & is difficult to meet. His suggestion that the details of cooperation would need to be very carefully studied is certainly pertinent.

Further details of our visit to the Viceroy. After our arrival at the yamen and without change of dress we were escorted from our quarters through the grounds by winding pathways and across an artistic bridge to the Viceroys reception quarters where he met us. His Excellency was very easy in his manner of welcome and throughout all our relations with him. He sat at the end of the table at the banquet with Prof Burton on his right & T.C.C on his left. Next to Prof Burton was Ensiguer the German who did some interpreting occasionally. Next to him was Wang followed by Taotai Wen. I sat next to T.C.C; on my left was Taotai Cheng who acted as chief interpreter throughout the evening. His Excellency asked a great many questions which kept the interpreter busy. Sometimes he spoke directly to the person addressed and sometimes he faced the interpreter. He asked me as a geologist if in America we found strata containing relics of former civilizations. I cited Mexico & the fact that it is supposed that this civilization came from Asia across Bering Straight. Some talk about stones with characters & inscriptions. His Excellency suddenly asked if the bluish green spots sometimes found on specimens of jade were produced by the influence of gold. A bad question to face. I replied that that was a subject about which His Excellency knew more than I. This reply provoked a general laugh. The Viceroy looked puzzled and apparently did not know what to make of it. This was the only time I saw him in the least ill at ease. The Viceroy then told how certain pieces of jade after being buried for a long time became brownish in color and the buried part became slightly lowered. A keen observation for later he showed such a jade. The discolored portion had lost a certain amount of matter in the chemical or weathering progress & so was slightly lower than the mattered green jade. His Excellency after the driver showed us a splendid collection of objects of jade ranging from watch charms to large vases. Also a fine set of bronze ware discovered only a few years ago in the province of Shansi. This dates from the 1st Han dynasty.

The Viceroy wore clothes which were entirely black and to us at least gave no indication of his rank. He was rather a large man for a Chinese standing about 5 ft 7-8 inches and being rather stout. At the table we noted his rather slow movements and dull eyes, but His Excellency was far from being well at the time of our visit. Judge McNally, American consul remarked at the banquet just before we left for Shanghai that the Viceroy did not look nearly so well as when he last saw him. The Viceroy spoke very slowly & deliberately. He did not stand on form; once when I was not quite near enough to see the bronzes to the best advantage he took me by the arm and led me up closer. During the early part of the dinner the Viceroy led us to drink toasts. He was always supplied with wine glasses only half full which he drained and then held upside down inviting us to drain our full glasses. Things looked serious but after a time he stopped, perhaps divining our wishes in that matter.

During the interview the Viceroy smoked a great deal from the typical long metallic Chinese pipe. He would put in a pinch of tobacco, light it with a burning stick of straw or punk which he blew into flame, and take (while lighting the tobacco) generally three puffs (though occasionally two and sometimes four never more) this was all the smoke he got from the tobacco. He then removed the metallic tube holding the tobacco and from the opposite end blew the partially consumed tobacco into a cuspidor. This tube he refilled with another pinch of tobacco and repeated the operation. This operation must have been performed some forty times during the interview of an hour & forty minutes. It impressed me as an enormous amount of work for a very unsatisfactory smoke.

The Viceroy wore black silk cloths trimmed with pure white fur. His hat was a dark fur trimmed with red and included a tuft at the top. The officials present wore similar hats which were never removed. The Viceroy, however, apparently a trifle weary for he had been working hard did lay aside his cap for a short time but soon resumed it. On Tuesday morning the Viceroy formally closed the period of New Year's vacation and opened the period of work in the presence of many high officials and soldiers at one of the open buildings. He kept the assemblage waiting a long time. The ceremony consisted in "Kaotaoing" or kneeling down with his back toward the sun & his face toward Peking where the Emperor resides. The Viceroy kneeled down on cushions and bowed very low three times as an official behind him called out in a loud voice each time "kaotao, kao tao, kao tao" (bow down, bow down) This was repeated by threes until the Viceroy had prostrated himself nine times when he got up, went over to another kneeling place and kao taoed 3 x 3 again. This ended the ceremony. When we went to the reception & banquet Wednesday morning we drove in the vice regal style – mounted officers, two wagons of lackeys, the two light red standards in front. The arrangements could hardly have been better if it had been a visiting Viceroy who was being entertained.

Friday Feb 12th. 1909

Off the China coast, 2nd day from Shanghai. Water clearer but not of typical Pacific blue. The lower quantity of silt probably due to our getting further south from the yang tze and being at the same time farther from land. Mostly out of sight of land during the day. Passed an occasional island. Weather slightly warmer, clear, gentle breeze N. Easterly.

Saturday Feb 13th. 1909

Approaching Hong Kong harbor at 7 AM. Rounded, rather steep contours of the islands. Seen at a few miles distant the slopes appear to descend without change of curve to the water level. No sign of raised beaches or sea cliffs discernable on the most careful search with glasses. On closer approach even to the fraction of a mile no raised beaches could be detected. The present beaches were scarcely more than the bottoms of small sea cliffs. Little or no horizontal extension of the outer beaches was seen. The sea cliffs were distinctly limited not appearing to be over 20-30 ft. though this estimate must be taken with allowance. At places the gullies and gulches did not seem to be truncated by the sea cliff but to hold their configuration as if they had been formed when the slope extended farther down. In short every feature seemed to imply a coast depressed in quite recent times. This is quite in harmony with the inlets and the isolated islands of the coast. Next the harbor of Hong Kong there is more evidence of foots lope and of aggradation at the water level but this is limited being confined so far as we observed essentially to the lower edge of the city of Victoria and that of Kowloon opposite.

What we observed during the three days of our stay at Hong Kong relative to the geology of the vicinity may be put down together. The main and at the same time the oldest formation observed is a granitic mass of soft largely disintegrated nature which shows very little evidence of structure. It embraces numerous large boulder like inclusions which are sometimes surrounded a concentric foliation extending for a few inches, rarely more than six, with the adjacent disintegrating mass but beyond that do not seem to affect it. In many cases in the upper portion of the disintegrating mass the boulders are well isolated and well rounded. At some points in lower portions shown by deep excavations the masses were more closely associated and had the appearance of grading into a mass of undisintegrated rock except along joint planes. The undisintegrated rock so seen was a gray or slightly bluish porphyritic granite of course texture. It showed little or no evidence or structure other than massive and should probably be classed as massive igneous granite of the batholitic type, though not necessarily constituting a batholith. The disintegrated granite had a reddish hue and the contrast between this and the gray granite was often striking and sharply defined. Occasionally there were boulders of reddish or pinkish hue.

On the hills back of Kowloon opposite Hong Kong there were at places numerous large boulders ranging up to a considerable number that were 20-30 ft in maximum diameter with a few of larger dimensions and one at least 50 ft in length and probably not much less in breadth and depth. Although a mile or thereabouts back of the center of Kowloon this boulder could be distinctly seen from the heights of Victoria on the opposite side of the harbor. These boulders which were weathered out and lying on the surface were sometimes perched and had clean, fresh looking surfaces giving them an appearance quite sharply in contrast with the disintegrated granite on which they rested, but this may be due to the removal of the exterior as fast as it weathers. The boulders and disintegrated granite are best exhibited back of Kowloon, but they may be seen in certain portions of Victoria. The question early arose in inspecting the formation within and back of Kowloon whether these boulders were merely the centers of blacks of a common massive granite which had disintegrated about them in the well-known concentric fashion and left them as the relatively undisintegrated nuclei of the common mass, or whether the more disintegrated mass had once been an arkose accumulated as an aggradation deposit at the base of mountains of granite into which boulders of a firmer character had rolled from the mountain heights thus producing a boulder bearing bed of arkose which had again somewhat solidified by metamorphic action and is now undergoing denudation and a second disintegration. There are some evidences that support both hypotheses and both may possible be true in different portions observed. Perhaps the most pointed evidence supporting the second hypothesis was seen in the cut of the railway now being constructed from Kowloon to Canton at a point perhaps a mile North of the former where, near the base of a deep cut two alternated beds of claylike material were seen. These looked much as though they were lens like sheets of clayey material that had been deposited in the arkose while it was accumulating. These claylike lenses had a minute texture as though they had once embraced orthoclase crystals which have since disintegrated giving a speckled whitish cast to the reddish mass. It is therefore possible to interpret even these masses consistently with either of the above hypotheses. The mountainous portion of the mass back of Victoria so far as seen near the peak which was the only portion visited was found to be formed of basic rock of diabasic or doleritic aspect.

On the northern slope at points within the city this has the appearance of having been intruded into the granite material above described. We saw a little granite about the peak. Where the basic rock intrudes the granite it appears very much fresher and either it is much more resistant to weathering (which is probably true to come extent) or is very much younger and perhaps intruded the granite after it was already partially disintegrated we did not have time to satisfactorily determine. Aside from what might most probably be regarded secondary deposits from the formations above described we saw no sedimentary formations, either old or young. The slopes of the mountain back of Victoria are generally steep but on the north the gradient becomes notably more gradual as the water is approached leaving a narrow foothold for the city. The disintegrated character of the granite which seems to underlie most of the city and the lower slope of the mountain greatly facilitates the cutting of the beautifully curved roads and the building of terraces upon which most of the residences are placed. The configuration of the mountain has been much as to give to the roadways and paths that have been laid out upon its slopes with skill & good taste a naturalness & beauty which no art could probably have given them unaided.

I know of no city whose roadway & paths equal those of Victoria in real beauty and this is markedly enhanced by the semitropical vegetation with which it is associated. Between the harbor, the mountains, the roads, the gardens, lawns & terraces and the picturesque architecture with abounding porticos, loggias and colonnades, the city is on the whole, I think, the most beautiful I have ever seen. This attractiveness together with the high attitudes immediately accessible and the climatic effect of the ocean make it a suitable site for a great institution of learning. When the Kowloon & Canton railway is finished and the Canton-Hankow R.R. is also finished, it will have direct railway communication with eastern Asia and Europe at once, and with its abundant water way connections will be a convenient center to which a great mass of population might be made tributary. From what I have thus far learned I entertain the view tentatively that the Cantonese and perhaps the people of South China generally are peculiarly well adapted to become a leading people in the development of the tropical zone particularly in Asia and Polynesia and perhaps throughout the globe. They appear to have an industry and frugality which is phenomenal for a people in so low latitude. It is true that the climate of South China within the tropical zone is cooler in winter than most regions of the same latitude and altitude, but it also appears from such testimony as we have as yet been able to gather that the Cantonese retain their activity, industry, frugality and reliability even in the heart of the tropical belt where many of them now occupy important places in competition with the native populations and other Orientals.

This is a matter to be studied further and independently of the problems which center in Hong Kong but the matter is here introduced because it gives importance to the problems of Hong Kong and has been a subject of study in connection with various features of the geographic situation and physical features of Hong Kong. It appears to me that one of the great educational opportunities of the Orient lies in developing here an educational system completed a university of a high order so shaped as to develop the better element of the people of South China into material fit for assuming an important function in solving the great problem of the evolution of the human race in the tropics. Our observations on the Chinese of Hong Kong and vicinity are chiefly confined to those engaged in service as waiters, the jurikisha men, chairmen, porters and the people seen in the parks, gardens and streets on Sunday. Of these the porters are probably the most representative for they seem to be of various classes, some in employ & some on their own account. They were engaged in carrying all sorts of commodities from telegraphy poles and lumber down to fruits, flowers and cakes. Almost without exception they were brisk in their movements and seemed almost wholly free from the indolence that is so common among workers in employ. They were generally quiet and respectful, helping to yield the way even when the more heavily loaded. On the whole civility was very marked among all classes of Chinese met. Those seen in the parks were quiet and courteous. The rickshaw & sedan men where conspicuously less persistent and annoying in their efforts to secure patronage than those of Japan, and very notably less so than those of Nagasaki where they were very persistent and annoying. The percentage of pleasant and attractive faces among the Chinese is notably high. Faces showing dissipation or bearing an evil aspect were extremely rare.

Monday Feb 15th. 1909

Made arrangements for trip up West River to Wuchow and saw about return to shanghai on the S.S. China; visited West Hong Kong including Queen's College which we found surrounded by Chinese settlements; called upon Consul General Amos P. Wilder and later received a return call from him; arranged with him for statistical meteorological data; discussed with him qualities of the Chinese and in the afternoon took boat for Wuchow. The boat traveled west-ward, then northward and then westward amid hills until the channel debouches into the lower part of Canton Bay. Darkness here cut off further observations.

Tuesday Feb 16th. 1909

When observation began we were ascending the West river and the surrounding country was an alluvial flat. Well rounded hills were in sight ahead and from this time to midday when we reached the entrance to the Pearl or East river near Sam Shui hills were in sight nearly constantly on both sides of the river though more abundantly on the west side. In general they increased in numbers and in height to the northward. The alluvial flats lay among these hills and joined their bases at a rather sharp angle. The sides of the hills next the river frequently showed cliffs of moderate height

due apparently to river cutting. Otherwise there were no evidences of sea cliff or elevated terraces. The alluvial flats were generally 15-20 feet above the river at its present stage but are said by the officers of the ship "Lintan" to be occasionally submerged at high water stages. The hillslopes carried only a scant tree vegetation consisting so far as could be seen with a glass, of Chinese pine of small size. The surface was generally covered with grass which was usually gray; only a small amount of greenish vegetation was seen on the slopes. The higher hills were generally gullied, particularly the range west of Sam Shui which was very notably creased by erosion; even its crest lines were sagitate or crenate apparently from the meeting of gullies on opposite sides. The most of the gullies and ravines were turfed with grass but at some points fresh gullying exposing soil and rock was observed. The amount of destruction due to gullying was not pronounced though sufficient to be worthy of note. The scantiness of the hills is a matter of surprise when the amount of rainfall particularly that in the summer – unless I am in error – is considered. The problem of utilizing the hills seems to be a very important one if the full reach of vision upon both sides of the river observed during the forenoon somewhere near one half is occupied by hills and of the hill surface very little seems to be cultivated. Some terracing was observed but the amount was small relatively. It does not appear that the timber produced is of more than trivial consequence. The pines were small, slender and singularly scattered. They were rarely clustered so as to produce a thick grove. Their foliage was apparently little more than a bunch at the top. We could not see signs of underbrush of any appreciable [amount]. The rock of the hills could not usually be detected. In some part it appeared to consist of igneous intrusions of the greenstone type. In a few cases stratification could be detected feebly and this appeared to be inclined. The hills were without any conspicuous alignment or systematic arrangement. We could not detect any uniform summit heights or any traces of an old peneplain. If such once existed the erosion appears to have quite destroyed it. With the exception of the range west of Sam Shui I should guess the hills rarely reached 1000 ft and were mostly below 500 ft.

The range west of Sam Shui probably reaches 1000-1200 ft and perhaps at points 1000 ft. The lower hills were often well rounded with clean smooth slopes. Very little talus was seen on any of the slopes. Apparently the soil covering is thin and this is probably a radical factor in the limited vegetal covering and the scantiness of the cultivation. The mate of the ship stated that he thought the soil was poor & thin and that this was the reason the hills are not cultivated. He also thought the hot sun and the small rainfall in certain seasons was the cause of the scant tree growth. He said that the Chinese were chiefly disposed to raise water crops, that they would not raise potatoes though they would grow in a dry soil that these habits were one reason for neglecting the slopes. We noted that the north slope of the high ridge west of Sam Shui was scarsely more clothed with trees than other exposures, but if the summer sun is the essential factor in limiting the tree growth this might not be a significant fact as the sun is here vertical at and near the summer solstice. On the alluvial flats and some of the very low hills fine trees of several varieties were common. Among those noted were the banyan, camphor tree, and the joss tree. The joss trees were naked; the others in full leaf. In Sam Shui we saw several significant camphor trees. Many of the houses and villages had tree clusters about them giving an attractive aspect to the plains. About the houses were fruit bearing trees known as lychees. We saw little or no shrubbery fruit bearing or otherwise; bamboo thickets were rather common. We saw no bamboo growing on the hills. Mulberry plants cut back to the ground and just beginning to send up shoots were pointed out.

This is said to be the practice here presumably to secure a thrifty leafy growth accessible for collecting to feed the silk worms. The soil of the alluvial flats is of a buffish hue and so far as seen at hand loess-like texture. It appeared to be better drained than the flats of Japan and of the Shanghai region but this may have been due to the point of view. A notable feature was the frequent occurrence of tall square windowless towers pierced with loopholes, which are known as pawn shops which function they really serve but which is quite subordinate to that of the safekeeping of valuables of various kinds. The structures are made with a view to being proof against burglars, robbers and enemies of all kinds and to be suitable for defense by guns used through the loopholes. It is said that jars of vitriol are kept on the top and are thrown upon assailants. Another singular feature was literary poles, resembling ships' masts with square platforms on them. These stood always in fairs in front of some of the larger houses and served to indicate the classical degree obtained by some member of the family. Poles with one platform signify Ku Yan (promoted men) which are equivalent to our Masters of Arts. Poles with two platforms belong to the Tsun Sze (Entered Scholars). Examinations for this degree are held triennially in Peking. It corresponds to our LLD. Three platforms belong only to those who have passed the fourth and highest degree, called Hon Lum (Forest of Pencils). This is more of an office than a degree. Examinations for this degree are held triennially in Peking in the Imperial Palace at Peking in the presence of the Emperor himself. The number passing is variously stated from 14-40. The highest graduate on the list is regarded as the greatest scholar in the world and his fame spreads throughout the empire. This chief scholar is said to be invariably a millionaire or else a Manchu.

During our stop of several hours at Sam Shui we were piloted through the shops and temples of the city by Mate and Chief Engineer of the Lin-Tan and saw the Chinese who are here said to be relatively poor at their various occupations, the details of which are too tedious for record here. We also strolled across the fields to the nine storied Pagoda which stands half a mile outside the walls of the city and incidentally observed the dikes, paved paths and other features of the region. A railway from Canton has been constructed to this point and is said to be destined to go indefinitely farther westward. The traffic by junks sanpans & other boats on the West river and the branch of the East river is notably large and the cluster of boats at Sam Shui was very considerable. The ingenuity displayed in giving these boats almost incredible loads by attaching reed rafts to their sides and by other devices is very noteworthy and the activity shown in handling them equally so.

The observations made on the West river to the westward from San Shui made in the late afternoon will be included with those made farther west tomorrow and those added on the return trip. Numerous photographs were taken during the day which see for further record.

Wednesday Feb 17 th. 1909

The geological observations of the evening of the 16th and of the 17th and 18th are here merged because they relate to sections of the West River and constitute a practical unity. The whole tract from the mouth of the North river near Sam Shui westward to Wuchow is a hilly submountainious tract with a very few points exceeding 1500 ft; quite a number between 1000-1500. But the average hills range from 100-500 ft. In all the portions passed by daylight on the up and down trips the valley is a trench in a hilly upland ranging roughly from a mile in width measured at the surface of the floodplain, down to perhaps an eighth of a mile in the narrows the so-called "gorges." The popular descriptions which make these gorges vertical sided clefts are quite erroneous.

The riverward side of the hills is almost everywhere a slope & is not appreciably steeper than other slopes. The hills are everywhere much dissected and do not appear to constitute definite ranges but merely be erosion remnants of a rather easily degraded rock. The lower hills are somewhat more notably rounded than the higher hills. The slopes are generally notably high. The more eastern portion seemed to be possibly composed of igneous rock of dark type, but the western portion is chiefly made up of reddish rock which rarely shows definite bedding or other declared structure. Where examined close at hand at and in the vicinity of Wuchow the material was found to be made up chiefly of a reddish sandy, clayey material of rather nondescript type with here and there dark bluish portions that did not seem to differ much in constitution. I incline to regard the whole as an alluvial aggradation deposit of great thickness. We saw no fossils nor anything to give definite evidence of the age of the deposit but the suggestion that it is a member of the Jura-trias series has perhaps some slight grounds for preference tentatively.

On the north side of the river near Wuchow the surface is but scantily covered with vegetation leaving much bare surface exposed and giving the whole a patchy reddish aspect. The surface so exposed is not however hard rock but either semi indurated material or stormy soil. There is much exposure of the soil or rock eastward on the north side of the river. On the south side the surface is more fully clothed with vegetation and considerable wood covers the surface but this rarely reaches a dense forest. Usually it is an open scattering of small pines of the Austrian pine type so far as seen near at hand. We saw little other arborous vegetation on the hills. Occasionally bamboos were seen on the lower slopes.

At one point on the Wuchow peak we saw a small cluster of bamboos at 630 ft above the river – perhaps 800 above sea level. We saw very little shrubbery and that of little appreciable use. A coarse reedlike grass seems to be the chief vegetation in addition to the pines. I could see no reason in the nature of the case why practically the whole surface should not be covered with trees or with profitable grasses for the rock is apparently soft enough to permit the penetration of roots and to disintegrate into soil readily. Why there should be the observed difference between the north and south sides of the river in respect to vegetation is naturally referable to the exposure of the north side to the sun in greater degree than on the south side with its north exposure.

Observations from the Wuchow Peak 1200 ft (aneroid read 1180) did not seem to support this view very well. For the views eastward, northward and westward showed about equal exposure of soil to the full distances of satisfactory observation. The erosion in the vicinity of the Wuchow peak was very pronounced, developing everywhere sharp V shaped valleys with very straight side slopes and practically no talus or aggradation until the river level was approached. Wherever practicable the lower parts of the valleys were graded into paddies for rice fields. Very little slope cultivation was seen though there were a few instances. The cultivation is practically confined to the alluvial bottoms. These are not notably large and the impression given is rather that of a sparse population than a dense one. Even the low slope did not seem to be terraced in general for cultivation and the extent of bamboo and other trees on the alluvial ground suggested that even this is not forced into cultivation as fully as it might be. I am much more impressed with the magnitude of the slope & hill problem in this region. At a rough guess I should say that not more than 5-10 percent of the country adjacent to this section of the West river outside the West river bottoms themselves is under cultivation and the hilly ground while worth something in its present condition is yielding but a minor fraction of its probable possibilities.

Physiographically the most striking feature of the country about Wuchow is the highly dissected topography which almost constitutes a type in itself but is closely allied to badland topography where the rock material is essentially uniform. It is certainly not a very old topography. It is perhaps to be regarded as a topography near its maturity and hence having the maximum relief and steepest slopes. No clear indication of the original surface out of which the carving took place was detected. So far as we examined closely enough at hand to identify the rock material we found no indication of intrusions though not a few observations made at some distance with field glasses gave the impression at the time, of intrusions. I am however inclined to regard these with skepticism. The topography does not lend much support to the suggestion of intrusions. Sufficiently washed. (written in pencil)

Thursday Feb 18th. 1909

Interviews with Capt. H.W Holmes of the SS. Lintan 1st Officer, Thos Donaldson, Chief

Engineer T.H. Gibbison of the Lin-tan with Van Aalst, Commissioner of customs, acting British Consul Harding, Dr. C.A. Hayes, Dr. J.G. Meadows, Mr. Trifton and Mr. Clive, harbor master. The officers of the ship were decidedly pro-Chinese in their general attitude, so also in general were all the others with perhaps the exception of Consul Harding whose general attitude respecting recent movements seemed rather pessimistic. The interview with commissioners van Aalst was the most instructive. Socially he regards the Chinese as an incompatible element but he believes that the new movement in education and reform has come to stay. He expressed his views in a statement that preeminence moves with the sun; that in early times it lay in the near east, moved westerly into western Europe; is now centering in America which is leading the world in inventions and will later pass to China which will be the foremost nation of the earth. Respecting the apparent sparseness of people along the West river he found a cause in piracy which he says is little more than petty thieving by people who make their attacks and make their escapes by boat. He cited an Emperor two centuries ago who ordered the people to withdraw from the coasts and main rivers for some distance perhaps 15 miles to avoid these attacks.

Subsequent statements made by Consul Harding and others did not seem to wholly confirm this view and seemed to support the general impression gained from the river view that this west country is not very densely populated compared with China in general. He stated that a school of forestry & agriculture had been established about 1907 at Kwei-lin, the capital of Kwang si and that they had imported Japanese instructors but that they had recently left alleging treatment as hirelings rather than as equals as the reason. In the line of productions he cited the superior equality of the Kwang-Si rice. He believed that the camphor tree might be cultivated with profit though this was said rather with reference to the province of Fu Kiev than Kwang Si. The views of meadows, Hayes & Tifton were of the usual missionary type. They did not give much testimony from the medical point of view & I gathered the impression that they had not yet come to a representative medical or surgical view. They spoke favorably of the physiological condition of the Chinese as shown by the usual progress of recovery after surgical treatment.

Messrs Hayes & Tifton took us to see one of the middle schools recently established which indicated some appreciable progress in education. The fact come out that temples are being converted into schools. A large normal school has recently been constructed but this we did not see. Military drill was in progress at the middle school. We saw anatomical charts, stuffed birds, mineralogical specimens which indicated some modernization. Commissioner Van Aalst gave us a tiffin at which the British Consul Harding & harbor master, Clive, were present.

The West river recently rose 67 ft above its low stage submerging the lower floors of the best residences in the city. What we saw in traversing the town indicated prevailing poverty which is indeed the acknowledged condition of the province of Kwang Si generally. Wood & wood products, chickens & nature cattle seemed to constitute the main traffic downstream. An antimony smelting plant has be erected here but we could learn little about its success or the origin of its ores. It was reported that the ores were surface finds & were uncertain in supply. The impression prevailed that the mineral deposits of the back country are considerable & varied. Iron, silver, lead, tin and antimony were mentioned but the information was vague and uncertain in value. As indicated above in the geological notes the supreme problem of this region seems to be the utilization of the slopes. Our impression is that there is a problem which can be solved here with a high measure of success by suitable investigation and by persistent & well controlled effort. The establishment of the school of agriculture & forestry at Kwei-lin is a step in the right direction, but the length & breadth of the problem is probably far from being realized by the government here and perhaps this might be said of governments universally, all of which have the problem of the slopes before them as yet unsolved satisfactorily.

Rev. J.G. Meadows Missionary of the South Baptist Board studied at U. of C at one time. Mr Thomas Donaldson, mate of the lintan says that near Lung Wun Tung up the Yang tze toward Chung King coal is obtained that is the equal of the best Welch coal. Gives little smoke or ash. Kwang Si is thought by most of the people seen to be rich in universal resources. Capt. Holmes said the average summer temperature in the neighborhood of Wuchow was 97°-103°. Said Hong Kong was much cooler. Both Capt. Holmes and Mate Donaldson stated that during the summer months the heat was more oppressive at Hankow than at Wuchow or Canton. Air Still (dead they called it) and no clouds in sight day after day. This question of Hankow climate is an important matter. We shall see it only in the spring and will not be able to judge of the summer climate. Perhaps have work done in Hankow in the winter and move to the hills during the hot season. Two separate terms with two sets of instructors (one foreign, other Chinese). Foreigners at Hankow in winter; Chinese there in summer.

Friday Feb 19th. 1909

Went from Sam Shui to Canton by train & spent the rest of the day in the study of the city. In the first half of the distance between Shui & Canton the railway crosses several low ridges or rather clusters of hills making cuts in them. A few of these showed indurated rock in their lower portions the character of which was unidentifiable from the train. The beds were usually inclined. The upper part of all the cuts and the larger part of most of them was made up of scarcely coherent sandy, clayey, sometimes gravelly material, the deeper part of which was usually stratified. It did not look older than tertiary or even old Quaternary. Apparently the hills are remnants of a widespread thick mantle which was extensively eroded before the present stage of alluvial aggradation was inaugurated.

These observations raised some question as to whether these hills should be classed with the high & much eroded hills of the West river country or not. It does not appear from any present positive evidence that they might not all belong to one great formation, but on the other hand these less coherent, more rounded and lower hills may be the remnants of a mantle derived from the formation of the West river country, and from the North river country. The country along the route from Sam Shui to Canton except those hills is occupied by a low alluvial flat generally covered with rice fields & similar water crops. This was notable true of the portion toward Canton. In this part the hills which were generally lower & had gentler slopes were partially occupied by terraces which were cropped. Otherwise the slopes showed little but grass. They have not suffered much from gullying and bare surfaces were not very common or extensive.

Saturday Feb 20th. 1909

Spent most of the day in visiting the White Cloud Hills N by N.E of Canton. The chief purpose was to see what topographic possibilities there might be in the vicinity of Canton for securing relief from the heat of summer and from the wetness and unwholesomeness of the flat lying country. The White Cloud chain of hills was found to really begin in the northern suburbs of the city. The five storied pagoda which rests on the north wall of the city between the two north gates stands on an eminence belonging to this chain. A temple surmounting a hill to the S.W. of the five storied pagoda lies within the wall. It is perhaps 100 ft above the flat land lying between it and the river and perhaps not more than two miles from the river. We found the general topographic aspect and the exterior of the whole chain of hills very similar to those near the West river. The original rock which was only seen in a decomposed or highly weathered form was of the granitic type but the exterior of the hills except in a few places chiefly in shape gullies were deeply veneered with decomposed rock forming what was rather a crude soil than an indurated rock. There appears to be no reason in the nature of the mantling material why the hills should not be densely clothed with forest.

Nearly the whole chain of hills is covered rather thickly by tombs or perhaps rather by peculiar movements that commemorated entombment but whose full significance we do not know. They consist of concentric horseshoe-like walls partially surrounding on the uphill side stone platforms which projected somewhat in advance and was terminated by a low wall so as to form a terrace like platform on the downhill side. See photos for other details. Some were bluish or grayish, some pink & some white. They appeared to be constructed chiefly of brick so covered with cement as to appear monolithic. On the whole they appeared new rather than old, though some were in decadence and some had evidently been torn out. These bear upon the possible occupancy of the hills nearer the city by an institution of learning. At the heads of the wooded ravines on the south side there were monasteries embowered picturesquely in trees. They were located near the points of issuance of springs giving rise to small streams. They are about half way up to the summit which is stated to be 1200 ft. above sea level. Tombs were not numerous much above these monasteries and on the several summits considerable ground might be made available for an institution without embracing many graves and no cultivated fields or buildings of any kind. The ascent of the hills is moderately steep say 20°.

Our general impression was that the site is scarcely eligible for an institution of learning intended to be near enough to Canton to serve as an effective educational factor in its development and it is doubtful whether the climate effects of this degree of elevation would be of much movement. We found it on this the 20th of February oppressively warm for such exercise as was required to inspect it. The coolies 4 each of which bore us to the foot of the hills and only carried their chairs to the lowest monastery wore only thin cloth pants reaching from the waist to the knees. The upper part of the body lower legs & feet being entirely bare and even then perspired freely. This is perhaps rather warm for the season but it suggests oppressive heat in midsummer which such moderate elevation probably would not greatly reduce. If elevation in this region is sought it might perhaps be found along the East river where by the use of launches it might be more accessible to the city than are the White Cloud hills. So far as the mantle of these hills and their topography bear on the problem of the utilization of high slopes their testimony is essentially the same as that of the hills laying to the westward & previously discussed. We see no reason why they should not be made several times as productive as they are.

So far as we have been able to study the Cantonese our conclusions coincide with the majority of observers to the effect that they are a very active industrious people and on the whole peaceful, contented and good natured. Their ingenuity is manifest in many things and they would probably develop originality & initiative under favorable conditions. We are still favorably impressed with the idea that they may become by proper development a leading factor in the development of higher civilization permanently in the tropics. We do not get the impression that there has been a coming together of Chinese & Europeans into a cooperative effort here to a degree equal to that seen at Shanghai. Doubtless we saw the latter in an exceptionally favorable aspect and the situation here less favorably, but this is the older field of contact and other things being equal should be in the more advanced state. We suspect that there is here a larger degree of incompatibility than in the more northerly latitudes. This inherent difference may however render the Cantonese all the better suited to developing a dominant tropical type.

Sunday Feb 21st. 1909

Spent the day at Christian College. Rained all day and limited outdoor observations. Attended chapel conducted by one of the staff. General appearance of the students prepossessing five or six women students present. Only one permanent building which is excellent; brick with cement floors, desks & seats of the standard American pattern. Apparatus for physics & chemistry considerable and serviceable; an iron lathe and other appliances for making apparatus implied knowledge & skill; drawing room and drawings in progress indicated good work in that direction; military drill given the students. Temporary buildings of inexpensive kind, but temporarily serviceable. Dormitories closely packed Lavatory, bath facilities-one bath for four students. The students take kindly to the system of baths & make good use of them. Have a football field. Grounds embrace about 40 acres running back from the water front over a gentle slope to a hill about 40 ft above water level. To obtain grounds about 300 separate deeds have been required thus far. A large number in addition will be required to make the grounds continuous. A definite price somewhat above current value is offered to holders but nothing more. Some owners obviously holding for high rates. Two villages lay adjacent to the grounds & limit extension, without excessive expense, in these directions but cultivated grounds lie in other directions.

General impression made by the members of the faculty seen-Graybill, Dr. Joseph Mc Cracken, Brownell, Groff, Motley Kinney, C.N. Laird and one other was favorable. They are all relatively young men Mc Cracken being the only one married. Their conversation indicated familiarity with modern movements and some attainments in Science. We discovered no special appreciation of the peculiar function which science must, in our judgment, play in the regeneration of China but should judge the faculty would be fairly receptive in that direction. Attended service in the city in the evening Sermon & service typical of the strictly orthodox type but with liberal tone within the limits implied.

We do not gain the impression from our observations at Canton that the missionaries have made any profound impression upon the Cantonese but rather that the results are relatively limited. The Cantonese seem to show much more effects of European commercialism than of higher influence. Our observations on the Cantonese concur in the common view that they are very active, enterprising, thrifty, frugal, rather noisy and aggressive. They seemed less uniting and congenial than other Chinese heretofore met. Perhaps this may be due in art to the personal squeezes which we met at every turn. Canton does not impress us particularly favorably as an eligible site for a dominant university in South China. The low grounds and moderate elevations have pronounced climatic disadvantages and the high grounds are not sufficiently convenient & accessible to the altogether desirable. Probably rather great difficulties would be encountered in securing adequate grounds on the better topographies. The members of the faculty go to a mountain some 60 miles eastward, having an elevation of 4000 ft, to escape the heat.

We incline to think that Hong Kong or some point in its immediate vicinity is much more eligible than any point seen in the interior for a dominating institution partly because the climatic conditions would apparently be appreciably better, partly because we incline to think that Hong Kong will be dominant business center when the railway system is developed, partly because available ground could probably be secured with less expense, delay and annoyance under the British system and because when secured it would be less subject to future contingencies. We incline to think that Hong Kong is the strategic center of South China and that it is therefore likely to be even more than now educationally strategic. The environment & control furnished by the British is itself an educator. If as heretofore intimated the Cantonese are to be an influential emigrating elements, influencing the eastern tropics, Hong Kong is most admirably fitted as a radiating center for this influence.

Monday Feb 22nd. 1909

Left Canton on SS. Kinshaw at 8 A.M. and reached Hong Kong a little after 3 P.M. The French gunboats of the Shameen in Canton harbor, gay with bunting subordinated to the American flag in recognition of Washington's birthday. Throughout practically the whole 100 miles from Canton to Hong Kong, hills rising from the alluvial plains, or from the waters were within the range of vision. This combined with what we saw on the north westerly route to Wuchow gives us the impression which the charts confirm that the whole tract is to be regarded as a hilly region which has been relatively depressed and partially filled with alluvium, forming what might be called an inset delta traversed by an intricate plexus of distributaries. It differs from a typical delta in that the alluvium has not pushed out into the sea as the term delta implies but is rather a partially filled indentation of the coast, the unfilled portion constituting Canton Bay. It appears to be an excellent case of a contest between a relative depression of the bottom and a relative rise by aggradation in which the rise in the river portion of the valley has kept the surface a little above the water level, while in the outer portion it has failed to do so leaving the bay & its arms as the result. Wherever the hills were near enough to be well observed they showed evidences of loss of material from wash resulting in patches bare of vegetation which were quite numerous & pronounced on the more mountainous portion north of Hong Kong. Clinometer observations on some of the steeper hills, 400-500 ft high indicated slopes ranging from 28-34°. There were of course much more numerous slopes or lower degree ranging down to mounds & gentle swells. In some places, terracing covered appreciable portions of the slopes, but this was exceptional rather than general. As elsewhere in this region the hills were generally bare of trees or merely covered with scattered pines of smaller type. There seemed to be somewhat less vegetation & more bare patches on the southern than on the northern aspects of the hills.

Tuesday Feb 23rd. 1909

The day was spent in getting up our notes, preparing synopses to send to Pres. Judson and others; in calling upon Consul Wilder and in making arrangements to Shanghai. This was largely an enforced day of delay as the S.S. China was advertised to sail at noon but did not sail until the following morning Went on board the S.S. China at 5 P.M.

Wednesday Feb 24th. 1909

When we took our bearings we found we were sailing westward with islands on either hand. We continued in this direction through Lan tan channel until we were off the end of Lan tan island when the steamer to our surprise came to anchor, the west end of Lan tan island lying in the stern quarter starboard and the island Chung Chow lying on the left quarter stern. An inconspicuous buoy chiefly submerged appearing to be formed of a cask lay near the point at which the steamer came to anchor and seemed to be put there for a mark of anchorage rather than a mark of school.

Shortly afterwards 5 boats approached from the westward, i.e. the direction of Macao about 20 miles distant. The boats consisted of a coast steamer flying the British flag and towing a junk together with two tugs and a coast guard gunboat. When near the China the steamer cast off the junk and sailed on toward Hong Kong. One of the tugs brought the junk alongside the China while the other tug and the gunboat lay off. The junk crew loaded boxes perhaps 2 ft x 18in x 8-10 in. labeled "Superior Opium" and on another side "Opium Prepared at Macao China." They were said to be consigned to San Francisco. They were passed in by two men at each shift and from the handling and the fall we guessed they might weigh 70-80 lbs each. They were something over an hour. A guard of men, apparently Portuguese soldiers, about a dozen in number, occupied the deck of the junk during the unloading and were taken off by the gunboat when the opium was all aboard the China. The first tug then shipped its cable and followed the gunboat back towards Macao while the other tug previously idle made fast to the junk and towed it in the same direction.

The China then turned eastward but did not pass the longitude of Hong Kong until somewhat more than 24 hours after the hour advertised for sailing. We thus lost a full day. A little but significant feature of the case was the presence on board of a young man who was given precedence to the passengers at the table the evening of leaving Hong Kong and was given a special tiffin on the morning (12 noon) of the opium transfer and who was taken by a Pacific Mail tug when the China reached the S.W. entrance to Hong Kong harbor. This and the whole transaction indicated that the passengers some of whom had come in from Manila, Canton and elsewhere to take the boat, at the date advertised as well as the week's American mail, were after all secondary affairs to an opium Cargo and an opium agent. Observation on the configuration and surface of the islands west of Hong Kong tallied closely with preceding ones on the hills about the S.E. entrance and in the Canton Bay. Weather, drizzling rain.

Thursday Feb 25th. 1909

At sea returning to Shanghai. Day occupied in writing up details of proceeding observations. Stormy weather as on preceding day.

Friday Feb 26th. 1909

Completed synopses of notes on Honolulu, Japan and south China ready to be mailed at Shanghai. Weather over cast with some rain.

Saturday Feb 27th. 1909

Reached Shanghai 10.30 AM. Got mail; called on Consul Denby; prepared baggage for shipment to Hankow; made arrangements for trip to Hankow; went on board S.S. Kinling in the late afternoon. Made short visit to old native city of Shanghai.

Sunday Feb 28th. 1909

Steamer sailed at midnight. The morning found us in the wide portion of the Yangtze with distant a low shore to the S.W. and land barely visible to the N.E. In the vicinity of Tung (see map) eminences appeared on the N.E. side of the river and others nearly opposite to the S.W. Otherwise alluvial flats prevailed in all directions. The steamer took the channel north of the large island west of Tung and was at times near enough the shore for inspection of the general nature of the alluvial plane. Eminences or sharp hills again appeared near Kiling as indicated on the map. They also appeared to the S.W. as China Kiang was approached in the evening. Our map is quite accurate in representing these hills.

A notable feature of the Alluvial plain throughout this day's trip was the trees chiefly clustered about the houses or arranged along the ditches or border lines some of which had considerable dimensions. These were so abundant that on the average one could see scarcely half a mile back from the shore even though the trees were bare of leafage. The cottages were generally scattered instead of being clustered into compact villages as noted near Canton. They were largely thatched and appeared to be of a cheap, rather temporary sort. The fields partially green with winter crops, the nature of which could not detected beyond the fact that it was pretty continuous as winter barley would be. The fields were not generally flooded. The meaning of the hills standing out from the alluvial plain seems here to be the same as that noted in the region of Canton Bay. The alluvial flats wrap around the hills and join their abrupt slopes in the same fashion previously noted. The hills near Tung showed some precipitous faces which were no doubt rock cliffs though too distant to be positively identified as such. Toward the great bend in the river between Chui Kiang and Nanking the hilly tract coming up from the south becomes denser set with hills. It is doubtless this tract that deflects the river to the northward. It appears to be continued on the north side by numerous hills for some distance. The topography and drainage features between Suchow and Wuhu suggests that possibly the river once discharged through that tract.

Monday March 1. 1909

From Nanking to a point beyond Wuhu, Generally through this stretch hills were in sight on the right hand (eastern) side of the river while plains predominated but not exclusively on the western side. The plains in this stretch are notably less covered by trees than in the region seen yesterday. It was only in distant views that the plains had the appearance of wooded tracts. It was at first suggested that the flood plains were here more subject to overflow than in the lower region where the river is notably broader but the correctness of this is open to question.

The hills bear the same relations to the alluvial plains as previously noted with one modification. That arises from the present of a higher terrace which was first noted a short distance above Nanking. This terrace is notably older than the alluvial plain next the river as shown by the ravines on its edge and by occasional notches in its crest. It seemed to gradually rise up the river until it reached perhaps 80 ft (possibly at some points 100 ft). At some places it seemed to rise gradually toward the hills and grade somewhat into them i.e. the hillslope and these terraces seemed to have the relations more normal to adjacent hills and plains doubtless because both their configurations have been shaped by erosion and gradation jointly for a considerable period. The terraces were generally or frequently in view as far as Wuhu. Beyond that they were lost for a time but reappeared. A fine example with hills lying immediately back was seen at the second northward turn of the river west of Wuhu, forming a very attractive and picturesque sight-One of the best seen below Kin Kiang. All the terraces seen today and yesterday seemed to be formed of rather fine silt; coarse sand or gravel was not certainly detected.

The hills of this region more often show indurated rock than those of South China and the beds of this rock seemed generally to have high angles but the character of the rock could not generally be detected though probably sedimentary. The hills were nearly bare of trees but generally covered with grass. Breaks and gullies in this were not uncommon but rock was not generally displayed. The hills are practically uncultivated and little terracing even of the lower slopes was observed. The hills are practically unoccupied by dwellings and tombs and other structures were not detected though the distance was usually such as to make this observation doubtful.

Tuesday March 2. 1909

The first observations were on the north-south stretch above Nan King and extended thence to Kiu Kiang. On the S.E side of the river hills and sub mountains prevail throughout this stretch and give a very picturesque aspect to the uplands. Their summits are notably irregular in height and are made peaked or knobby by numerous sub summits where the hills are clustered so as to join one another and form a complex mass as is generally true in this section. It is not apparent that the hills form a definite range of structural origin. Their aspect toward the river is somewhat that of a NE-SW range but this is possibly assignable to the erosion of the river rather than any inherent structural feature in the uplands themselves. No summit level or any approximate equality of height was observed. If the hills have been carved from a base plain the erosion has apparently gone so far as to destroy the plain completely. Perhaps observation from the summit might throw the extreme heights into an approximate plain.

A notable isolated rock in the river occupied by a low pagoda and a temple was perhaps the most picturesque feature seen and was photographed. It stands opposite a ridge on the right hand side of the river from which it had probably been dissevered by the river. A walled town identified as Pong tze situated in the valley was covered by smoke issuing from numerous points suggesting that smelters or furnaces were in operation. (To be inquired into) The wall ascended and descended the steep slopes of the hills among which the town nestles in a picturesque valley.

The terrace noted yesterday was less observable today but it probably represented by the undulating surface on which Kiu Kiang is situated. This is not wholly clear however for the material of the latter is of a high reddish color not observed in the previous terraces equally and the undulatory surface raises the question whether it is not simply a very low expression of the hill tract. Some of the hills east of Kiu Kiang are notably sandy and are much eroded giving rise to fans of bare sand at the base of some of the ravines and wind drift accumulations on the higher parts of the hills. The suggestion is that these are parts of a sandstone formation outcropping here. The alluvial plain has gradually arisen above the present water level and is 30 ft or more in the vicinity of Kiu Kiang.

The mountain south of Kiu Kiang is said to be occupied by a notable summer resort – perhaps the most notable in Central China. Its elevation is given as 1800 meters on our map. Capt. Newcomb of the Kinling gave it as 4800 ft. It is said to have considerable comparatively plain ground on the summit and to have an advantage of 10° temp. during the summer months. The nights are said to be cool and the summit generally above the clouds and mists. The temperature at Kiu Kiang in summer is said to be extremely hot, one of the hottest points in China. This is assigned to the mountains to the southward & eastward which cut off the summer monsoons which blow from that direction. A tramway extends from Kiu Kiang to the base of the mountain but not to the summit as yet. It takes about 5 hours to reach the summit from Kiu Kiang. A rival summer resort is said to have been started on the Hankow Peking railway, 5 hours from the former. The elevation is said to be about 3000ft. In this connection it may be noted that there is an elevation about 100 mile E NE of Hankow which is given an elevation of 2500 meters, Kan-Chung Shan. This near a possible railway line from Hankow eastward & northward to Tientsin, parallel to the Peking line. The British Consul at Kiu Kiang in conversation with other gentleman stated that there is an American mission (Catholic?) at Kiu Kiang which gives it chief attention to education. It has a school for boys & one for girls with about 6-8 foreign teachers with some additional Chinese.

As previously noted the Yangtze runs much closer to the hills on its right hand or south side than on its left, which latter is generally occupied by a very broad alluvial plain. Here and there hills are cut off as it were so as to appear on the left hand side but the general fact is as though the river has been gradually shifting to the south and east. This comports with the general conception of continental creep which would make the movement of China southward and south eastward and eastward radiant to its periphery. The low banks of the Yangtze are generally very steep affording excellent sections of the laminated alluvial deposits. The upper portions of the banks are invariably of a brownish color indicating an oxidized condition of the material. The lower portion of the banks were generally of the familiar dark gray or bluish gray color which is so characteristic of the lower portions of the older drift sheets in Iowa and Minnesota. The difference here as in the drifts is largely a matter of oxidation. But here it would seem to be deoxidation instead of Oxidation. For the mud (note the yellow color or the river water) is deposited in the oxidized condition. After being buried and protected from the oxygen of the air etc & in the presence doubtless of organic matter it appears to suffer reduction of ferric to ferrous iron. Question. May not the tints of the different portions of the older drifts have been produced in a similar way. Perhaps deoxidation may have been as important or even more important than oxidation, though both processes probably have gone on. All depends upon the original condition of the material follow this matter up further. The British Consul at Kiu Kiang stated that the British (the only concession) concession there measured 1692 ft along the river and about one third of that in depth. The concession upon the mountain top is limited.

Wednesday March 3. 1909

Reached Hankow at 1 P.M. Saw the country along the river for about 50 miles below Hankow. For the greater portion of the distance only the alluvial plain was seen on either side. Hills as represented on our map of moderate height had the usual grassy aspect seen eastward. The slopes on those hills near enough to be well seen was considerably broken by erosion patches. A feature not much seen lower down consisted of low hills of flowing contours somewhat resembling an old terrace but showing rock in the river bank had some notable development in the first half of the stretch seen. The rock had the appearance of sandstone with rather high dips say 45° +/-. Some of the hills were terraced for cultivation. Not very far east of Hankow on the left hand side of the river there was a considerable stretch of the higher terrace perhaps 100 feet above the present water level. In general the left bank is more abrupt than the right bank and is suffering considerable erosion. Recent slumping was obvious. We saw a mass actually undergoing slumping. The alluvial plain in this section is but slightly wooded. Afternoon engaged in arrangements for the upriver trip. Li San reported with cook and two helpers. He had met Prof. Burton at Tientsin and was acting under his direction. Prof. Burton, Mr. Reed, Mr. Wang returned from Peking at 3.30 P.M and reported excellent success.

Thursday March 4. 1909

Under the guidance of Mr. J. H. Deuring, Mr. W.D. Gates we first went eastward along the Bund to the east edge of the Japanese Concession and examined a tract between this concession and the Belgian concession which has a face on the river which here runs north easterly, of about 1500 ft and extends back to the railway a third of a mile on the average. Perhaps the tract way include 70 acres. To bring the tract up to the level of the Bund as now established would perhaps require 4-5 ft of filling on the average. On the river front the slope would require considerable treatment which might be cutting and filling conjoined or might be largely filling if the extension of the land justified it. If the frontage of the Japanese concession were extended without change of alignment it would require extensive filling on the N.E. border. The Belgian concession lies considerably back of the Japanese frontage projected. It would probably be most economical and at the same time most attractive to give the tract a curved frontage continuing the Japanese front line for a distance & then gradually curving it back so as to make connection with the Belgian frontage.

This is the most eligible site for a university which we have thus far found about the three cities. After examining this section we rode along the line of the old wall to its western limit, crossed the railroad near its terminal station and drove some distance beyond the city settlement to see the general character of the country adjacent to the left bank of the Han river. It is the common alluvial flat of the region except that at a few points in the distance low swells rose above it but these are not near enough to be eligible sites for a University.

We returned to the western angle of the old wall and went southward to the river bank. There taking a [sampan] we went down the Han river to a point opposite the iron works and passing through these ascended the hill or rather ridge north of Han Yang. The iron works form a quite extensive plant with enlargements in progress (for general aspects see photograph). The iron ore is a mixture of hematite and limonite of irregular rather loose texture whose value could not well be judged by its appearance. The plant is said to be capitalized for $20,000,000 and said to employ 20,000 men who are paid from $7-$100 Mex. per month and who work 12 hours per shift and on one day in the week 18 hours which I believe gives one day holiday per week.

The ridge north of Han Yang has a height above present water stage of 290 ft. It is formed of a quartzitic conglomerate with heavy beds dipping to the northeastward say 20°. The ridge has a sharp crest line; the south slope formed by the broken edges of the layers has about the same inclination as the north slope. The eastern extremity of the ridge is occupied by a temple and there are numerous graves on the slopes. The hill is said in addition to be sacred. Even aside from this the proximity of the iron works at its north base and the rumor that the south base is owned by the same company who propose to tunnel the ridge and use the flat on the south side in connection with the iron works constitutes a serious objection to using the ridge as the site of a University. Beside this the sharpness of the ridge and the hardness of the rock would make the reshaping of the topography into terraces suitable for buildings and roadways difficult and expensive. On the whole therefore it seems excluded from serious consideration. A rock bottom is said to extend across the Yangtze to Wu chang connecting this ridge with the central ridge in the latter making the bridging of the river at this point practicable.

Descending from this ridge on the south we crossed the flat to the portion of Han Yang lying N.E of the walled city and visited the compound of the Baptist Mission with which Messrs Denning and Gates are connected where we took tiffin and glanced through the premises including the new building for the girls department. Afterwards we crossed the Yangtze and entering Wu Chang by one of the westerly gates went through the northern part of the city to the Boone College where we hastily inspected the buildings, met and took tea with Pres. Jackson; met also Bishop Roots, and Prof. who is to take charge of the college in Pres. Jackson's absence on a vacation. We also met Bishop Brent here. We passed out of Wu chang by the north entrance, crossed the plot of ground laid out in rectangular squares with straight macadamized streets, stone curbs on distinctly American plan with streets about the usual wide for streets in American cities. We than crossed Yangtze to the British concession and returned to the terminus Hotel. By this trip we essentially reconnoitered the topographic and general geographic situation of the three cities with the exception of portions within the walled cities which are probably not available for an institution requiring large grounds without excessive expense. The result points to the left hand shore of the Yangtze N.E. of the city as the most available ground for an institutions site (see blue print map of the three cities)

Friday March 5. 1909

In the morning, Prof. Burton and myself called by appointment upon the Prefect of the province at the Yamen in Wuchang. Owing to the illness of the Viceroy he was unable to receive us and designated the prefect to act in his stead. The reception by the Prefect was cordial and he expressed a desire to further our object as far as he was able and said among other things that the Chinese regarded the Americans in a light different from Europeans. Beyond the terms of politeness and cordiality nothing of radical moment was said. He introduced us to two officers to show us such of the schools of Wuchang as we had time to visit. He placed the state carriages at our disposal and we were driven first to an elementary school which we found to surround a court 200-300 ft on a side which was pleasantly laid out with a mound as a central feature. We first visited a room where a Chinese lady sitting at a reed organ that might well have been of the usual American make (Mason & Hamlin for instance) before which was gathered a group of boys 20-30 in number who were being taught the intonations which we were told they were to use in reading. These were given first by the teacher and the organ and were repeated in concert by the boys.

It much resembled the exercises of an elementary singing class. The intervals were, I should say, chiefly thirds, major and minor though I did not at the time pay particular attention to this. The intervals were several in number and I should say ranged from the key note to the fifth above and the minor third below though this is not to be taken as strictly accurate but merely representative statement. The teacher had a very peculiar almost instrumental voice. The responses of the boys were fairly good and better I should say on the whole than the singing exercised of average American boys of the same age, say 8-10 years. The boys were generally fresh faced, fat and hearty and seemed bright. We visited other boy's classes where the work was somewhat more advanced. It represented nothing specially notable. It was orderly and decorous and neither here nor elsewhere have I as yet seen that pell mell babal like procedure which is so often described as the typical Chinese school method in use in the school classes. I did see it in rooms provided for study by students themselves and this raises the question whether it is not merely a practice of studying aloud to acquire the sounds and associate them with the forms rather than a school method as such. Elsewhere during the day we were shown rooms set apart for the pupils' studying where desks etc. were provided with candles for use after dark. This was chiefly in the school of languages visited later and in these students were pronouncing their lessons aloud.

In the elementary school we visited two or three classes of girls of say 10 years downwards. The girls occupy separate rooms and recite by themselves but are not kept separate in the court which serves as a playground. The lowest class of girls were quite inferior to the boys of corresponding age in appearance. They were less well formed and appeared notably less bright. This has been noticed elsewhere and is probably a representative fact. The women seen on the streets are generally much inferior to the men in both physical and mental appearance. In one of the girl's rooms, ages perhaps averaging 8, a reading exercise was in progress. One girl read a sentence and the whole school repeated it. So far as I noticed each school room seemed to be occupied by a single grade and all the pupils constituted a single class. It is to be noted that the exercises in this and the other schools visited were without doubt prepared for our inspection as it was definitely indicated by the officials. They are therefore to be interpreted on that basis and are to be taken as representative in kind rather than efficiency. My notes as to the mental qualities are based on the appearance and manners of the pupils, not on the character of their responses in the matter of accuracy of which I could not judge. It may be noted that the children were tidy in appearance but this may be special rather than representative. It is also to be noted that the school buildings and the court in particular were decidedly more attractive than the other portions of the city, even more attractive than the enter courts of Yamen itself.

We next visited the school of languages. Here as at all of the three schools visited we were first taken to a reception room of rather large size in which there were rows of chairs and little tables placed opposite one another 12 ft +/- apart where tea was offered. This seems to be a common feature of the schools and is perhaps significant as showing the place which the social element and the courtesies of life hold in the Chinese school system. In the school of languages and still more notably in the normal school subsequently visited the windows, lamps, and some other features of these reception halls are decidedly artistic and might well be studied by western architects & decorators. They were however associated with other features not wholly in keeping with these and sometimes quite out of keeping, as a rough poor floor or a shabby ceiling. In the higher schools aside from the two rows of chairs there was a third row transverse to them thus forming three sides of a square and these were raised and distinguished from others. They are obviously intended to mark special honorable distinction. We were invited to occupy these even though we stopped for a few moments merely. This was doubtless intended as a mark of courtesy. In the school of language we visited a room where a Russian was writing Chinese Characters on the board and the students were reproducing them in Russian. We visited a room in which a German teacher was conducting a reading exercise in German but was not translating at the time; so also a room in which a Japanese teacher was giving instruction in that language. The master of the school took us to his own room where the students were alone but who were studying English; an exercise in English history was read in English. We also visited a room in charge of a French teacher. The above five languages beside the Chinese constitute the branches taught. I think an English teacher is employed though we did not meet him. If so each language is taught by an instructor to whom it is the mother tongue. The German instructor gave a good impression; the Russian a poor one; the French rather commonplace; the Japanese only fair, but all this is superficial judgment.

The general appointments were of the typical rather crude Chinese style so far as buildings are concerned but the courts, the topography (on a slope) and the general arrangement of buildings and courts were pleasant and might be made decidedly attractive. We were given an elaborate tiffin in the reception room of the normal school, the head of the school presiding. Afterwards glanced rapidly through some of the rooms. The Normal school occupies a tract said to be about a mile square; the buildings are placed between two lakes and so it is known as the College of the two lakes. In one of the rooms a Japanese teacher was giving a lecture on porcelain manufacture with a Chinese at his side translating his Japanese into Chinese, a sentence or two or three sentences at a time. In another room geometry was being handled the students drawing the diagram placed on the board in their notebooks preparatory I judged to writing out the demonstration. We stopped for a few moments for other rooms where exercises in different lines were in progress. We were shown several study rooms in which studying aloud as noted above was in progress but it was always suspended and the students rose to their feet on our approach. We were also shown through the dormitories which have glass partitions in part; 10 cots per room seemed to be the rule. They were simple but not uncomfortable apparently. At the present time the students receive tuition and board free. Formerly they were also paid an allotment. This is to be noted in contrast with the practice at Boone College where tuition, board and room rent are all paid for by the student.

We inspected the physical and chemical rooms where considerable apparatus and material was gathered but the facilities for work are yet very limited. Chemical laboratories are however, being prepared and will soon be occupied. I counted tables for 72 students already placed. Several rooms were wholly bare as yet and our time did not permit us to inquire in detail as to the uses to which they were to be put. A plant for the manufacture of gas for the laboratory is being erected. The chemical tables were of the usual style though plain and inexpensive. There was also some museumistic material in mineralogy & zoology. It should have been noted in the sketch of the elementary schools that there were mounted birds, insects, fish and a collection of rocks and minerals of the usual school type as well as specimens of handwork in different fabrics. It should be noted that although the main work of the institution of the Two Lakes is the preparation of teachers there is a division of general science and to this division as I understand the chemical laboratory is mainly adapted. The buildings of this school are poorly kept as seems to be common with Chinese institutions but the grounds are large and susceptible of beautiful development and the existing buildings can easily be replaced, part by part, as may be practicable. So that the whole might be transformed in time to a very attractive institution.

It seemed to us very clear that the authorities are making a genuine effort to develop Western education in connection with Chinese education. They seemed to be succeeding in some measure but this apparently has its limitations. The difficulty of replacing the old with the new especially in the matter of teachers seemed obvious and probably must inevitably be so. The old teachers cannot well be dismissed nor can a complete supply of teachers of a new education be found and hence a period of transition attended by any imperfections must probably ensue inevitably. A leadership, example and supervision seemed to be greatly needed everywhere.

The afternoon was spent in completing arrangements for the upriver trip, and in the evening we went aboard the SS Tachi Maru for Ichang. During the afternoon I had a short interview with the American Consul, Mr. Martin, who gave briefly his general impression of the present educational movement. He seemed to regard the missionary institutions as a vital factor.

Saturday March 6. 1909

Hankow to Yochow Steamer Tachi Maru left Hankow at 7 A.M. And reached Yochow about the same time next morning. Country on either side of the river was chiefly the alluvial flats with banks ranging up to 40-50 ft. At rather rare intervals low rounded hills were in sight and also more considerable hills but both these were relatively scattered. Some of the lower hills formed continuous elevated tracts resembling the upper terrace previously seen on the lower river but it was not wholly clear that they were such for they might have been merely low portions of the hilly uplands.

Sunday March 7. 1909

Left Yochow soon after 8 A.M. and entered upon the meandering portion of the river to the N.W. We continued to sail until about midday when the boat ran aground on a sand shoal where we remained until the following morning. The alluvial flat prevails almost exclusively in this tract. The banks show increasing height and apparently also increasing sandiness. The phenomena observed on the sand shoal as the result of currents set up by the boat were the most instructive phenomena of the day. Purposely or incidentally the boat was thrown athwart the stream, the anchors cast while the propellers were still kept in action for an hour or two. Soon the current concentrated by the vessel cut out the sand at the prow and stern and at certain points amid ships these latter enlarged and shifted variously permitting the vessel to shift downstream. The cutting out of channels in the shoal by these concentrated undercurrents through the pressure of the boat on the intervening ridges of the shoal. These were in consequence bulged upward at the side of the vessel and were cracked caused to fault block upon block and to fall to one side or the other into the adjacent currents which came boiling up on the downside of the hill. These currents also cut into the ridges as they were swelled by the pressure of the boat and this gave rise to sliding, caving, etc. The phenomena of cracking and breaking of the swelling embossments of wet sand as it rose above the surface afforded many fine illustrations of fractured blocks. One phase of fracturing consisted of two sets of oblique lines crossing one another at large but not right angles dividing the sand into lozenge like blocks which were pushed in the direction of longest dimension. This phase of the phenomenon seemed to be an expression of the principles of fracture and shear advocated by Van Hise & Leith as the lines were oblique to the side of the vessel which represented the face of the active force. This however was by no means the only phase of fracture and shear. In some cases the fracture lines were nearly transverse to the vessel's side and sub parallel to one another. This seemed more nearly an expression of the principles of fracture and shear advocated by Becker. There were also cases in which the fracture lines were nearly parallel to the vessel's side. There were also cases in which the upper segment of the mound like mass of sand was detached from that below and shoved over it giving a projecting cap. There were also phenomena of creep as for example this dissevered and projecting cap crept down the sides of the truncated mound lying beneath it. In connection with the various forms of blocking there were differential movements between the sand blocks illustrating different phases of faulting. These sand mounds were successively produced and destroyed by the joint action of the under currents and the side pressure of the vessel. A flat broad bar was formed a little farther off from the vessel by the sand cut out from beneath it by the currents forced under it and this took the two winged fish tail form the wings of which extended fore and aft to 2-3 times the length of the vessel. The whole phenomena was very suggestive as to the possibility of removing bars by controlling and concentrating the river currents so as to cause them to cut away the bar and carry it downstream. Apparently so simple a devise as the laying of the vessel alongside the head of the shoal and thwart the current and the holding it in that transverse position would be sufficient to cut a channel whose breadth was somewhat greater than the length of the vessel through the bar and that at a rather rapid rate where the current was of the strength shown in this case and the material was as amendable to water action as the sand of this case. Probably a suitably constructed raft might produce similar effects. The phenomena suggest that a raft of special construction with sloping undersides so shaped as to best concentrate the current might be substituted for a more expensive vessel. It is also suggested that shafts might be traced transverse to the raft armed on the upstream end with screws adapted to catch the current and rotate the shaft while the end of the shaft on the downside of the boat might be armed with blades adapted to give the maximum agitation of the sand with the minimum of resistance. The suppose effect of this device would be to disturb the sand shoal so that the currents passing under the raft or vessel would have their maximum effect in washing away the sand.

It would seem that with some such combination of mechanical agitation and current force that the sand, mud or other shoal material might be rather rapidly shifted downstream. No doubt this would lodge a short distance below and would have to be agitated and shifted again but as the current furnishes the chief power and does the work of transportation this successive shifting would not be a serious matter unless the shoal became a complete bar rising to the surface and shutting off the current action. In this case however the current action would be lateral and this would carry the sand to the two extremities of the raft & discharge it on either side of the channel in process of cutting and the sand would thus be disposed of. This is but a crude first suggestion. Other devices for controlling currents so as to make them keep their channels open had come into mind previously and the accident of the day gave a concrete object lesson on this subject. The more general question is raised whether or not the currents of a silt bearing stream may not be manipulated by rather simple and cheap devices so as to become over loaded at short distances above the points where they are cutting and so transform the cutting part of the current into a depositing habit. So cannot the depositing phases of the current be so manipulated by concentration as to become cutting currents and thus make the current itself fill where it should fill and cut where it should cut to preserve the integrity of the central channel and avoid the shifting of the channel by cutting here and barring up younger. At some points low bars were seen some of which had elevated heads, truncated by erosion in front and tailing out very gradually in the rear. The forms had some resemblance, though in reverse, to the erosion phenomena of glaciers. These bars had been formed originally during higher stages of the water. At the present low water stage they have come above water and the upstream ends have suffered erosion.

Monday March 8. 1909

Our steamer managed to get clear of the bottom without apparent difficulty at daylight. Why it could not have done so yesterday afternoon was not apparent. The day was rainy keeping the party below decks much of the time. We would right and left around various bends in the river. There was however very little to note. The banks of the river were somewhat lower than those seen yesterday, as if apparently the river had been able to spread out to a greater extend in this region when it overflowed and hence did not build up its flood plain so high.

The general plain due to the aggradation of the Yangtze is of great width along this portion of its course. We go day after day with only an occasional hill or mound in sight in the distance. This great flood plain of which we can see little for the banks are as high as the upper deck of the steamer affords only monotonous scenery. The formation of large lakes from the damming up of tributaries' mouths by the more rapid deposition of silt by the Yangtze is one of the most notable features of this great flood plain.

Tuesday March 9. 1909

During the morning we steamed slowly up the river between banks perhaps a trifle lower than those of yesterday but generally not notably different. We are out of sight of hills. About noon we sighted the Jardin-Matheson steamer Kiang Wo either anchored or a ground around a bend in the channel. The river is here well filled with low sand bars and there is only one channel in which the water is said to be very shallow. Our steamer dropped anchors and we waited the action of the other steamer while our launch explored the channel ahead. Nothing happened and we thus waited all the rest of the day. The weather was misty so that most of the day was spent indoors upon reading the Yangtze literature abroad and attending to various details.

Wednesday March 10. 1909

When we awoke in the morning we were still anchored where we had lain yesterday afternoon. About the middle of the morning the other steamer began to slowly advance downstream and after getting stuck a ground once finally passed by us into deep water downstream. After some delay we proceeded slowly upstream and passed through the critical part of the river without material difficulty. The question arose: why could we not have done all this yesterday and thus avoided this delay of nearly a whole day? This is a Japanese steamer affording us an opportunity to study both the actions of Japanese and Chinese. The Japanese officers did not show much ability in handling the ship. Their language sounded extremely harsh in comparison with the Chinese. In all cases the language of communication between the Japanese officers and the Chinese water sounders and pilots was English. The Japanese do not learn much Chinese nor the Chinese Japanese both learn a little English.

In the afternoon we passed through a strip of country which appeared much more prosperous than any we had seen on the Yangtze. The banks were almost continuously lined with houses of substantial appearance. What little we could see of the vegetation and crops suggested greater fertility of the soil. The river banks in many places have been protected from stream erosion by covering solidly with roughly hewn blocks of stone – apparently limestone. In some places they are paved with flat slabs; in other places there is at the present time only talus piles. But even these nearly obscure the clay bank so that the stream can do little eroding. Good devices for protecting the banks. We reached Scha Sahi or Sha-sze at 5.30 P.M. and anchored for the night.

Thursday March 11. 1909

Left Sha-sze at 6.30 Am. Jeties run out from bank to protect bank by deflecting the current. Tung tze, a fine appearing town. Chi Kiang a city with fine appearing buildings. This region looks far better than lower down the river. The hills put in appearance making the country seem unusually attractive after the monotonous flood plain of the last few days. Strata at their first appearance dip downstream at an angle of 10-15°. They later became horizontal and further on dip upstream. Some limestone. Much reddish formation (perhaps Permo Mesozoic?). At I-tu there were many large circular lime kilus. Town shown much evidence of activity. Between I-tu and Ichang a comparatively persistent higher terrace or remnant of pen plain was in view most of the time. Because of its persistence it seems more like a general peneplaination than a river terrace. In some places the truncated red strata come to the plain level. Elsewhere a coarse yellow brown gravel deposit runs to the top level. This feature resembles in general appearance the tertiary base level in the Appalachians. Nearing Ichang the bluff became steep and rugged due to the unequal weathering and erosion of a course brownish conglomerate. A natural bridge, sharp Knobs (Tiger's Teeth) etc. Reached Ichang at 6.00 P.M

Notebook
No. 3

Friday March 12th. 1909

At Ichang. Mr. Reech met us on our arrival and reported arrangements essentially completed subject to some election. Everything found unexpectedly satisfactory. Completed a few outstanding preliminaries and the house boat moved at 1.30 P.M. Most of the intervening time given by Mr. Burton & myself to visiting the missionary schools and meeting foreign residents. Among the schools visited one where elementary work in trades was being attempted chiefly in metal and wood work. Quite crude but still a beginning. The girls in the schools particularly the older girls did not show that worked inferiority in brightness noted at several previous points. At the girl's school tuition was being met by lace work for which a market without effort was found. Last year the lace product was about $200 in excess of tuition expenses and this is being used in the erection of a new building. Were piloted about by Rev. Deans of the Scotch Mission. Took tiffin with the faculty of women at the girl's school.

At 2 P.M. met perhaps a score of foreign residents, men & women at the chapel for foreigners. By request. After a formal introduction Prof Burton made a statement of the purposes of the commission to which I added a few words. Questions were then asked chiefly relating to purposes and views. After this and the completion of the money arrangements took the red boat and joined the house boat a short distance above Ichang.

Saturday March 13th. 1909

Fair day with favorable breeze. The Ichang gorge was entered shortly after our start at 6.30 A.M. The gorge differs from what I had anticipated in the more retiring character of the walls which are chiefly made up of steps offsets, bastions, terraces with buttress ridges at the base. The general aspect of the rock is dependent on weathering which gives to the prevailingly dark limestone a reddish buff or gray color which is much modified by dark coating due to wash. The combined effect is a dark reddish brown or gray hue relieved by patches & streaks of brighter slightly pinkish hue. The ledges and slopes are generally covered with grasses and small shrubs. The terminal portion of the grasses is usually a reddish buff color graduating downwards to deeper dull colors or to subdued green while the shrubs mingled in small patches with the grasses are generally green giving to the whole combination an external soft harmonious effect singularly in keeping with the age and solid aspects of the great rock masses.

In this respect it far surpasses anything seen before. The retiring angle is such that the walls are ascendable at numerous if not most points. Both the lower and the higher terraces and summits afford extremely picturesque sites for country places and similar structures where retirement and scenery of lastingly attractiveness is desired. This general character extends with numerous variations set forth by turns & angles in the stream as far as the village of Nanton. Here the basal granitic series rises rapidly in an arch and the Paleozoic series above it are carried upward to a battlemented border beyond which granitic topography replaces that previously described and is in marked contrast to it. Vertical erosion lines are here dominant and the topography is made up of peaks or irregular height and more or less bunchy but on the whole rather regular slopes.

About noon we reached Nanton and spent an hour and a half visiting the glacial beds described by Willis and Blackwelder. A large part of the time was spent in finding the exact locality and little of the material was seen in situ. It is typical tillite but we were not successful in finding markedly striated slopes though considerable number typically smoothed and of typical form were seen. A further study is reserved for the return. All that was seen is in harmony with the observations and interpretations of Willis and Blackwelder. Above Nanton granite forms the rock series to the limit of the day's trip, 31 miles, with the exception of the high cliffs of Sinian (Ki-sin-ling) Cambro Ordovician limestone which are seen as steep walled hill tops in the distant view for some distance above Nanton. The influence of the character of the rock upon the erosion topography of this general region was splendidly shown on this days' trip. Sinian limestone gave nearly vertical cliffs; Mid Paleozoic (Sintan) shale grassed slopes of comparatively regular character, while the Huang-Ling granite developed grass covered slopes of irregular, bunched hill, dissected appearance. Tied up for the night at the Ta-tong rapids through which we passed before coming to anchor.

Sunday March 14th. 1909

Started from Ta-Tong rapids about 6.30 A.M. The granitic series continues to Kong-ling chou. Here the Paleozoic series descends on the western side of the granitic arch at an angle similar to that of its rise near Nan-ton and with similar erosion and stratigraphic phenomena. What appears to be the Sinian limestone forms the first gorge cliffs and extends to the angle northward and a little beyond. The cliffs extend about a mile and a half, beyond which the gorge is more open and the slopes more receding and the middle Paleozoics (Sintan series) appear. The shale series extends along the river's edge to the western end of the village of Sin-tan.

Immediately above Sin-tan the Wushan limestone forms a steep walled gorge early two miles in length. The appearance of softer sandstone formation just beyond this hard limestone has resulted in a widening of the river together with sandy banks from which the strong wind blew clouds of dust against our boat. While sailing before a good breeze at Hoang-tsien the rope holding the sail suddenly broke, allowing the sail to fall and by swinging to one side nearly caused the boat to capsize. Our baggage was thrown in a heap at one side of the boat and some of the party a bit frightened. The boat quickly drifted against some rocks but though it struck with considerable force it was not stove in. We remained on the rocks for an hour or so and after getting off with the aid of ropes was towed a short distance upstream and anchored for the night. Day's run 16-17 miles making a total of 47 miles from Ichang. This is exceptionally good time for this mode of travel. (Lost several hours at the Sin tan rapids).

Monday March 15th. 1909

Started from Hoang-tsien; passed by some dark dike like projections which had the appearance of being either very fine grained siliceous sediment well indurated or else conformable igneous rock of the dark doleritic type. Specimens collected later indicated that the former interpretation is true. These and similar hard layers stand out on the slopes which are here quite retreating in general, (say between 20°-40° roughly). Landed opposite Kwei chow and followed the footpath around the promontory on the south side of the gorge below which are rather difficult rapids caused probably by the indurated layers mentioned above. Horizon of these layers doubtful. The alternating series of indurated and soft strata known as Kwei Chow continues with a V shaped valley for about 13 miles where it is replaced by a gorge like stretch of 3 miles lying east of Pa-tong shien.

The valley resumes its open V shaped for about 7 miles westward where it is replaced by the eastern end of the Wushan gorge. This presents an abrupt eastern entrance. The strata here are high dipping but traced upwards curve rapidly toward horizontality. Following the gorge upward the river soon assumes the general direction of the strike, minor undulations aside, for about 17 miles (to Chin-Si tong). Here it turn at an angle slightly over 90° and runs N.W.ly across the axis of the range for about 3 miles where it curves again to the westward more nearly into the direction of the strike for about 5 miles where it emerges from the range. Seen at this point the N.W. side of the range stands forth prominently, the strata dipping 40°-50° by estimate. Only a comparatively small part of the gorge has walls that are really sheer. For the most part the sides are slopes ranging 30°-40°. At many points portions of the slope are adorned with cultivated patches. Where the gorge crosses the axis the sheer faces rise to great heights on the east by a series of steps and form a really impressive assemblage. Some of the summit portions have rectangular faces; other are worn to pinnacles. These are the only heights with approximately sheer faces that rise beyond 1000 ft. by estimate. The change from the gorge to the more open and lower country about Wushan and westward is very striking. (The last of the gorge was passed on the following day). Today's run was 43 miles making a total of 90 from Ichang.

Tuesday March 16th. 1909

Started from Pei-sze at 6.40 A.M. and passed out of the gorge at Wu-shan in the middle of the forenoon. For the features of the gorge seen during the morning see notes of yesterday. The course of the valley at Wushan turns to the W.S.W. essentially parallel to the face of the fold which forms the Wushan gorge and the alignment of the N. Western face or both sides of the river is distinct. The slopes adjacent to the river and much lower and quite generally cultivated. Some of the fields and orchards, interspersed with banyan trees, bamboos and smaller trees probably including orange trees, gives to certain portions very attractive aspect.

The river appears here to be running the strike of the upper or red series (Mesozoic ?). From Wu-shan westward the river follows near the north side of the Wushan arch which remains in sight for a considerable distance. The Mesozoic series consists of red sandstones and shales with some gray and other colors. The topography adjacent to the river is rounded in outline and the slopes relatively low (say 20° and downward). The slopes are largely cultivated in patches with irregular areas between left unused because too steep or rocky. At a point about 8 miles below Kwei Chow the river valley turns to the northwest and the Wind Box gorge is entered. The strata arch upward and appear to belong to the Wushan limestone. It soon became too dark to follow the details. We stopped for the night near the west end of the gorge at the village of Koei-men about 1 ½ miles below Kwei chow fu. It was at Wushan that Mr. Willis' party first struck the Yangtze, coming down the tributary valley which joins the Yangtze at this point. We did not stop at Wushan but continued on up the river for a couple of miles. The day's run was 35 miles.

Wednesday March 17th. 1909

Got up just before we were reaching Kwei chow. The boat started at day break T.C.C. got up at once but it was still too dark to make out the stratification. But so far as could be seen in looking backward after full day light it would appear that the north west side of the Wind Box gorge is formed of the descending limb of the limestone (Wushan) arch. The topography accords with this. Near Kwei Chow on both sides of the river salt is manufactured from brine which probably comes from the Mesozoic series. Willis' has called the Permo-Mesozoic series between Sintan and Wushan gorge the Kwei chou series but this name was given from the other town of Kwei chow farther downstream and not from this larger town of Kwei Chow fee though apparently the rocks here belong to the same general series. Willis did not reach Kwei Chow fu (Sze chuan) but named his red bed series after Kwei Chow (Hupeh). Series probably the same however.

Kwei chow was once a town of considerable importance but it seems to have declined. We spent a couple of hours ashore making some purchases and seeing the sights. Westward from Kwei Chow the river valley lies in the line of the strike. For a considerable part of the afternoon's sail a hard formation of this series constituted the south side of the valley, single beds almost forming the slope from crest to river's edge, for say 1000 +/- ft. while lower dips appeared on the opposite side. These beds seemed to be the more central parts of a synclinal on the south sides of which the valley has been eroded. Pyramidal, hilly and submountainous forms were often developed on this side while saw tooth topography prevailed on the south side. This continued to the end of the day's sail. Today about 30 miles were made notwithstanding a stop of 2 ½ hours at Kwei Chow. This was due in a large part to the good easterly wind. Easterly winds have favored us on each day thus far. This continued piece of good fortune is said to be remarkable. At Kwei–chow, Mr. Pratt a missionary came on board and brought a young Chinese student who intends to go to America to school. We had a long interview with him (his name is Wang also) and gave him the best information we could. Spent the night near Miao-Ki-tse.

Thursday March 18th. 1909

Started at day break from point about 11 miles below Yun Yang Hsien. The formations continued through most of the day to be similar to those of yesterday. The pyramidal type of terraced hills was a marked feature till the latter part of the afternoon when the valley became somewhat more open and the configuration more rounded. The pyramidal buttes are due to a rather regular alternation of more or less inclining beds of red and grayish sandstones and shales which give rise to the steps similar to those of the pyramids of Egypt and not radically different in relative size though they were larger 500-800 ft. Aneroid measurement to road way & estimate above gave 700 ft. as the height of one of them. Seven of these were seen in a row facing the river on the North. This might be called the land of pyramids. The terraces are quite generally cultivated Yun Yang Hien stands on a promontory on the North side on the river. Opposite this city and standing at the angle of a pyramid is a temple of unusually picturesque architecture. This is said to date back to the Han dynasty. Mr. Wang gives the name as Chang Won Heh Miao (for details see photo) No 47 Temple built by people in honor of this Marquis Chang.

At 3 P.M we reached the Sin lung rapids. These rapids were caused by a landslide and are among the most dangerous. About an hour before this a boat went down in these rapids. Of the 9 men aboard 8 were drowned. We say this boat suddenly rise above the water just as we arrived, it having been kept under for this length of time by the powerful eddies. We saw the one survivor wrapped in blankets in one of the thatched houses. Li San talked with him and learned that he was not much injured. It would apparently not be difficult or very expensive to greatly improve the rapids here. Perhaps the same may be said of these rapids in general. Earlier in the trip it seemed to T.C.C. that a combination of short railway around the rapids and in the more open portions of the valley (which includes most of the rapids) might best solve the problem of transportation along the Yangtze for the immediate future, leaving to the more distant future to complete the railway system, but later observation incline him to think that improvement of the rapids is better as it would seem to be very much cheaper. Apparently the outlay of what wreckage, porterage and delay now costs annually would so improve the rapids as to soon make the river comparatively safe to good boats well managed. The rapids are not so formidable from the engineering point of view as we had supposed. However since the rapids change with the varying height of the river the problem may be more difficult than it appears at this stage alone.

Our boat passed these Sin lung rapids without much difficulty though the captain delayed the attempt as hour or so possibly because of the fate of the other boat. Just above the squalid village beyond the Sin lung rapids a new school house of large and attractive appearance stands on the hillside. It may be noted also that a notably large, new schoolhouse also stands near Yun Yang Hien. Toward the end of the day's journey we passed buttes capped by hard layers. The topography became less pyramidal. Darkness closed in when we were near the upper end of the N.W. trend above Yun Yang. We stopped for the night near the village of Siao Kiang Chang at the mouth of a tributary from the north. Day's run was 28 miles which leaves about 20 miles to Wan-hsien.

Friday March 19th. 1909

Started from a point 20 miles below Wan Hsien and completed the upriver trip. The formation so far as could be seen still seemed to belong to the Mesozoic series but not to the markedly red-bed portion. Massive layers of pinkish gray dull colored sandstone prevailed. In some portions the river channel at this stage was a mere trench in the rock for 20-30 ft in height. Generally above this the valley receded even more widely than on the day previous. The butte topography changed from the pyramidal type to more ordinary class, higher buttes being of the order of 1000 ft, the lower slopes were more extensively terraced and better cultivated than below. Somewhat extensive and well pronounced terraces of natural origin developed progressively upriver. At first they seemed possible equivalents of the alluvial terraces farther downstream but further observation seemed to indicate that they are structural. The finest of these stands opposite Wan Hsien and stands forth from the high submountainous background perhaps half a mile. The topography toward Wan Hsien becomes progressively butte like. This is the first day since leaving Ichang that the wind has blown down stream. But we are now past the gorges & rapids. Beautiful weather but a little hot. Reached Wan Hsien at 6 P.M.

Saturday March 20th. 1909

Forenoon spent in organizing for trip across country to Cheng tu, 400 miles. Started at 12.15 P.M. Arrived at night station at 10.15 P.M.

Westward from Wan Hsien pronounced butte topography with well developed, highly cultivated valleys prevail for perhaps 10 miles. It then gives place gradually to erosion ridges of the sub-mountainous type. Heights guessed at 1000-2000 ft. The valleys are persistent and well cut and no topographic difficulties were passed during the day that would seriously interfere with a railway. The valleys are well terraced, the irrigation system highly developed; the crops unusually fine; the roads paved with cut sandstone with retaining walls above and below bridges of massive cut stone, the reaches of which were often 2 x 2 x 18 ft. and piers of similar type. The country seemed well developed and more prosperous than most parts of China thus far visited. Darkness set in about as we reached the col leading to the next tributary valley. Rode in darkness to village of Fen-Shui chang where we arrived at 10.15 P.M. Wasted much time deciding between two inns. Finished dinner at 12.30 A.M.

Sunday March 21st. 1909

Started from Fen Shui at 7.15 A.M. After passing through the village we quickly rose up the hill slopes to N.W. The beds were dipping at high angles during the first 500 ft climbed. Across the river to the S.E. the dip was much less (20-30°) and to the S.E. We crossed through the first high ridge along a stream course and reached 900 ft above Fen Shui before we emerged onto a flatter, wider portion of the valley. The ridge is composed for the most part of a generally buff colored, fairly well indurated sandstone whose greater hardness is undoubtedly the cause of the formation of the mountain ridge. This buff sandstone formation was micaceous where first encountered. At a point along the canyon across the ridge we passed the rock slope of a small coal mine. The pit mouth was only about 2 ft. 6 in. in height at its highest point and perhaps a yard in width. The coal was said to be reached at about 200 ft. in. Did not see much evidence of coal in the strata out crops but there was a large pile of coal at the pit mouth. Fair grade of bituminous coal.

After pass through this sandstone ridge we turned to the westward in the general direction of the strike ascending gradually along the slopes. The divide was reached at a point having an elevation above Fen Shui according to the aneroid of 1240 ft. A railroad to Cheng tu following this road would have to cross at this height. We followed the slopes up to 1760 ft. above Feng Shui which is itself 1400 ft. above sea level. From these slopes views to the North and Northwest showed a considerable lower area of typical red beds comprising buttes and low hills. The strata dip to the N.W at moderate angles. Beyond the red bed area there could be distinctly seen a buff colored formation apparently a sandstone which overlies the red beds. This appeared in the next ridge several miles away. Most of the afternoon's journey was over sandstone (buff & (gray) slopes. The general dip was to the Northwest. We descended a comparatively steep slope from the high ridge to the plain upon which Liang-Shan Hsien is built.

A short time before reaching Liang-Shan we passed through 7 finely constructed arches within half a mile. These arches were dedicated to widows who never married again. Many very attractive houses were seen on the afternoon's journey. The houses are generally constructed of pine with plaster covering between the wooden beams. For lathering strips of bamboo interwoven are used. These are covered with a poor sort of mortar over which is placed a thin veneering of white plaster. The general appearance of these dwellings indicated greater prosperity than in most of the other parts of China visited. We reached Liang-Shan Hsien at 5.15 P.M. and put up at a much better inn than we had at Fen-Shui. Mr. Thompson of the China Inland Mission East called upon as and kindly invited the party to dinner. The magistrate sent us his card in the evening.

Monday March 22nd. 1909

Breakfasted with Mr. Thompson and started on the road at 7.30 A.M. Our course today was W.N.W and so instead of being nearly parallel with the strike as on the last two days we crossed the mountain ridges during the afternoon. The morning's journey was across a wide plain (perhaps 15 miles in width) to Lao-yin Chang where we had tiffin. The first part was amid an occasional red sandstone hill or butte of nearly horizontal beds. But nearly everywhere were the paddy fields without rock in sight. Rock seen in a creek bed in one or two places.

This broad plain between Liang-Shen and Lao-yin may possibly be a broad syncline throughout the greater portion of which the strata (much of them red beds) are nearly horizontal. The view of the mountain ridge to the N.W. from Lao-yin obtained just before reaching that village is strikingly like that of the Swiss Jura from Geneva. The general crest line as far as the eye can see is of the same elevation with but little variation from the original pen plain. It is a splendid illustration of a base leveling. It differs from the Kittatiny base level in Pennsylvania in not having the straight line, uneroded crest line. Instead the formerly level crest has been notched by gullies heading back so that it now presents a bunchy appearance in detail just as the Jura. As we ascended this ridge after tiffin the beds were found to dip to the S.E. at angles of 20°-30°.

Part way up the slopes we visited a lime burning establishment. The material used was a brownish gray crystalline metamorphosed limestone containing many large crystals of calcite. The fragments of limestone are mixed with round masses of briquet coal and the whole burned in a large excavation. Farther on was a coal mine in which the coal was reached by a long rock tunnel. The coal is brought out in baskets set upon wheels which run upon a small wooden track. These baskets (usually two together at a time) are pushed out by a man entirely naked except for breechcloth. Each basket holds about 80 lbs of coal and the total output of the mine cannot exceed a couple of tons a day. After being brought to the surface the coal is carried away in baskets a la pole.

The aneroid gave a reading of 2840 ft. at the top of this ridge where we crossed it. This was at a col perhaps 100 +/- ft below the hillocks on either side. Call it 3000 ft above sea level for we have the elevations of the chief villages from Mr Beech's map and set the aneroid at 1650 ft at Liang Shan. The view to the East looking over rice fields innumerable was very attractive. The region looked almost like one great marsh.

Cross section of the structure between Lao-yin and Yen-La yi. The vertical scale is exaggerated. The coal seams on opposite sides of the two ridges appear to be the same. The same metamorphosed limestone was found above each coal seam on the opposite limbs of the anticlinal fold. As we descended to Yen-pa yi the angle of dip steadily lessened and the red beds reappeared, the counterpart of the east flank of the other limb. The most interesting feature of this fold is the erosion & removal of the axial portion, an excellent illustration of the principle that streams tend to change over to and develop along the anticlines in preference to synclines.

There are two mines in operation in the seam on the western limb of the fold. At one of these the coal was reached through a rock tunnel 2000 ft. in length. The coal was said to have a thickness of 2 ½ - 3 ft. The pit mouth was as large as many mine mouth's in the U.S. The coal as in the mine seen in the other limb of the fold was brought out in baskets on trucks, each basket holding about 80 lbs. The total output of this mine was said to be 30-40 baskets per day. There were four men at work. Thus 4 men mine about 1 ½ tons of coal daily. The coal appeared to be of good grade. We reached Yen-pa yi at 6.15 P.M. This village appears to be near the eastern edge of a basin analogous to that in which Liang-Shan is located. Red beds prevail; the dips are low. Note: The total output of this coal mine amounts to only about $.75 gold a day.

Tuesday March 23rd. 1909

Started from Yen-pa yi at 7.15 A.M. and proceeded in a westerly direction across the plain. Red beds at first dipping gently to the N.W. When about half way across the plain the strata became visible in several hills capped by temples and were seen to be nearly horizontal. As the western boarder of the plain was approached the strata (red beds) were found to gradually assume higher dips. The dips were now to the S.E. The plain is clearly a syncline (like the one in which Liang shan is located) the greater portion of which contains very low dipping strata with red beds at higher angles on the borders.

At about 8 miles West of Yen-pa yi the plain comes to an end in the slopes of the next ridge. The series is similar in general to that observed in the other fold to the east. Foothills of red beds. Higher up is a coal mine. Altitude 1665 ft. Yen-pa yi, 1400 ft where aneroid was set. Beds dip 49°-51°. Direction of dip S46°E. Coal seam said to be about a yard in thickness. Higher up on the slope (50 ft perhaps) is another mine working on the same seam. Higher up is a thick limestone formation. The top of the ridge consists of a mass of hummocks. Toward the west side of the ridge the limestone strata suddenly begin to dip to the N.W. at very high angles. There appears at first a slight overturn apparently. The limestone strata then begin to dip at lessening angles as we descend the N.W. side of the ridge. At first after the limestone comes a yellowish sandstone followed by the familiar red beds. We were total while crossing the ridge that there was no coal on the N.W flank. The coal seems should apparently be on this flank as well as on the other. Possibly it is simply because it has not yet been found. At Ta-Chu where we spent the night there was a pile of coal behind our inn that was said to have come from the side of the ridge at a point some 20 li to the south. This was very good bituminous coal which does not leave a great deal of ash.

After reaching the red bed plain we proceeded perhaps 8 miles by a winding course amid exceedingly picturesque country scenery with garden like terraced fields (on low hills) to Ta-chu Hsien where we arrived at 5.30 P.M. The country seen today like that of yesterday seemed to be cultivated practically up to it's the maximum capacity. The mountain sides are thickly covered with bamboo thickets. The lower hills are almost completely terraced; the ravines have had their bottoms filled in and rounded, followed by terracing which allows by their utilization as rice fields; while on the odds & ends of the land along the roadsides etc there are growing heavy crops of mustard, beans, and other vegetables. The plains between the ridges afford exceedingly attractive and always interesting views.

Up on the ridge where the bamboo grows thickly was a paper manufacturing plant which was bamboo fiber for paper making material. The strips of bamboo are first soaked for a period of time in lime until it rots to a certain extent after which it is pounded to a pulp. The paper made from this bamboo fiber was of a bright yellow color. It is easily torn and does not appear to be very good grade. Bamboo thickets on the hillsides protect the soil admirably but they are so thick that they prevent the growth of other plants. Work somewhat like pine forest. The soil on the hillside appears to be good and of good thickness. This seems to be due in part to the extensive system of terracing, one above another, which prevents gullying altogether and does not allow slope wash except of the most limited sort.

Wednesday March 24th. 1909

Started from Ta-chu Hsien at 7.05 A.M. Traveled over red bed hilly plain for about 2 hours. Beds dipping to the S.E at increasing angles. The first strata in the mountain ridge are a buff sandstone which stand out as harder than the younger red beds. At an elevation of 1440 ft (9.40 AM) the aneroid having read (1420 ft on map) 1075 ft at Ta-chu when we started, we reached a coal mine at which there was much activity. The aneroid has been changing toward better weather this morning so that we may have actually climbed more than is indicated by these figures. The strata at the mine dip 35° in a direction about S 50° E. The coal seam is said to vary from 1 – 1 ½ ft in thickness and to have been worked in perhaps half a mile. About a quarter of a mile further up the slope as we go is another coal mine which is clearly in a different seam since the projection of the other coal seam would carry it into the air before reaching this point. There may be 200-300 ft between these seams. The coal is brought out of the mine in long shallow baskets on bamboo runners. The entry is so low that the man is forced to crawl along using wooden shoes or skis for his hands. These he slides along the ground in front of him. The passage is said to be so narrow in places that the man cannot crawl along with clothing on. The miners were all naked except for small breech cloth.

We ate lunch at the village of Chin-pa ship on the ridge where the aneroid read (map gives 3020 ft) This ridge is broader than the others, the limestone beds still dipping to the S.E. for some distance west of Chin-pa. At length the beds begin to dip to the N.W at high angles. Beautiful view of the plains from the brink of west face of the ridge. At the brink the beds are buff sandstone resting up on the thick limestone. Because of their softness they have eroded readily resulting in the steep western slope of the ridge. We had hoped to find something unusual at the contact of the red beds with these highly inclined strata but the red beds themselves come part way up the slope of the ridge. There is a gradual lessening of the angle of dip until the ridge is left behind and the red bed basin type of topography & strata prevail.

We reached the town of Li-tu ho located on the Chu Ho at 4.10 P.M. The windows of our inn afforded views out over this river upon whose bank the inn is located. I took advantage of this early arrival to develop negatives.

Thursday March 25th. 1909

Started from Li-tu Ho at 7.15 A.M. Boarded boats and were ferried across the Chu Ho and carried downstream some distance since the stream here flows in the general direction of the Cheng tu road for a mile or more. Aneroid read 675 ft (Map says 960ft.) at the rim and 600 ft on the river. This is quite a river at this point being perhaps 200 yards across. We gradually climbed up from the river level during most of the morning until the aneroid read 1000 ft. At perhaps a mile from the main stream we encountered a tributary which has cut a sharp canyon for itself. Where we first struck it there is a waterfall of 40-50 ft □All of the rock strata visible were red sandstones. I could detect no outward difference in the hardness of the beds which might have caused the formation of the falls but undoubtedly there must be some such difference which has been operative.

We lunched at Wu-chia Chang. The country west of here is much poorer than the further east. There are fewer people living here, while beggars become much more numerous. Mr. Beech says the soil is not so good here. Perhaps they do not make so good use of it. We have been noticing during the last two days that often wheat and beans instead of being raised in separate fields are put together in the same field. Often alternate rows of beans and wheat. Often both mixed together. We have observed that when the two are grown together the wheat grew much higher and more luxuriously than when it was alone. This is undoubtedly due to the fixation of nitrogen in the soil by the bean plants. By quizzing it was found that the Chinese generally knew that better results were obtained in this way but they had no idea of the reason for it. We reached Chin-hsi-chin at 3.15 and stopped for the night.

Friday March 26th. 1909

We started from Chin-hsi chen at 6.55 A.M. At 8 o'clock we began to ascend to a small plateau upon which the aneroid read 1310 ft. At Chin-hsi-chen it read 930 ft. (Mr Beech's map gives not given). Steep walled canyons have been cut back into this plateau. Standing up above this semi-plateau area are several high peaks which are clearly remnants left after the extensive erosion had swept all else away. Later we saw more of these peaks as well as numerous buttes standing up from the basal plain to this intermediate level.

The strata throughout this region are largely red beds lying nearly horizontally. The highest level probably corresponds to the base level seen in the summits of the various ridges crossed since leaving Wan Hsien. This we would put provisionally at the end of the Cretaceous in correspondence with the main base level seen in the Appalachians. The folding of the region probably occurred at the end of the Jura Trias since the red beds are incorporated in the folds. This was probably essentially base leveled (perhaps local base levelling due to obstruction of the drainage system downstream) by the end of the Cretaceous or Eocene. Perhaps the second uplift came somewhere along in the Miocene. Since then it may be that this second level was reached by base leveling during the later Tertiary. It may however be that this second level is due entirely to structure. The streams cutting canyons back into this level would appear to be due to rejuvenation unless the general erosion of this formation takes place by formation erosion. We passed over the divide between the Chu Ho and the Chia Ling Ho systems.

At 12.10 P.M. we had launched at village between Lo-chia chang and Hsin lung chen. In the afternoon we crossed a country with numerous scattered buttes or [monadnocks] belonging to the second level. See photo (No.72) showing the buttes and the high base level in the distance to the east. The country seen toward the west is lower than that to the east as would naturally be expected since the divide lies due east while in the west a large river is approached. This day's travel was through a more prosperous region than that of yesterday. Beggars were less numerous. A quite apparent change in the appearance of the peoples was noticed. As one member of the party expressed it, we are now getting into a white man's land. We saw many faces with quite light complexions and frequently red cheeks. With them went round black eyes. Another type was a pale faced, very angular type or countenance. These changes we assign to the mingling with some of the aboriginal races such as the Lolos and others. Many of the people, especially the children, seemed bright and acute. We reached Chiao-tien pa at P.M and stopped for the night having made 105 li.

Saturday March 27th. 1909

Started from Chiao-tien pa at 7 A.M. Our course was a winding one among low hills and rice fields but with little to be seen with which we were not already fairly familiar. Tung-kian chang passed about the middle of the morning is a town of some 10 000 inhabitants. This part of the country is much flatter and with less relief than that farther away from the river. Early in the afternoon we came upon a generally level plain of coarse gravel whose attitude where we reached it from the east was 1140 ft. This gravel plain was perhaps 2 ½ miles wide ending at its western extremity in the high river bluff of the Chia Ling.

This gravel plain sloped steadily toward the east since at the western edge the aneroid read 1250 ft. The aneroid carried down to the river read 970 ft. At the river bluff the gravel was found to be a superficial deposit amounting to 15-20 ft. This rests directly upon the undistributed red beds. The gravel is clearly the work of the Chia Ling river sometime during the Quateruary. This river at the present time exhibits much understanding. Apparently from its windings shown on the map and the slope of this gravel plain to the eastward it is entirely reasonable to suppose that the river flowed for some time on the eastern extremity of this plain. The flood plain of the present stream is abundantly strewn with gravel much of which is coarse. From the river bluff a splendid view of the river its highly cultivated and the city of Shun Ching Fu was obtained. The width of the present valley is perhaps a mile. We reached the city of Shun Ching Fu at 4.15 P.M. and went to the China Inland Mission where we were entertained by Mr. Evans and Porter.

Sunday March 28th. 1909

Day spent at the China Inland Mission in Shun Ching Fu. In the morning we walked along the top of the city wall led by Mr. Porter. Sky overcast but the lack of wind made the sight of the quiet city beneath is enticing because of its peacefulness. The city has two walls, an outer and an inner. We afterwards visited one of the government schools at which no work was in progress today since all government schools close on Sunday in China. Visited also many shops especially the silk manufacturing establishments. Silk is one of the specialties of Shun Ching. The silk looms show great ingenuity in their construction.

Had services at 11.30 Prof. Burton presiding. In the late afternoon I crossed the river with Mr. Wang and visited the 13 story pagoda on the opposite river bank. The river water is very clear so that we could see the bottom all the way across. Maximum depth perhaps 7-8 ft. Water of a dull green color. On way back followed the city wall again after crossing river by bridge. In one tree saw 18 large birds which Mr. Evans said were hawks, though Wang says they were eagles. Many others in other trees.

Monday March 29th. 1909

Left Mission in Shun ching Fu at 7.10 A.M and rode through city until we came out on the open terrace. Aneroid at city read 900ft (street level). Mr. Beech's map gives 1000 ft. After a mile or so across the terrace we began to ascend the hillslopes rapidly. There is little evidence of the higher terrace or gravel plain which was observed on the other side of the river at a height of 280 ft above the stream. Above 12oo ft we saw none of the gravel. The lack of a corresponding terrace on this side rise at once up to considerable elevations on steep hills, strongly favors the theory previously raised that the river formerly had its course further to the east than at the present and that the gravel plain was largely on its western bank. We climbed up to a point where the aneroid read 1490 ft indicating a rise of nearly 600 ft only a short distance back from the river.

For a couple of hours we traveled through a strongly hilly country. The strata were as during the past few days entirely of that red bed series with which we have now become so familiar. The beds are nearly horizontal with perhaps a very slight dip toward the N.W. At 10.30 reached a col to the North of which is a knob 60-80 ft. higher than the col. The upper 40 ft of this knob consist of a light ocean colored micaceous sandstone which does not exhibit the characteristics of the red beds. I could find no evidence of unconformity. The red bed shales suddenly turned to a light gray shale. Directly above the shale came the sandstone. This sandstone being more indurated than the strata below forms an abrupt wall perhaps 12 ft high above which the slopes rise gradually to the top of the knob.

On the face of the cliff I found a deposit of [travertine] indicating the presence of calcareous material somewhere in the series above. The aneroid read 1495 ft at the contact of the red beds and the sandstone. Further to the west on account of the slight dip this cream colored sandstone came lower in the hills and it was then found that above it came more red shales. It therefore is included in the red bed series younger rock formations than which we have not yet encountered. The most striking feature of the topography seen on the mornings journey was perhaps the steep sloped cols connecting the higher hills, the valley heads at these cols were cirque-like being well rounded instead of sharp V shaped gullies. Apparently these cirques are the result of weathering & erosion by formations. Softer layers below became eroded allowing the harder strata above to split off and tumble down leaving steep cliffs.

We took lunch at Chia Feng Chang at 1.30 P.M. After this the topography showed less and less relief apparently because by getting farther and farther from the river the valley bottoms became higher and higher and the summits are all at the original pen plain level. We reached Peng Chi Hsien at 6.45 P.M. Aneroid read 1200 ft.

Tuesday March 30th. 1909

Left Peng Chi Hsien at 7 A.M. Aneroid read 1195 ft. Crossed the stream and climbed the banks. Same red bed series. The region traversed during the morning was characterized by numerous buttes. Butte topography perhaps better developed than that which we have been seeing during the last few days. Strata weather by formations. Cols steep sided; valleys wide bottomed and comparatively level due for the most part probably to artificial cultivation. The red beds on this days journey showed more irregularity of bedding than previously seen. Some contorted layers underneath undisturbed horizontal beds.

The most interesting feature of the day's sightseeing was the great number of salt wells. These extended practically throughout the whole distance traversed. The brine come from deep down in the red bed strata and is reached be boring or drilling holes 600-800 ft. deep. The wholes are perhaps 3 inches in diameter. Above each salt well is a large bamboo wheel generally about 9 ft in diameter (see photo No The rope used is spliced bamboo strips. A bamboo basket, long and narrow, is let down into the well. The pressure of the water in the well opens a valve in the bottom of the bucket. When the bucket is pulled up the weight of water closes the valve. We visited a brine evaporating plant. Grass used as fuel and the brine evaporated in large shallow basins. The brine is purified by treatment with a mixture of clay and the ash from the grass fuel. The calcium and magnesium salts are perhaps precipitated by potassium carbonate in the ash. For details of the process see notes of T.C.C who inspected the plant most carefully.

We saw many rice power chain buckets raising water from lower rice fields to those at higher levels. In the afternoon we passed two large water wheels run by the water power of the creek and which raised the water to the top of the wheel where it was poured into a trough. From the trough a bamboo pipe carried the water to an adjacent field. These water wheels are said to cost about $ 15.00 gold but when once installed run without much attention. Near the periphery of the wheel are the paddles which contribute the power & turn the wheel, and the buckets which carry the water. Launched at Tang-chia pan at 1.45 P.M. Shortly after 5 o'clock we descended from the hills to the broad plain of the Sui-ning ho. This plain was highly cultivated and appeared prosperous. We ferried across the river & reached Tai-ho chen at 6.50 P.M.

Wednesday March 31th. 1909

Started from Tai ho chen at 7 A.M. Aneroid read 1245 ft. Crossed rest of flood plain (less than a mile); then a rock shoulder, and followed a tributary westward rising gradually. Strata red beds with some beds of gray micaceous sandstone and some grayish shale. Many small fragments and patches of $CaCO_3$ deposits here and there. These take the general form of chalk rather than ordinary limestone. The topography seen in distant views from the uplands is in no essential way different from what we have been seeing for the last few days. Scenery rather monotonous. Lunched at Cheng-Ku-dong.

Upon the red beds are quite different from them and may possibly belong to the Jurassic. No fossils were seen. A short distance further we visited a cave dug in the side of a steep cliff. Said to be very old. Ground plan shown in diagram.

Main entry goes in straight for 22 paces. Tunnels 7 ft high and perhaps 8 ft wide. Dug in a soft calcareous sandstone. Such a cave would be an admirable fortress since the entrance is small and in the side of a steep cliff. We reached Kuan-yin chiao one after another between 4.30 and 5.15 P.M

Thursday April 1st. 1909

Left Kuan-yin Chiao at 7 AM. Aneroid read 1350 ft. Red beds now appear more irregular. Gray and buff layers appear more generally. Increasing calcareousness apparently. Aneroid read 1800 ft on one of the higher shoulders. Lunched at Pai-Shu wa. Just west of here on the hilltops and cols bright buff micaceous sandstone beds give a pleasant change & relief after the monotonous red beds. Botryoidal weathering with large boulders resulting. At some distance below the butte summits we saw a horizon of conglomerate grit apparently with more or less calcareous cement. Both below and above this horizon there are gray layers. The grit may mean a local unconformity but it does not appear to be any general horizon marker or formation division point.

In the early afternoon when we were at the highest part of the day's journey there were exposed more than 100 ft of gray buff strata in sight. There does not appear to be any break in the whole Permo-Mesozoic series. There seems to be considerable lateral gradation from red into gray strata. But there is much difference apparent between the lower part of the Mesozoic series and the upper seen today and yesterday. The lower part was almost exclusively red; the upper some red beds with much of the gray & buff sandstones It may be that this upper part of the series belongs to the Jurassic. It is not unlike the Jurassic seen above the red beds in Arizona. In the middle of the afternoon we dropped down onto a lower country. The buff and gray strata were left behind. The strata are now altogether red. There may be a slight dip toward the S.E though the strata are nearly horizontal. We reached Ta-sheu-teng at 4.30 P.M and stopped for the night.

Friday April 2nd. 1909

Started from Ta-sheu teng at 7.06 A.M. Aneroid read 1700 ft. Country at first becomes less and less hilly. Evidently the erosion has progressed further here. Soon entered broad bottomed valley ½ - ¾ of a mile wide bordered by low hills. Further on the valley becomes narrower. Lunched at Hsin lung chang. Red beds in horizontal position during the morning; at the lunch point had become S. Easterly dipping beds. Soon after lunch we crossed over a low ridge, the result of a minor anticline. This first ridge is but an outlier of the main ridge beyond. The main range has a gentle front for the beds do not reach high angles-- not much exceeding 15°.

The fold is much smaller than the other folds toward Wan Hsien since it does not bring up the limestone strata below the red beds. The entire ridge is composed of red beds. At the point where we crossed it the aneroid read 2800 ft. For a time it appeared as those the ridge were a monoclonal fold but after passing the crest the beds became horizontal and further west began to dip to the N.W. At one point near the beginning of the plain the beds seemed to dip to the N.W. at high angles for a short distance but how local this was we did not discover

We emerged upon the famous plain of cheng tu after walking down the gulch for several miles. The ridge rises abruptly up from the plain on this side for the plain is quite flat and there are no foothills at this point. The slopes however are not very steep. The plain supports exceedingly luxurious crops. Fruit trees – oranges, peaches, cherries etc were abundant. Sometime after 4 P.M we reached Chao chia tu and crossed the Lu Ho. A couple of hours more though the highly cultivated fields brought us to Yao Chia tu.

Saturday April 3rd. 1909

Started from Yao Chia tu at 7.10 A.M. on the last stage of the overland journey. We crossed both the plain and various low eminences which have not yet been brought down to the plain level. These low hills exhibited the red bed sandstones and shales in nearly horizontal strata. They are clearly remnants. The general plain appears to be due for the most part to sedimentation by streams from the mountains. This part of the country appeared dry and dusty in comparison to what we have seen farther east. Many rice fields without water. This is due to the fact that the irrigation controlling works at Kwan Hsien have only just been opened and the water has not yet reached all the irrigation ditches throughout the plain. This region was therefore seen under unfavorable conditions which in addition to a hot, lifeless day, made it seem less attractive than we had expected. The region is cultivated to a high degree of perfection.

The roadway, however, was much poorer than any strip traveled since Wan Hsien. This is due to a great extent to the wheel barrow traffic which is very heavy here. Men are carried on wheelbarrows far more than chairs or rickshaws. The wheelbarrow wheels which have narrow tires rapidly cut deep grooves in the stone pavements thus spoiling the streets□ We followed the dusty road through suburbs and entered the north gate into Cheng tu the capital of Sze Chuan. We crossed most of the city following along fairly wide streets to the Methodist Episcopal Mission where we arrived after 4 o'clock and became the guests of Mr Beech.

Sunday April 4th. 1909

At Cheng tu. We attended the Chinese church service at 11 A.M. held in the Mission church room. Large attendance. In the afternoon we took a stroll in company with Mr. Beech along the city wall beginning at the south gate. Saw the "city water works" A large brick reservoir had been built but after much money had been spent upon it it was found to be defective and is not used. At present the water is raised up from the river by water bucket wheels and poured into troughs which feed into bamboo pipes. This water works was pointed out as an example of the inefficiency of the Chinese system for undertaking public enterprises and public improvements. Mr. Beech had made suggestions to those in charge of the construction of the brick reservoir but they were afraid to follow his suggestions since he is a foreigner. The reservoir failed because of ignorance of some of the common principles of dynamics.

We walked along the wall westward from the south gate. Saw the great crowds just outside the wall who are going and coming from the fair now being held near the city. Various styles of conveyance-chairs, rickshaws, wheelbarrows, pony carriages, horseback, by boat and afoot. We walked as far as possible until further progress was barred at the beginning of the Manchu city. Thence descended and crossed the athletic grounds to the Imperial University. Visited the old Methodist college property now being rented to the Y.M.C.A in charge of Mr. Service. Met today or last night, Dr. & Mrs. Canright, Mr. & Mrs. Newman, Mr. William, Mr & Mrs. Yost of the Methodist Mission, Mr & Mrs. Service of the Y. M. C. A.

Monday April 5th. 1909

Met Prof Burton with Dr. Hodgkin, his host, and Dr. Kilbourne of the Canadian Mission at the Commercial Press rooms and from there went to call upon the Chancellor of Education. Mr. Wang did the interpreting. Many courtesies exchanged. Prof. Burton asked if there were any ways in which our American Universities could be of service to China and what his Excellency thought desirable in this connection. His Excellency replied (1) Send more Chinese students to the University of Chicago. (2) that the American Universities should select better teachers to send to China. His Excellency seemed cordial and much interested. Arrangements were complicated for visiting the Imperial University later in the morning.

We next called upon the head director of the board of foreign affairs as preliminary to the call upon the Viceroy in the afternoon. From the foreign office we went to the imperial university where we were entertained at an informal tea and conducted about the institution by one of the acting directors of the University. The President of the University died only a couple of weeks ago and hence no real head at the present time. We spent a few minutes in the Chemistry lecture room where Mr. Sprague was describing the behavior of the halogen elements writing his chief points upon the blackboard in English while an interpreter nearly kept pace with him translating with Chinese upon the other half of the blackboard. To illustrate the principles simple experiments were performed before the class. Was very favorably impressed with the character of the work. The chemical laboratory room was large and very well equipped. The desks were practically new since the laboratory work has had to lag because of the lack of interpreters. The physical laboratory which is under the charge of Mr. Battdorf (grad of the U. of California) had considerable apparatus out on the tables showing that work was in progress though there was no class there at the time of our visit. Much first class apparatus in the supply cases. We saw the students at tiffin later. Table cloths were in use which is unusual in China. Everything seemed unusually clean for this country. The institution though only about six years old has a large number of buildings and all in all presents the best appearance of any institution which we have yet seen in China. On the scientific side it is much in advance of anything we have seen in this country.

After tiffin at the M.W. Mission we started at 2.40 P.M for the Viceroy's Yamen. Party consisted of Prof. Burton, Drs Hodgkin & Kilbourne, Messrs Beech, Wang Reed and ourselves. Caravan halted a couple of minutes in front of the Yamen while they were making preparations inside no doubt. Had time to watch the Chinese infantry outside going through a bayonet drill. Were met at the first door by Mr. Huang the Viceroy's interpreter and at the second door by His Excellency himself. Conducted inside and seated around a table at one end of which sat the Viceroy and at the other the Director of the board of foreign affairs.

The usual courtesies were passed back & forth. Prof. Burton asked if the Chinese students should be sent to America while quite young or after they had a good Chinese Education. The Viceroy replied that they should have a good knowledge of Chinese before going abroad since otherwise they would be of much less use to China when they returned. Prof. Burton asked if it would not be desirable to teach Chinese in America universities so that Chinese students could perfect themselves in Chinese while pursuing their studies of western subjects. His Excellency thought that this would be an excellent plan. Prof. Burton asked what subjects would be of the greatest benefit to Chinese students. Hus Excellency replied mining, the subject of manufacturing and other industries. The Viceroy asked T.C.C. how many mines he had seen in his travels in China. A vague question T.C.C replied that his studies were more upon educational & scientific lives than economics, and he had traveled so fast that he had not time to study mining conditions very critically. However he had seen considerable coal mining and had a high opinion of the richness and future importance of China's coal supply. The Viceroy ad only just received notification from Peking of our intended visit since we had come almost straight to Cheng tu from Hankow directly after prof Burton's party left Peking. He was therefore not expecting us for some time yet and was much surprised to learn that we were already here. He therefore at the opening of the interview asked for particulars of our routes and the trip from the U.S. to Cheng-tu. He expressed surprise and some admiration of our trip from Ichang to Wan Hsien, saying "Why we Chinese cannot do that." His Excellency throughout the interview showed much interest and cordiality.

The interview was brought to a close by Prof. Burton saying and holding to it that it was time to go. The general independent testimony of those of our party who understood Chinese was that the Viceroy wished to continue the interview as he was eager to have us talk. He is not a man who keeps the conversation going by his own contributions but is rather reserved though perfectly frank in stating his position according to Mr. Beech. He was therefore waiting for us to do the talking and keep the conversation going. Prof. Burton had asked him all that he wished to ask His Excellency directly and so when the lull came terminated the interview. Total length of interview 40 minutes. We were very favorably impressed with the appearance and bearing of the Viceroy.

From the Yamen we rode out through the south gate to the new University grounds where we were taken in charge by Dr. Davidson. The grounds are large, at the present time amounting to 65-70 acres. The location seems excellent for it is but a very short distance from the walls. The Chinese students belonging to the M.E. mission were engaged in a game of baseball which they played fairly well. At the request of Mr. Yost I pitched one inning for each side to give the batters some idea of how it is done in America. The batters knew nothing about curves which fooled the umpire as well. The catchers were much bothered by the speed as well as the curves. But the students played the game with a good deal of enjoyment apparently. After the baseball listened to the meeting held in Mr. Davidson's room. Prof. Burton & T.C.C talked.

Tuesday April 6th. 1909

Attended to arrangements for the trip to the mountains beyond Kuan Hsien. Then went out with Reed and Li San to make purchases. Found Cheng tu a fine city with many wide streets and attractive shops. In the meantime T.C.C. was busily engaged in conference with the representatives of the new University. The Chancellor of Education and the Director of the Board of foreign affairs returned yesterday's calls by calling at the new University. We all came together at 4 P.M. at the reception given in our honor at the University. Was greatly impressed by the number of Americans and Canadians present. Had not expected such an array of college graduates so far inland. There are 103 foreigners now in Cheng tu. Found those with whom I talked very much alive and in touch with outside affairs. After the reception we went to Mr. Yost's house where the discussion of the scope and proposed curriculum of the University was further discussed. Short talks were made by Messrs Taylor, Carson Beech and Davidson besides T.CC. and Prof. Burton. The meeting roused considerable enthusiasm and interested us exceedingly.

Wednesday April 7th. 1909

Most of party left the M.E. mission at 7.30 A.M; I did not get off till some 20 minutes later after everything else was on the road. Crossed through the Manchu city which afforded charming views in the bright early morning. Perfect day. In the Manchu city there is no crowding of buildings together. The houses are separated by small groves of imposing trees. Left the city by the west gate and joined the rest of the party at the stop for breakfast a short distance beyond the gate.

The day's journey was entirely over a plain gently sloping from the mountains toward Cheng tu. The plain is really one vast garden for it is very highly cultivated – probably one of the most highly cultivated tracts on the globe. Vast quantities of mustard were in bloom producing a bright yellow and green landscape. Along the roadside there are vigorous streams of water let into the irrigating ditches by the recent opening of the controlling works at Kuan Hsien. Apparently an excellent system of irrigation. Some of the ditches were almost small rivers. We passed an almost continuous stream of men bringing sacks of grain, apparently, on wheelbarrows. There were also a great many men bringing loads of coke on wheelbarrows. The coke was in very large pieces suggesting that the coal seam from which the coal came must be a fairly thick one. This coke is bound for Cheng-tu. The coking ovens are said to be near Kuan Hsien. This traffic all indicated much activity.

We stopped for lunch at Pi Hsien at 12.40 P.M. Started again at 1.15 P.M. Pushed on as fast as we could go throughout the afternoon. Wang, going on ahead to secure our entry into the city before the gates closed reached the gate of Kuan Hsien at 7.45 P.M. I arrived at 7.55; the rest later. Gates do not close till 10 P.M unlike Cheng tu which closes at dark. The plain over which we have come is a plain of aggradation resulting from streams coming down from the mountains. At many points there was a great deal of coarse gravel exposed in the irrigation ditches. Often in the afternoon we saw piles of large stones (6 inches in diameter) in the fields. A plain due to erosion chiefly would be far less regular. At 3.30 P.M. the gradient of the plain increased noticeably. The irrigation streams descended many short falls at points where there had been slight terracing.

Thursday April 8th. 1909

Yesterday's hard journey proved too much for about half of our chairmen and carriers who gave up the job and returned to Cheng tu. On account of the general prosperity of this region and apparently abundant work to keep the inhabitants employed our head man had much difficulty in engaging men to replace them. Because of this we were unable to leave the inn until yesterday 8.45 A.M. This fact of the scarcity of men especially when we remember the great abundance of local men who were so frequently seeking to relieve our chairmen between Wan Hsien and Cheng-tu, is of much significance in comparing the general economic conditions and relative prosperity of these districts.

The aneroid read 2690 ft at Kuan Hsien just before starting. The elevation is given as 2500 ft on Mr. Beech's map. We climbed over a rock ridge which runs from the mountain side to the river's edge where it ends in a nearly vertical cliff. The wall runs along this ridge. This ridge is the result of a hard conglomerate formation which stands at an angle of approximately 80° dipping toward the S.E. This conglomerate looks as if it might belong to the red bed series. It is several hundred feet in thickness. The next younger formation appearing in a second ridge and still dipping to the S.E. at angles of 70-80° is a hard grayish sandstone. After continuing along the east bank for ½ - ¾ of a mile we crossed the river on a bridge consisting of a board walk suspended by heavy bamboo ropes. Just above the bridge is the dam which deflects much of the water from the river into the irrigation ditches and controls the whole system of irrigation which waters the plain of Cheng tu. The walk along the east bank of the river afforded splendid views of the west. These constitute the first range of the Tibetan uplands. Some of them rise 3000-4000 ft above the plain and terminate in sharp peaks. They are real mountains and afforded a pleasant relief from the monotony of the level topped ridges of eastern Sze Chuan. Soon after turning to the north on the west bank of the river the strata were found to dip to the N.W. at high angles. Strike was N.E. & S.W the direction of dip being nearly due N.W. These beds were a hard indurated grayish sandstone which in some places was coarse enough to be classed as a grit. Saw men washing the river sands for gold.

At the bend in the river there are three coal mines. It was not apparent whether they are in different seams or whether they are all in one seam for they are approximately in the line of the strike. The average thickness of the coal in the three mines is said to be 1 ½ ft. Just beyond the bend are what appear to be lime kilns. Beyond the great bend in the river we proceeded along the strike of the beds for most of the afternoon. On the North side (left bank) a great limestone cliff is a prominent landmark. This is a gray limestone which has under gone some metamorphism so that calcite facets are prominent. The beds dip to the N.W. All the beds now in sight on both banks dip to the N.W. Examined some of this limestone as the right bank and found several specimens of the genus Products. This indicates Carboniferous age. Probably this great limestone formation is to be correlated with the Wushan limestone of the Yangtze gorges. This limestone continued all the way to Tzien keh ching.

Friday April 9th. 1909

Left Tzien keh ching at 7.05 A.M for a day's excursion up the Hsi valley into the mountains. To facilitate travel T.C.C's four man chair was left behind and Wang's chair fitted up for three carriers taking this three man chair and my light two men chair and eight chair carriers for relays, and leaving the boys and all the baggage behind, T.C.C. Wang & I hurried up the valley going almost due north. We abandoned the road leading to Ta tien lu since this road runs nearly straight west and is too nearly parallel to the strike of the fold to reveal much of the structure in a day's journey. The map is incorrect in giving to the mountain ridges such a N & S. trend. They really trend E.N.E and W.S.W. The formation just across the river to the North from Tzien keh ching is the Carboniferous limestone.

The river coming in from the north flows through a sharp gorge for ½ - ¾ of a mile just before the tributary joins it from the west. The walls of the gorge are of this limestone which is quite resistant like the Wushan limestone in the gorges of the Yangtze. The bedding planes are no longer very well seen, since the limestone has undergone considerable alteration since it was deposited. Whenever the bedding planes could be made out the strata were found to rest at very high angles, the dip generally being to the N.W. Beyond the limestone gorge the valley broadens out and the slopes are very generally covered with rock mantle and vegetation. It is only here and there that the solid rock is seen in place and on such a hurried trip could be inspected only at a few points. Wherever the bedding planes could be made out they were found to be nearly vertical. The strike taken at two separate points perhaps a mile apart where the direction of strike was very clearly shown in vertical layers was found to be N 65° E and N 68-70° E. Ripple marks were fairly well preserved on the sides of several of these beds. Vertical slabs of ripple marks! The striking feature of the morning's trip was the extraordinary persistence of very high dipping or nearly vertical beds for mile after mile as we crossed the axis of folding. There were some suggestions in one or two places of lower dips but they could not be shown conclusively to be bedding planes. Finally at a point perhaps 6 miles in a straight line from Tzien keh ching we suddenly came upon massive granite. The first suggestion of the granite was the fact that comparatively few pebbles of sedimentary rocks were found in the stream bed of the tributary which comes in from the east at this point. Instead most of the pebbles were a gray granite together with some pinkish or reddish granites, gabbro diorites and a variety of red porphyry. Beyond this tributary the granite was quickly found in situ. This granite in many places shows secondary alteration with the formation of [serpentine]. Pebbles of what appeared to be a chlorite schist were found in the bed of the tributary just referred to. We followed the path on into the granite area until at the point where the main road from Kuan Hsien joined our path the party split. This is perhaps a mile from the beginning of the granite.

T.C.C. and Wang continued on (passing through the village of Yin hsin wan shortly) for about 2 miles. They report various local changes in the character of the granite. This makes about 3 miles of this granite actually seen. How much further it continues we cannot say. From this junction of the roads I followed the Kuan Hsien road ascending rapidly on the hillside until nearly to the col through which it crosses to the next valley. Then climbed straight up the grass slopes to the North through thickets and brambles to an elevation of 5650 ft. or 1975 ft above the junction of the roads (aneroid read 2970 ft at Tzien keh before starting). This peak consists of the same gray granite throughout. From this elevation secured a good view of the neighboring peaks to the West, South, and East though the view to the north was cut off by higher portion of the same mountain. The peak opposite across the river must be in the neighborhood of 10000 ft in altitude. The toothed mountain in the front range south of Tzien keh, seen over a lower mountain (5500-6000 ft) apparently attains a height of at least 7,000 ft above the sea. The general appearance of these mountains is peaked. Their great difference in height and individual character makes them unusually attractive after the monotony of mountains carved from former base levels in which all the summits have the same level. (see photos). They are worthy outliers of the greatest mountain system of the globe. We came together and returned to the tributary valley where we first saw the granite. We could not find the contact between the sedimentary and igneous rocks. (There is a gap of some 100 yards between the granite seen in place and the first sedimentary rock seen in place. This is a very hard indurated shale of nearly black color. Between are grass slopes. In the bed of the tributary I found many pebbles of a reddish porphyry which I did not see within the main granite area from which I judge that a red porphyry occurs between the main granite and the sedimentary series. Whether the granite belongs to the basement complex or is a later intrusion, perhaps contemporaneous with the great uplift of the strata, could not be definitely determined. It did not seem coarse enough to be a batholithic intrusion. It is a granite of medium granularity. There was also too much local variation apparently to be consistent with the hypothesis that the mass is one great intrusion. Some specimens of the rock were granites, or more strictly, quartz diorites with an abundance of quartz; others were diabasic. Perhaps several separate intrusions might be taken as the explanation of this variation. But because of the great extent of the formation and the fact that it is at the base of a great series of sedimentary beds, we are inclined to regard this granite as the Pre-Cambrian Complex brought up by the great folding. We have come through the entire Paleozoic series from the red beds of the Cheng tu plain to the granite in these mountains. The beds have nearly universally been found to dip at high angles and in many places were practically vertical. At the town of Kuan Hsien a coarse reddish conglomerate suggested the Permo-Mesozoic red bed series – probably the base of that series. Then came sandstones and shales with coal seams followed by a hard resistant limestone containing specimens of Productions. This limestone must be 3000-5000 ft in thickness and where crossed by the river produces a gorge. Beyond this come softer sandstones and shales, followed by more indurated shales and coarser grits. Then the granite. In addition there may be other strata of significance which were overlooked since we often were compelled to travel some distance without any outcrops. It seems impossible, however, that the gorge making Carboniferous limestone can be repeated in the succession as would have to be the case if the great extent of vertical beds were the result of repetition of folds. I interpret the succession of strata to mean one gigantic fold of which we have seen only one limb.

If we allow 2 miles of vertical beds South of Tzien keh to the beginning of the upturn and 6 miles north from Tzien keh to the beginning of the granite, there must have been some 8 miles of nearly vertical sedimentary beds in the limb of this anticline. This would mean a thickness of something like 40,000 ft for the sedimentary series here. How much granite there is we cannot say. The whole anticline must be one of tremendous proportions. While there was some local contortion of the strata we saw no evidence of down turning of secondary folds. The nature of the fold tends to force the beds upward. We saw no evidence of faulting. Apparently the great front of the Tibetan uplands is not a fault face as some authorities have guessed it to be. We reached Tzien keh at 4.45 P.M. earlier than we had expected.

Saturday April 10th. 1909

Left Tzien keh at 7.10 A.M. for the return journey. The river follows the strike of the folds for about half the way to Kuan Hsien. For most of the distance it has cut its course through the less resistant shales. Shortly before making the sharp bend to the South it is working in the limestone & cutting a narrow channel. Several large lime kilns near the bend. Just at the bend where the shales appear above the limestone are four coal mines. These now appear to be in different seams. Between the great bend in the river and Kuan Hsien there appears to be a charge in the direction of strike.

The rock exposures here seen along the road were generally such as not to give good opportunities to determine the direction of strike and hence the figures obtained are to be regarded as less curtain than those found yesterday. The following strike readings were obtained between the bend of the river and Kuan Hsien N 38º E. Hard indurated sands N 25º E at local anticlinal contortion N 25º E 100 yds from anticlinal " this in a shale formation N 24º E Sandstone layer further on N 65º E Shale beds at the bridge crossing the river to Kuan Hsien. Those beds dip 57º N.W. They stand out much more conspicuously than those from which the previous figures on this page were taken. Hence I give more weight to this last reading than to the others N 50º E Shale layer near the bridge from the bridge the bearing of the lofty peak south of Tzien keh which we have been using as a sort of landmark is S 67º W Further strike readings N 37 E Sandstone near bridge N 60 E Shale The last from a clear cut face. The dip here was 55º-60º quarter of a mile South of the bridge was an exposure having a strike N 70º E. The dip was 77º S.E. Of all these readings those in the neighborhood of N 60º + E were from the best developed beds and are far more reliable than the others. There is no question of their reliability. Those exposures from which the figures N 25-30º E were obtained were generally such as to make the value of the readings uncertain but they were taken for what they might be worth. The apparent strike may not always have been the true strike. These may be some local variation in the strike just above Kuan Hsien. But the main trend of the fold from Kuan Hsien to the granite is in the neighborhood of N 65º E. The trend of the ridges on Stieler's map is erroneous. The ridges are only partially dependent upon the geologic structure. Near the plain there is a conspicuous chain of serrate peaks rising to 7000-8000 ft parallel with the general strike. Obviously due to resistant strata. Just inside of them (to the N.W) is a long valley tract cut in the softer shales. Then a ridge composed of the Carboniferous limestone. The further back into the axis of the fold the less, apparently, is the topography dependent upon the structure. The erosion probably has not yet progressed to the stage where the influence of structure reaches its maximum. This will come later when the softer strata are mostly cut away and it is chiefly the more resistant strata which remain as ridges. In the granite area the peaks show little order or grouping.

To the west of Kuan Hsien there were outlying peaks, low but sharp in outline which extended farther out into the plain than any at Kuan Hsien. We appealed to the river to have removed the low outlying hills near its delta out onto the plain. There were some low hills to the east but they were less conspicuous than those toward the west. Near the bridge across the river just above Kuan Hsien is a beautiful temple erected in honor of the engineer who devised the system of irrigation for the Chang tu plain. This temple is in reality a series of temples built one above the other on the

hillside which are so connected by flights of steps as to seem like one building. The whole effect is both picturesque and imposing and to me was quite unique in conception.

To shorten tomorrow's journey and lessen the toil we pushed on past Kuan Hsien and followed the river banks down the gently sloping alluvial plain to Hsing Chang where we arrived at 4.50 P.M. Took photos of an open air theater by setting up tripod on a table in the rear. Almost instantly every face in the audience (perhaps 300-400) was turned toward me. Actors on stage were completely forgotten and sank into insignificance in comparison with a Yankee photographer.

Sunday April 11th. 1909

Commenced the return journey from Hsing Chang to Cheng tu at 6.55 A.M. Reached Pi Hsien at noon delaying many times on the road to secure snapshots of street scenes. A long and extremely dusty walk brought us to the west gate of Cheng tu at 5.30 P.M and the M.E. Mission at 6 o'clock.

Monday April 12th. 1909

Dined at 12 o'clock in the Yamen of the provincial treasurer, Mr. Wang, who had sent out invitations during our absence. We were most cordially received and treated in a friendly and informal way by the Chinese officials present. The officials present were the provincial treasurer, chancellor of education, taotai of military department, taotai of foreign office, assist. director of education, official interpreter of viceroy, Mr. Cheng, teacher in foreign office school & provincial University and taotai Chow, head of industrial department. The foreigners present were Dr. Hodgkin, Kilbourne, Canright, Messrs, Beech & Davidson, Burton, Wang, T.C.C. & R.T.C.

After the dinner the host sent out for a photographer who took a large group picture of the assemblage in the garden of the yamen. We were conducted through the extensive and very picturesque gardens which form an important part of the whole estate. Artificial lake with gold fish, handsome peacocks and a Szechuan deer. The general effect of the open houses set in between carefully planned gardens which are arranged as a sort of labyrinth was most agreeable. Our host is contemplating a tour of Europe & the U.S. in the near future to examine & study the financial systems of the different countries.

Tuesday April 13th. 1909

Made arrangements for the return journey down the river. Took both kodaks and strolled about the Manchu city and thence through the main Chinese city of Cheng-tu. The Chinese city looks very crowded after the open courts and breathing spaces of the Manchu city. The Manchu women do not bind their feet and appear generally superior to those in the Chinese city. After tiffin went out to the University. Busy meetings in progress. T.C.C. gave a lecture on "Some Geological problems of Asia" at 4 P.M. After this came final meet of the organization committees of the University and the fare well ceremonies.

Wednesday April 14th. 1909

Our complete party assembled at the M.E. Mission as a rendezvous and commenced the return journey at 8.10 A.M. On account of the low state of the water in the river our large boat (the one which brought Mr. Beech's family up from Ichang) could only come up to Kiang Kon and hence we are obliged to make the first part of the journey by chair. Left the city of Cheng tu by the South gate and followed a generally South westerly course though with considerable winding. The first part of the journey is across a flat country not unlike the plain crossed on the way to Kuan Hsien. The streets in the first few villages were fairly clean and no beggars were seen suggesting that these villages are under the same police control as the capital or else that they demand similar conditions. Before we reached Hsing tsing beggars became numerous.

We had lunch at Hsing tsing and were obligated to wait a long time for the baggage carriers to arrive. During the afternoon a terrace of reddish material paralleled our course to the left (S.E.) Later hills or red beds appeared to the west. Soon after 5 P.M. the chair carriers went on strike because of the prospect of a long day of it. Finally forced them on after much time was lost. The distance from Cheng tu to Kiang kon instead of being 120 li as we had been informed at Cheng tu proves to be 165 li by the main road though less by a narrow shorter cut. We were therefore obliged to stop for the night at Tung lung chang where we arrived about 7.30 P.M. after crossing several good sized streams. These were close together. Whether separate streams or merely arms of the same river was not determined in the darkness. Tung lung chang is said to be 95 li from Cheng tu and yo li from Kiang kon.

Thursday April 15th. 1909

Started from Tung lung chang at 6.50 A.M. Hills of red beds which are generally horizontal back of the town (to the west). We followed the west bank of the river. A high gravel terrace appeared on the east side. This may possibly be the local equivalent of the extensive high gravel terrace at Shun King. The stream here has a well-defined valley between hills or upland country. Farther north it flowed across the great Cheng tu plain. Probably the Cheng tu plain before the extensive filling from the mountains to the W & N.W began was characterized by topography not essentially unlike that now to be seen in the neighborhood of Tung lung chang and below. Was probably a well eroded area with wide valleys and remnant ridges of hills between the stream courses. But with the great uplift of mountains to the West & North along such a sharp steep front there began at once a rapid deposition of course material at the base of the mountains which filled up the irregularities of surface in this low area and has finally produced the Cheng tu plain. As we get further and further away from the mountain front the masking of the former topography become less and less. It is not impossible that there has been a slight uplifting of the plain to the N.W. has caused rejuvenation of the streams down here.

During the morning we saw many fields of poppies in bloom. Plant about 2 ft high; flowers white or purplish pink in color. Shortly before noon we ferried across the river to Kiang Kou and got aboard our boat which is to take us to Ichang. The boat started downstream at 2.45 P.M. Pyramidal forms appear soon on the left bank. Red bed series in approximately horizontal beds. The day was very hot.

Friday April 16th. 1909

Aboard craft all day without a chance to go ashore. Descending the Min ho by drifting, rowing and sculling. Throughout the entire day the red bed series continued to be the only rock formation seen. Beds generally horizontal though at some points there is a dip of a few degrees upstream. The river bluffs and hills near the river rise up to heights of 300 ft. at the maximum; many of them are lower. We could only see the hills close to the river but from their general appearance I judge that the topography of this region is the low hill-butte topography which is so characteristic of the red basin of Szechuan.

While the scenery was attractive to the traveler this strip of river afforded very little of geologic interest. The water was low so that we ran aground twice. We lost considerable time in getting off the rocks late in the afternoon and had to send men ashore with ropes. I put in a heavy afternoon developing negatives taken at Cheng tu and on the Kuan Hsien trip. As yesterday, the weather was oppressively hot. About noon we passed a fleet of small fishing boats whose owners use a kind of black duck to catch the fish. The birds dive and catch small fish in their hills. When they come up the men cause them to disgorge.

Saturday April 17th. 1909

In the middle of the forenoon the scenery became quite picturesque; later the valley widened and the banks less abrupt, Red beds, exceedingly red in places, and generally horizontal. We reached Kia-ting about 2.30 P.M. and went ashore supposedly having an hour's shore leave.

Kia ting is an average Chinese City. Many houses were fairly new. Saw one large house in the process of construction. The city wall instead of being constructed of gray brick is built of blocks of very red sandstone. Many of the blocks of this sandstone have suffered considerable wear. Kia-ting is situated at the junction of the Min ho and the Tung ho in the acute angle between them. We walked along the wall fronting the Tung ho and marveled that this stream is so much larger than the Min whose name and direction are imparted to the combined stream below Kia-ting. The Tung comes down from Ta-tsien lu and the high mountains to the west. It was carrying much more water and running much swifter than the Min.

At the junction of the two rivers is a notable spit which follows the direction of the Tung ho and runs nearly across the channel of the Min. The water of the Min is forced over into a narrow channel against the left bank. Threw a stone from the split across this channel against the sandstone bluff. It was at this point that we tied up for the night. The bluff opposite is made of exceedingly red, massive sandstone, the face of which has been extensively carved. Surmounting the bluff is the usual pagoda. Many green trees offsetting the bright red sandstone. Altogether a very picturesque spot.

We returned to the boat at the end of the agreed hour but the captain did not appear. While waiting for him we witnessed a fight between two groups of longshoremen over the right to unload cargo from the boat next to ours. At first a boisterous war of words. Then pushing men about followed by grabbing the queues of the opponents and pulling their hair. It was a laughable but very exciting riot. Apparently nobody was hurt though in its way it was as fierce a fight as I ever saw. It attracted a great crowd who watched the progress of the squabble from the banks. The captain not returning the crew rowed the boat down to the above described where they tied up for the night. Prof. Burton paid a call to the Baptist Mission.

Sunday April 18th. 1909

To make up for yesterday afternoon's lost time the boat started very early. When I awoke the sacred mountain, O mei shan was in full view to the west. According to Mr. Beech this is unusual. We doubtless have to thank the thunderstorm of last night for the partial clarification of the atmosphere which made this view possible. The weather has been remarkably dry for a long time past. Day after day has gone by without any rain. But last night there was a great deal of lightning and a moderate rain. This morning the atmosphere still appeared hazy but distant views were possible, the distant outlines taking that clear cut blue tint which is so generally associated with rain in mountainous countries. Two isolated peaks were to be seen, the one to the right being O mei shan according to our map.

They were anything but impressive, either as to apparent height or character of outline. I should not have guessed them to rise more than 4000 ft above the plain. The slopes do not seem sufficiently abrupt to require a fault to explain them. I should think it more likely that they are parts of a fold whose adjacent portions have been removed by the Tung and its tributaries which flow past them. The view of these mountains was soon out off by the bluffs of generally horizontal beds of red sandstone. Further on is a gentle anticlinal arch which brings up the buff sandstones below the red beds. Saw one coal mine and another village where they were loading baskets of coal onto long rafts, within this area of buff strata. The coal mine was not at the river level but more than 100 ft up the slope.

Beyond this point the beds dip downstream at a angle (up to 10°) for a long distance bringing in the red series again. From the character of this fold we are inclined to consider it the prolongation of the ridge forming fold 1 ½ day's journey east of Cheng tu. This fold at the point where we crossed it east of Cheng tu, however, did not bring up the formation underlying the red beds. At 1.45 P.M. we came upon a sharper fold. The beds rapidly became inclined until they dipped 32° in a direction approximately N 47° W. The strike of the fold is therefore in the neighborhood of N 45° E. Within half a mile the inclination of the beds had greatly lessened and soon became zero followed by a dip in the opposite direction. The fold appeared to be rather symmetrical for dips of 30° to the S.E characterized the downstream limb. The older formations were not brought to the surface.

About the middle of the afternoon we passed the mouth of the tributary stream from the west which brought in water having a remarkably bright red tint. This red water did not mix with the fairly clear water of the Min for some distance below the debouchure of the tributary. Red color due to sediment from the red beds some of which are exceedingly red. Perhaps last night's storm has had a good deal to do with the amount of red sediment which has been washed into the stream. At 4.15 we passed a small local anticline in which the beds dip perhaps 8. This and the shaper fold seen at 2 pm we do not correlate with anything seen on the overland journey to Cheng tu since the second fold east of Cheng tu is too far away from the first to come in at this point.

During the later part of the afternoon we had as a companion all along the river a series of level topped hills which in places amounted to practically a rock bench. This may have been perhaps 150 ft above the river. As it extended back away from the immediate river channel we are inclined to regard it as a pen plain, probably analogous to the Tertiary base level in the Appalachians. It is very persistent and well developed. Between it and the river are ordinary river terraces. Beyond it to S.W. rises a ridge of fairly high mountains which were in view for the last hour before we tied up for the night. I guessed them to be perhaps 2000 ft. in height above the plain. We caught a glimpse of them seen edgeways shortly before 4 P.M. They were then seen to be the prolongation of the sharp anticlinal fold which we observed about 2. P.M. Most of the peaks then in sight were on the S.E. limb of the anticline as was evident from their profiles. On the extreme right of our limited field of vision however were two peaks which appeared to belong to the N.W. limb. We tied up for the night in a little alcove just as darkness was coming on.

Monday April 19th. 1909

Strata at first horizontal. At 8.20 (my time; T.C.C. has ½ hour earlier and has had for several days) the beds are dipping to the N.W. at an angle of about 10°. This dip continues until at about one mile above Sui fu the buff formation below the red beds is brought up. Opposite the northern end of Sui fu the fold turns sharply and the dip changes to about 45° to the S.E. The direction of strike is roughly N 45° E. This sharp dip quickly brings down the red bed series and the buff formation goes beneath the river. The angle of dip lessens to 35°.

We landed at Sui fu at 10.45 A.M. I went back to get a photo of the curved temple which follows the outline of the river bluff just above the city. On the hilltop back of this curved temple is another large temple toward which great crowds of people were going to pray for rain. Saw many gorgeously decorated boys 4-5 years old being carried thither some on ponies, others in men's arms. Sui fu is a fine city located on a terrace perhaps 60 ft above the river. It occupies the acute angle between the Min and the Yangtze Kiang. There are many fairly wide streets with very attractive shops. The city is said to have about 200,000 inhabitants while Kia Ting has 40,000-50,000. The city seemed to me far more attractive than Kia ting. There are more large attractive buildings in Sui fu and apparently some unusually interesting temples which would repay a longer stay. The hillsides about are dotted here and there with small temples. We saw four pagodas, 3 across the Min ho and 1 across the Yangtze kiang very picturesque view of the city between the rivers as we started down the Yangtze.

The Min ho seems fully as large as the Yangtze at the junction. The beds dip to the S.E just below Sui fu after which they become horizontal and soon dip N.W at angles up to 50° in places. The above diagram gives approximately the structure. The anticline to the S.E. of Sin fu brings the lower formation high above the river so that it forms a ridge. In these buff beds are a great number of holes dug for coal. Many dump piles of blackish or dark gray material seen on the hillsides. None of the workings seemed to be very extensive. The core of this anticline is very well shown in the river bluff. Beyond this arch the red beds come in again and continue to the end of the day's journey.

During most of the reminder of the afternoon the river generally flowed in a direction parallel with the strike except for frequent small bends. The beds were generally resting horizontally or at low angles. The valley became very wide in places with low hills in the distance. In other places the river flowed at the base of steep cliffs. These cliffs were usually composed of very massive layers of a dirty brownish pink sandstone which breaks off in great blocks and yields a coarse talus.

Tuesday April 20th. 1909

Valley fairly wide and bounded by hills ranging up to 300 ft in height. Same red bed series. The river runs close to the strike of the beds much of the time. Beds dip at low angles now in one direction, now in another but no notable folds encountered. At 10.05 AM. beds were dipping about 15° to the N.W. Have made sharp bend; were going N.E. are now going nearly due south. At 10.30 beds dipping 14° S.E determine the whole contour of the hills to the east. Difficult to get angle of strike. One reading gave N 44º E. Better say N 40º -50º E. Our course is now nearly due east. The valley has become wide and open. The dip to the S.E without much change for a half hour after which it lessens somewhat.

At 11.10 came to bluffs on the right bank while the left bank is low as far as one can see. The bluffs are 400-500 ft high, steep in the upper half but with more moderate slopes in the lower half. Our course is now nearly due east. The turn from the Southerly course made about 11.05. The beds are now nearly horizontal. The lower slopes of the bluffs are very extensively cultivated interspersed with groves of trees which give a brilliant green tint on this spring day. Patches of red soil show many of the layers in the precipitous cliffs above are of a bright vermilion color; others are brick red; the weathered surfaces gray brown. The whole combination is most pleasing to the eye. Bamboo groves here and there whose color has changed (perhaps with the season) to an olive brown color add that tint to the picture.

At 11.45 passed the end of the steep bluffs on the right bank. Our course has gradually changed until we are now going N 45º E or in the direction of the strike. The beds are seen to dip to the S.E at low angles. For the last couple of hours the Yangtze has been broad (500 yds perhaps) and the current has been much slower than usual. The water is still remarkably red in color due to red bed wash though I think I detect a slight decrease in the muddiness due no doubt to some of the sediment having settled owing to the more sluggish current in this strip. Still I find it necessary to have water boiled to coagulate the sediment and then filtered through cotton to remove the ferruginous silt before attempting to use it to develop negatives this afternoon.

At 12 o'clock beds in low hills on left bank dip to the N.W. at an angle of about 10º. Our course is now easterly. This generally open country through which the Yangtze is now flowing is apparently to be correlated with the stretch of open lowland country which we crossed on the overland journey before reaching the final ridge of upturned strata a day and a half east of Cheng tu. At 12.05 P.M. dip 14º N.W. at 12.50 beds dipping 10º N.W. Our course is due North. The dip is 20º N.W at 1.45. We are headed S 70º E. Have been coming through a wide, open valley.

At 3 P.M. we were opposite the city of Lu chow located at the junction of the Fu sung with the Yangtze. Back of the city is a wall running over hills and ravines like a miniature great wall of China. Within the city is a new type of Pagoda. Between the stories are two rings. Instead of tapering gradually toward the top it is large and apparently circular at the base and tapers rapidly in a curved line so that it roughly suggests the dome of the capital at Washington though proportionately taller and more slender. During the remainder of the afternoon we passed through a region of broad minor undulations. None of them were of sufficient magnitude to develop notable ridges. The region was characterized by low hills of red beds. The river was generally broad and the current slow with however an occasional small rapid.

Wednesday April 21. 1909

Boat started before it was fully light. Beautiful sunrise which I could watch from my sleeping bag without stirring. At 10.45 A.M. we passed the town of Ho-Kiang which means the junction of rivers. Small river comes in from the South. Generally open hilly country through which the Yangtze follows a winding course. Current moderate. More prominent ridge than usual seen about noon but even this ridge has been worn down to ordinary dimensions in the neighborhood of the river. At 3.25 P.M. we were obliged to stop at the town of Chu Kia deh while the captain purchased a cargo of rice and loaded it into the hold of our boat. We strolled about the town but saw little of interest. Just outside the town were some rice fields in which the bright green young grain stood four or five inches above the water.

Started on again at 4.45 P.M. after being followed to the boat by a large crowd of curious natives who made photographic work difficult. At 5.15 strata dipped 40°-42° to the N.W. At 5.30 the dip was 60° NW. Our course is nearly due East. This is only a minor fold though sharp for at 6 P.M the beds are dipping to the S.E at an angle of about 15°. Course somewhat north of East. The intermediate beds did not indicate very clearly just how they did lie. The fold does not produce any ridge which is worthy of the name.

Thursday April 22nd. 1909

Following a north easterly course. Started at 4 A.M. At 7.55 began to cross the core of a prominent ridge. Beds dipping to the West at an angle of about 35°. The carboniferous comes up. Two coal mines, one of which has a large pile of good looking coal beside the mouth. These are on the left bank. Across the river the hills are comparatively low. The beds near the water's edge on the right bank dip to the S.W. On the left bank the hills are 800-1000 ft high and peaked at the top. Limestone continues up to the peak tops. Lime kilus high up on the hillsides. Turning to the east in our course we are opposite red beds again at 8.12 A.M. These are dipping to the S.E. at angles of 30°-32°. The reason for these peculiar dips is now apparent. We are now facing a long ridge of parallel hills or peaks. We have apparently just crossed the fold near its end where it plunges down at an unusually rapid angle for a plunging anticline. We were at first wondering whether it might not be a turning of the fold upon itself, or perhaps a dome like folding of the strata. The plunging of the anticline which brings the resistant Carboniferous beds below the river level explains why there is no high ridge of peaks on the right hand side of the river. Only red beds occur on this side. We turned to the S.E. and then around a bend to the N.E. Red beds are now dipping to the E. or even N.E. We are abreast of them and their axis prolonged runs straight against the high ridge of limestone peaks. Their axis appears to be nearly at right angles to that of the main ridge. This observation made at 8.45. At 9.10 AM. going N 45° E. we can now see the high ridge of limestone peaks extending for miles to the N.E. There are a good many fairly sharp peaks in the distance standing up over the low hills of red beds through which the river is now flowing. The Trend of this ridge is NE-SW which makes it entirely consistent with the folds seen on the overland trip from Wan Hsien. This is undoubtedly to be correlated with one of these mountain ridges, pro 10 AM. running N.W on a long stretch. Ahead in full view is the high ridge of limestone peaks which run N.E. and S.W. Their base levelled crest is seen to good advantage. The beds near the river are now nearly horizontal.

At 10.30 passed town of Kiang tsing Chuan. At 11.15 were going south after passing around the great bend. The high ridge is still in plain view to the N.W. The beds near the river are dipping to the NW at an angle of 8°. At 12.15 we are following an Easterly or South easterly course. Ahead is a high ridge which suggests itself as fold No 3 of the overland series. At 1.30 we are running to the North nearly parallel with the ridge just mentioned. The beds dip to the West at angles of 40° approximately. At 1.45 we turned sharply to the East and cross the ridge. The ridge is composed apparently entirely of limestone. The outer portion is dark colored but the lower beds of the series are a light buff. A very resistant layer of limestone runs out 100 yards into the river just at the turn. Sighting along this I got the strike of the beds very accurately as N 10° W. The ridge sighted for a length of several miles just before reaching the turn appeared to run nearly N & S. but with a slight deviation toward the NW & SE rather than N.E. & S.W. as the folds have usually been running. Limestone beds sip 53° to W. Several coal mines on both sides of the river. With these are several lime kilus. Perhaps 10 lime kilus which constitute quite an industry. At 1.58 limestone strata have eased off to horizontality beds soon dip toward the East some contortions & minor folds. At 2.07 limestone dips 29° in a direction about S 75° E. In 100 yds the beds are again horizontal. Considerable contortion of the beds. Beds again assume the easterly dip. The coal bed reappears and with it are associated lime kilus. About 100 yards beyond the coal seam the strata become vertical and in one spot overturned a few degrees. A sharp ridge results. This ridge is the last of the limestone. Beyond to the east are low hills of red beds. The last ridge can be followed by the eye for several miles to the north. This abrupt front of the mountain ridge runs nearly N & S, or a few degrees to the NW & SE (possibly N 5°-10° W.) The high dips to the East continue for more than a mile across the fold and then decline toward horizontality. The red beds in this region cannot therefore be less than 5000 ft in thickness. Cross section of the fold.

At 2.45 a hard layer of rock standing out of the water enabled me to get the strike of the beds at this point. Found N 10° E approximately. At 3.50 red beds dip 24° to the west. We are now running nearly straight east and approaching another mountain ridge. This is the point at which the upturn really begins. I should estimate the distance to the beginning of the real peaks of hard rock at a mile & a half, At the end of half a mile the dip has increased to 60° W. Unfortunately for an estimate of the thickness of the red bed series the river does not continue further across the fold at this point but turns to the north and follows the strike. This continued all the rest of the way to Chung King. We passed the mint opposite the city shortly before dark. At 7.10 P.M we were abreast of the lights at the upper end of the city. We did not actually tie up and land until 7.45. This took place on the spit between the Yangtze and the Kia Ling; at the end of the spit rather more on the Kia Ling than the Yangtze. We went ashore and visited various shops and stores.

Notebook
No. 4

Friday April 23rd. 1909

Woke up at anchor at the end of the spit between the Yangtze Kiang and the Kia Ling. A rainy morning. Went ashore and spent the morning strolling about the streets of Chung King. Followed the wall throughout its entire extent (said to be 4 ¾ miles) going up the right bank of the Kia Ling at the outset and crossing over to the left bank or the Yangtze on the return. Fine views of the city and the two rivers from the hill at the south western extremity of the city wall. Some picturesque temple buildings on this hill. The city is very compactly built – far more so than Cheng tu whose wall is 9 miles in circumference. These are said to be some 500,000 people here according to the best estimates. The city does not look to me to be larger than Cheng tu though generally considered to be so by quite a margin. The shops and buildings along the principal streets present a substantial appearance. The buildings are higher than usual. The captain of our boat had to get a new crew since the old crew were up river men. We had hoped to get away by 1 o'clock but custom house arrangements & the slowness of the captain lost all the rest of the day for us. We tied up for the night near the German gunboat "Vaterland" just across the Yangtze from where we spent last night.

Saturday April 24th. 1909

Started at the first break of day and hence missed much of the ridge which lies just to the east of Chung King. T.C.C woke up sometime before me and has some of this part in his notes. The first ridge runs approximately N. and S. (NE & SW) Some coal mines but not much limestone apparently. Beyond this there does not appear to be any very distinct series of ridges. We turned South East through a small gorge cut through buff beds. The beds at first dipped toward the North West just before the turn. Then they became horizontal, and later dipped strongly to the East or slightly South of East. Red beds on both sides of the gorge.

After leaving the gorge (8.15) we followed an easterly course. Red beds dipping at high angles slightly south of east. Passing the face of a great exposed layer the strike of N 15 E was obtained. Further back considerable turning of the axis of folding was noted. These folds appear more complicated than farther north on the overland trip. 8.45 A.M. To the N. W. is now seen a smooth topped Appalachian like ridge rising up above the foot hills. A line sighted perpendicular to this ridge took the direction of N 70 W which makes the axis of the ridge run N20 E. The topography here strongly resemble that of the Appalachians. The smooth ridge in the distance corresponds to the Cretaceous level (in appearance, but not necessarily age) base level of the Appalachians while the foothills nearer the river which themselves show pen planation resemble the Tertiary pen plain of the Appalachians. 9.20

A.M. running East and approaching what appears to be another prominent fold ridge. The beds along the first part of this easterly stretch of the river are dipping 20º W. The strike is now nearly N. & S. Red bed series, which is clearly a thick one. 9.30 A.M. Dip 14º W. Then slowly increases. 9.45 A.M. Dip 43º W and quickly increases to 55º. We now are nearly to the mountain ridge and bend to the south for a short distance before turning east and crossing thru the ridge. 10.00 A.M. At bend toward the East. Axis of a sharp fold. Perhaps not the main fold. Across the river on the right bank is a coal mine. Seam said by captain of our boat to be 2 ½ ft thick. Tunnel ½ mile in length (2 li). Half a mile further on is another coal mine which is apparently in the same coal seam but on the other limb of the fold. The sharp turn just noted now turns out to be a minor infolding. Between the two coal mines the strata are chiefly limestones. The limestone beds become overturned. It was not apparent just where the overturn straightens itself out. However the red beds with easterly dip soon set in and we are past the ridge.

This is the most compressed fold seen on the down river. It forms the sharpest fold ridge and contains the most crumpling. The red beds on the east side are soon dipping at angles of about 20º. At 11 o'clock we are commencing on a long stretch of the river which follows the strike of the beds. The left bank is a dip surface of hard sandstone. The vegetation and soil upon this sandstone face are scanty, but these slopes appear to be cultivated to the limit. The smallest patches of lodged soil are supporting a few tufts of grain. A long stretch of the river in this notable strike valley enabled me to get the reading of N 23º E for the strike. We now follow the strike valley until 4.10 P.M when

we turn sharply to the south and advance toward the high ridge which has been on our right hand all the afternoon. Seen earlier in the afternoon this mountain ranged looked as if it might consist of two separate lines of hills – a lower even crested ridge nearest us and a series of higher peaks, more or less separated from one another which rose in the distance above the even crested ridge. At 4.30 P.M beds dip 30º in a direction approximating N 25º W. Lung Ki on map. River flows S.E. until a coal mine appears on the left bank at 5.10 P.M. River turns to S.W. Beds dip 48º S.E. Strike N 60-70 E several minor folds, both anticlinal and synclinal occur on this S.W stretch. 5.50 P.M. Strike N 55º E. Tied up at Li tu cheng at 9 P.M.

Sunday April 25th. 1909

The river turns to the S.E. shortly after passing Li tu cheng. At the turn we crossed an anticline which brings the coal bearing formation above the river level. A small coal mine is located on the right bank. Reached Fu chan at 7 A.M. This is a large well-built city located at the junction of the Wu Kiang and the Yangtze Kiang. The Wu Kiang is the artery of traffic into Kwei Chow province. Its relatively clear water maintained its purity for some distance against the red Yangtze. The Yangtze bends sharply at Fu Chow and follows a N.E. direction for many miles along the strike or cutting it at moderate angles. This was an uninteresting stretch of river. At 11 o'clock we turned to the N.W. around Ping sui pa island. Ahead to the N.W. is a ridge of peaks arranged in a N.E.–S.W. line. These are clearly the prolongation of the fold ridge which we crossed before reaching Fu Chow this morning early. The river turns to the east and then South East after which it bends to the North East course which it maintains with a few small windings according to the map all the way to Wan Hsien. This course is determined by the strike of the beds which is generally followed. As a result little new develops of the general structure of the region. We passed Fung tu Hsien in the middle of the afternoon. Several fine pagodas. Are following the strike of beds which are dipping to the N.W at angles up to 10°. Erosion has carved many pyramidal buttes out of the river bank to the left. The right bank on the contrary is a long gentle dip slope of 10° +/-. The pyramidal forms appear to develop best in red bed formations which dip away from the river at low angles. At various points during the afternoon's run a range of high hills has been in sight in the distance to our right (E or S.E.) This range is a new one which we have not yet reached. It parallels our course very closely. At 8.15 P.M we tied up for the night.

Monday April 26th. 1909

Landed at Chung chow at 7.30 A.M. Captain picked up some new men. Spent nearly an hour strolling about the city and taking a couple of photos of picturesque bits outside the walls. Beyond Chung chow are several sharp bends in the river. At 10.00 A.M. opposite Yuen ki chang. To the east and South East is a high range of hills perhaps 3-4 miles distant. They are running N.E and S.W. and appear to be the continuation of the range which paralleled our course yesterday afternoon. 10.10 A.M. Line projected perpendicular to the range of hills would have a direction approximating S.70° E. At noon we passed Shi pao chai a striking butte with nearly vertical sides resembling the famous Enchanted mesa of New Mexico. On the flat top is a temple. A 7 storied pagoda-like temple is built against the S.E wall of the butte and furnishes means of access to the top of the [monaduock]. The river flows to the East for a short distance from Shi pao chai. Ahead to the East is seen a range of high hills which seem rather higher than those further back but this effect may be due to the blue haze which makes the hills appear further distant than they actually are. We now follow a strike valley practically to Wan Hsien. Many pyramidal erosion hills along the river. During much of this course along the strike the river is broad and flows smoothly with few rapids. A very noticeable change in the color of the water appeared today and was welcome when it came to developing films. The water has become a light muddy yellow instead of strong red. We reached the familiar water front of Wan Hsien at 7.15 P.M.

Tuesday April 27th. 1909

Rained hard last night so that roof was leaking when we awoke. Rained all morning – hard at times – for the first time since leaving Hankow. Started from Wan Hsien at 8.20 A.M. The boat which brought us from Ichang to Wan Hsien spent the night next to our present boat but one in the innumerable line of boats tied up along the water front. It had been back to Ichang and is now en route to Cheng tu carrying a Chinese official. At one or two points during the morning hills higher than those immediately adjacent to the river were seen through gaps toward the north. Just before reaching Wan Hsien last night what appeared to be a possible fold ridge was seen running E. & W. beyond Wan Hsien to the north. We are wondering whether the strike of the folds may turn more to the east at this point. On the overland journey the strata near Wan Hsien were seen to be nearly horizontal. The high hills are erosion buttes. Perhaps the high hills which appeared to form a ridge north of Wan Hsien last evening may be only erosion forms cut out of horizontal beds. The hills seen this morning did not suggest upturned strata. 2.10 P.M. running S.E. Red beds dip 6°-8° in a direction about N 50° W. At 3.18 P.M. our boat ran the Sin lung tan while we watched it from the shore.

The strata are now dipping to the S.E at an angle of about 10°. Before reaching Yun Yang Hsien the beds show some irregular folding, especially on the left bank. Dips as high as 45° to the S.E are seen. On the South bank the strata dip rather uniformly at low angles. We reached Yun Yang Hsien at 5.30 P.M. and tied up for the night since the captain did not wish to pass some rapids below while it was raining and there was considerable adverse wind. Strolled about the town and was impressed by the dirty streets and the general dilapidated appearance of everything. Some allowance, however must be made for rainy weather.

Wednesday April 28th. 1909

Rained hard during the night and was still raining when we awoke. Boat crews do not work during the rain if it rains much and so we did not start from Yun Yang Hsien until the weather cleared which took place about 9 o'clock. We took advantage of the delay to cross the river in a boat and visit the famous temple of Chang Won Heh Miao which stands forth majestically just opposite the city. It is built irregularly and is far less impressive than when seen from the river. There are many small rooms containing objects of interest but nothing very imposing as in the magnificent temple at Kwan Hsien. The principle image of worship were those representing former kings and illustrious personages. Though a Buddhist temple there was no image of Buddha. It seems that images of Buddha are not very common in China even in Buddhist temples. This sort of religion while not really ancestor worship appears to be a sort of memorialization of illustrious historical characters whose spirits are supposed to be present as working force at the present time. The images of two financiers who are supposed to guard the present treasury stood side by side in a deft to the left of the ruling king. Mr. Wang explains that this is a Buddhist temple chiefly because the priests there are Buddhist priests and that they have a very imperfect understanding of what Buddhism really is. Prof. Burton agreed that they did not know very much of the real essence of Buddhism. Our room in the temple had its walls covered with extracts from the old nine books of classics. The characters being written in a flowing style appeared quite different from the printed characters commonly seen. Many people cannot read them. On account of adverse wind our progress down the river was slow. Our map proved very unreliable since it gives a nearly straight course from a little below Yun Yang nearly to Kwei chow fu whereas in reality there are several quite notable bends which would have aided us in locating ourselves.

At 12.40 we cut through beds strongly upturned and dipping to the N.W. Previous to this the journey had been through generally horizontal red beds cut into pyramidal forms which form has now become decidedly monotonous to us. The one notable feature was the fact that the river now occupies (at low water) a trench cut through the flat topped rock ledges which are entirely submerged at high water. In other words there are two channels – one for high and one for low water – instead of the usual channel and bordering flood plain.

In the early afternoon the Northwesterly dip continues at varying angles. We are running nearly parallel to the strike on the N.W. limb of the anticline which brings up the limestone and forms the Wind Box gorge just below Kwei fu. We passed the village of Ngan ping at 2.35 P.M At 3.55 saw a coal mine high above the river on the left bank. At the water's edge the beds appeared to be limestone but at the coal mine the color of all that was visible was distinctly red. Strata obscured by considerable rock mantle. Possibly the color has washed down from the red beds above but, it may be that the coal is actually in the red bed series. The strata at this point are much contorted with minor anticlines and synclines with varying axes. The valley then widens exhibiting fine erosion slopes as far as Kwei chow fu. The structure is somewhat complex. We were opposite Kwei chow fu at 4.30 P.M and went ashore at 4.48. Went up on hill behind the town and got a couple a views of the river Valley. Were detained and did not actually leave Kwei fu until 6.15 P.M. The wind though very light was now blowing downstream and we thought it imperative to make the most of every minute and get through the Wind box gorge which with an adverse wind would be our greatest difficulty before stopping for the night. Passed salt works which line both banks and constitute a very extensive industry.

Entered the Wind Box gorge at 6.40 and enjoyed what was easily the finest view in all the gorges. The cliffs are remarkably steep and actually approach verticality. A turn in the river which cuts off further view makes the whole quite striking. Regret exceedingly that I could get no photographs on account of the lateness of the hour. The gorge is cut through massive limestones which are sharply folded. Near the upper end of the gorge the limestone beds which close to the water at this point are less heavily bedded, have suffered transverse jointing to such an extent as to closely resemble bedding. This fracturing is clearly to be associated with the folding during the period of mountain making. The folds are somewhat complex and we could no longer distinguish detains well after about the middle of the gorge. While we cannot be very sure, the axis of the major fold appeared to be more nearly N. & S. than we would have expected to find it. We tied up for the night near the lower end of the gorge at 7.40 P.M. Saw numerous streams of water coming out of the solid limestone cliffs.

Thursday April 29th. 1909

Started from the end of the Wind Box gorge at 4.50 AM. The Wind Box showed finally on the left having a definite impressive South slope. From this point to the village of Wushan the river runs near the synclinal axis between the Wind Box range on the north and he Wushan range on the South. The Wushan range comes into clear view on the right soon after leaving the Wind Box gorge and is seen at intervals all the way to the Wushan gorge. A short distance below the Wind Box gorge a tributary from the South cuts across the Wushan range showing the thick limestone layers in vertical section on either side resembling the appearance of the similar layer in the Wind Box gorge. The course of both these ranges is a little N. of E. In the syncline some small part of the red series appears but it is not a dominate feature. The dark layers of sandstone above the Carboniferous play a notable part in the secondary topography. In the syntaxes there are many minor undulation & some rather abrupt twists indicating that the folding of the 2 main ranges was felt in a secondary way throughout the whole syncline. Near Wushan the Wind Box gorge range could be seen on the East of the tributary that joins the Yangtze at Wushan. So far as could be seen the two layers continue then parallelism to the E.N.E. There are at the gorges features of dip & strike that seem to be inconsistent with the general trend of the two ranges but these are probably assignable to local twists or to oblique outcrops and do not probably mean any notable flexure of the main range. The secondary ranges in the syncline lie in general to about the height of the 2nd pen plain redoing the summit plain as the 1st.

We reached the town of Wushan at 7.30 A.M. and soon entered the Wushan gorge. Just before entering the gorge a retrospect shows the Wind Box range running from the Wind Box gorge to as far as could be seen to the right of Wushan. It may be 3 miles away from the Wushan range which it parallels. Just after entering the gorge terraced farms were seen on the right bank and a few cultivated fields on the left bank. Strike in gorge N 66° E. At 8.05 passed a splendid illustration of the "controlling bed's" influence upon topography. The controlling bed is a resistant limestone. The hillslopes assume the angles of dip of this limestone ranging from 30° at the river to horizontality on top.

Large boulders of black [dirty] limestone along the water's edge. At 8.20. Small syncline. " 8.30. Some weaker layers near the river have been greatly crumpled & contorted while the "master beds" have not been greatly affected. As in the case of the controlling beds just referred to the weaker layers adjust themselves to the master beds. 8.40. Crossed the axis of the fold. Peaks rise on the left bank abruptly to a height of 2000 ft. These are the sharpest peaks in the gorge. In about 1/3 mile the river bends sharply to the East and follows the strike through the midst of the limestone formation. Occasional houses and cultivated fields. We emerged from the gorge at 10.20 and entered a broader valley with grassed slopes. We quickly turned from an easterly course to the S.E. and encountered another anticline which produces another gorge though possibly the two are generally grouped together as the Wushan gorge. At 11.00 A.M. the strata are dipping 57° N.W. The strike was N 62-65° E. This dip is a persistent one running high up on the hillsides which are more than 1000 ft above the river. It is the N.W. limb of a large anticline followed generally along the strike until at 11.50 the river turned toward the NE and we crossed the layers, returning to the N side of the fold instead of crossing it to the South side. We shall therefore have to cross this fold in another gorge further on.

At 12.18 we actually left the gorge at the sharply defined contact of the limestone with the red beds. The country opens out immediately with the beginning of the red beds, A strong adverse wind soon sprang up which caused the captain to tie up and wait for it to subside. Late in the afternoon the boat started and made slow progress until dark. There was little of interest to be seen. At night we were still 30 li from Kwei Chow. The great importance of the wind in this river navigation was strongly impressed upon me. In the morning without more than occasional use of the oars, but with a strong wind at our back we made surprising time; in the afternoon with the wind against us & the current with us we often could not go.

Friday April 30th. 1909

Boat started about 4.30 A.M. Passed through the Mitan gorge where the river cuts through the Wushan limestone. The strata dip steadily to the N.W. at angles of about 20-25°. We are steadily going down the stratigraphic series from the Permo-Mesozoic red beds to the granite since this north westerly dip continues for a long distance as I remember from the upriver trip. This Mitan gorge appears to be cut into the same fold as the lower Wushan gorge into the N.W. limb of which we penetrated for a distance and then came out again on the N.W side. If so this would simplify the structure of these gorges. About 7.45 we went ashore at the village of Sin tan and walked around the rapids. The approximate contact between the Wushan limestone and the Sin tan shale is seen at the upper end of the village at the point where we went ashore limestone cliffs above; grassy slopes with protruding layers of reddish and gray shale below. Lower in the Sintan formation farther along there is much shine green shale in these beds, some of which show fine examples of ripple marks. Considerable greenish shale seen across the river. We went aboard our boat again at 8.20. At 8.40 we passed the contact between the Sintan formation and the Ki sin-ling (Cambro Ordovician) limestone. The limestone cliffs begin at once so that we are soon in the Lu Kan gorge. The structure is still a monocline with N.W. dip. This cambro-Ordovician limestone produces the Lu Kan gorge in which are some very steep walls.

After passing out of the Lu Kan gorge the country becomes low and open. Rounded hills take the place of the limestone cliffs. This is the Pre Cambrian granite area. A retrospect from some distance below the gorge shows a high ridge of sharp peaks rising far above low rounded foot hills in the foreground. The high peaks (see photo No 135) represent the upturned edges of the Cambro-Ordovician limestone while the foothills represent the Pre Cambrian granite. The fact that limestone makes the peaks and granite wide areas of low foot hills is very suggestive and would furnish the topic for a first class piece of research. The granite suffers partial decomposition and disintegration at an astonishing rate probably due to chemical action along the planes between the component crystals. Possibly carbonation of the ferromagnesian minerals which sets loose the feldspars and the quartz; possibly chemical interaction between the silicates themselves. Keep in mind also the case of the Pike's Peak granite and follow this matter further if occasion permits.

Cliffs across Yang tze kiang from Nanton showing unconformity between the granite and the quartzite, and the hills above which represent the glacial horizon. The top formation is the Ki sin Ling (Cambro-Ordovician) limestone.

At 2.15 P.M. we passed Nanton and entered the Ichang gorge. Cambro Ordovician limestone (Ki Sin ling) during the first portion. The way in which the limestone erodes and weathers into somewhat characteristic forms is well shown. Here a sheer cliff, there a gentle slope. At the point where the river after following a southerly course, turns toward the east on the final stretch of the gorge, the Ki Sin ling limestone dips below the river and the Sin tan shale is the formation at the water's edge for a short distance. This is a thinner formation than the limestones and the dip soon carries it out of sight. The Wushan limestone makes the rest of the gorge. At a short distance above the custom's station there were many men engaged in quarrying out blocks of a dark gray limestone apparently for building purposes. These dark gray beds fracture in layers of about a foot in thickness. This rock would seem to be a very good building stone. The gorge plays out gradually to the east. The bluffs & hills become lower & lower. The limestone is followed by the Red Beds with diminishing dips. We reached Ichang about 7.30 P.M. Went up to the China Ichang Mission to find out when our boat started for Hankow.

Saturday May 1st. 1909

Ichang & Vicinity Went aboard Kiang Wo and completed arrangements for voyage to Hankow. After sending letters and a little business on shore, made an excursion on foot east and north East of Ichang. For a distance of less than two miles out there are abundant indications of old river deposits chiefly in the form of quartzite gravel extending up to heights of between 200-300 ft above the river. The summits of the higher gravel covered hills correspond with smooth terrace surfaces stretching to the S.E. adjacent to the river. These are the same as noted on the up trip. Back of these gravel covered hills lie other hills and ridges of comparable heights and higher ones farther to the E.N.E. These hills were found to be essentially erosion remnants of the red series. The topographic forms were of much the same type as seen in middle Szechuan except that they are of a much lower and milder order. The valleys are broad, flat bottomed and occupied by rice fields. In general the region is well cultivated with two exceptions.

The one consists of the graveyards in which the mounds were scattered so that if single graves as we suppose, they occupy considerably more ground than an average grave in an American cemetery. The total area occupied by graves near Ichang is an appreciable fraction of the total cultivable land. The second uncultivated factor consists of certain ridge summits and slopes which were merely occupied by grass or by bare slope gullies or demanded surfaces. Among the graves freshly constructed a striking similarity to the Eskimo snow hut was noted in the fact that the form is nearly identical and the outer part of the grave mound is made by rectangular blocks of grass sod.

The Yangtze river emerges from the Ichang range by so constricted a valley that its location was very difficult to detect at 3-4 miles distance and was only positively located when we were near enough to look down upon the river itself. The face of the Ichang range stretches from the west point to a point east of north with practically unbroken face corresponding measurably with the dip slope. Somewhat to the east of north in the distance, say 8-10 miles, a valley seems to cut across at least the S.E. portion of the range and to have a rather broad valley. N.E. of that the range was conspicuous as far as the N. 60° E point where it dropped out of vision. The meaning of the above valley was not clear and suggested questions regarding the former system of drainage. It also connected itself with the statement of the Cheng tu official that there is a practicable route for a railway north of the gorges and connecting with Ichang. Off the face of the Ichang range as far as could be seen the border ground is made up of hills & ridges of the red series eroded to heights generally less than 500 ft, mainly less than 300 ft apparently. Looked at in another way the mountain region of the gorges grades away toward the plains through the red series in a quite normal typical way. There is not the slightest indication of a fault face or any unusual phenomenon of that class. To the S. & S.W. beyond the Yangtze notably higher butte like hills and submountains occur but these die away in a direction normal to the mountain range. Directly west from Ichang there is a broad open tract occupied by hills of the same order as those East of Ichang. In the distance at the limit of vision in the hazy atmosphere a range of hills & mountains was indistinctly seen which apparently had a somewhat N-S trend.

In general it appeared that the Ichang axis probably runs E.N.E only until it dies down in the direction of the Han valley. Our inference is that the Wushan and other ranges parallel to it are limited to the eastward in similar ways. Why the Yangtze did not keep its course eastward from Wan Hsien parallel to the ranges between which it there lie to valley of the Han is an outstanding question. Not quite satisfactorily settled by the hypothesis that it occupies an old pen plain and took a course on it across what the mountains arose.

The seed plots of rice were in brilliant green, the plants being 3-4 inches high. They were being planted out in the hills in the paddy fields by men who thrust small bunches into the mud rapidly without any particular care as to the roots. Later we are told they press the roots further into the mud with their feet. In the evening we took dinner with Mr. & Mrs. Stockman at the American Eposcopal Mission and met Lord William Cecil and Lady Florence Cecil. Went aboard the S.S. Kiang Wo about 10.30 P.M

Sunday May 2nd. 1909

The Kiang Wo started about 5 A.M. so that we were steaming through a flat country when we came on deck. The water is higher so that we made very good time about 5 P.M while we were making some great meanders a long range of low hills was sighted to the east. Later we came close to them. The river here as elsewhere is cutting against hills on its southern bank while everything is plain on the north. Prof. Burton and T.C.C. spent most of the day in conference with Lord Cecil.

Monday May 3rd. 1909

A brilliant moon shown last night so that the steamer ran all night and we have made splendid time. The conference with Lord Cecil continued. As a result of the discussion with Lord Cecil yesterday and subsequent conference with Mr. Burton I formulated the following scheme for an International University which after conference with Prof. Burton was formally Submitted to Lord Cecil and accepted by him individually but with the reservation that he must submit it to his principals and was individually without authority to act. At his request the scheme was formulated definitely and a type written copy furnished him. A copy of this memorandum is herewith attached. The run down the river was made without hindrance so that we reached Hankow shortly before 4. P.M.

Tuesday May 4th. 1909

At Hankow. The morning was spent in making various arrangements. In the afternoon in company with Messrs Deming and Gates the party drove out to visit the London Mission compound. This is located to the west of Hankow perhaps 3 miles from the center of the city and about a quarter of a mile from the Han river. The country crossed in reaching was so level for long distances and had so few houses upon it that it strongly resembled the land in the neighborhood of Chicago. Much of the land was uncultivated and resembled pasture land in the U.S. It was however land which is now vacant because owned and held by real estate speculators.

The London Mission school compound consists of one large main building of brick with several smaller ones adjoining. In front of this group of buildings are two football fields upon one of which a dozen Chinese were practicing at the time of our visit. We met Mr. McFarland who is at the head of the institution and who showed us about. We were unfortunate in coming on a day of vacation but saw the general character of the institution.

On the way back to the hotel we passed close to the antimony smelting works which were closed. They are a large plant. On the way out some other antimony works were pointed out by Mr. Gates in Wuchang opposite the Hankow bund. Apparently antimony is an important product of this region. We were impressed on this side with the weeds along the roadsides and general lack of close care. The people here seem hardly up to the standard of the Szechuanese. The numerous smoke stacks seen today point toward Hankow as the great industrial and commercial center of China.

Wednesday May 5th. 1909

Forenoon and midday given to miscellaneous business, personal conferences etc. of merely incidental nature. Late afternoon given to conference with committee on Medical School. Time given chiefly to discussion of situation, fundamental ideas, preparation actually received, preparation desired etc. Considerable time also given to location of hospital, relations of hospital to school & to proposed university. Location north of old wall near junction of native city and British concession favored. Location of University in Hankow favored. River frontage east of Japanese concession most suitable. Location on river front east of Wuchang, opposite Hankow thought probably unavailable because of Chinese military projects. Location in Wuchang obviously not favored by medical gentlemen. Fundamental ideas of medical gentlemen not advanced or incisive. Prospect only for a gradual evolution of ideas as well as capabilities

Thursday May 6th. 1909

Forenoon spent in conference with Rev. Sparham, Dr. Gillison and Mr. on matters to be considered at afternoon meeting of Wu Han committee on University. Matter of location to be avoided because of differences likely to arise (it is clear that there is somewhat sharp controversy in progress on this point). Meeting of committee on proposed University in the afternoon developed sharp differences on making religious requirements prerequisite to election on staff in the form phrased in the Lord Cecil printed scheme which see. Controversy developed into discussion of academic freedom.

Vote finally taken approving Lord Cecil's scheme including requirement of strong Christian principles and sympathy with missionary ideals as prerequisite to membership in faculty including proposition for nominating committee as specified in Lord Cecil's scheme. General impressions formed from above meeting and subsequent personal conferences. There is an almost complete of true University conceptions. Narrow views of the old ultra-orthodox religious type put to the front and higher scholarly ideas quite to the rear. General lack of sympathy with scholarly progress with fundamental theistic conceptions and with little international and inter institutional cooperation sadly lacking.

The British element overwhelmingly dominant. The American element being the most British of all. While there is a general external disposition to get together there is a real lack of harmony and of confidence in one another. Physical situation fairly favorable except in the matter of climate which I think is rather serious. Business transactions even of a trivial nature are excessively slow and indicate inefficient business methods implying lack of energy and vitality. For further statement of opinions see letter to Pro Burton.

Friday May 7th. 1909

Had a long interview occupying all of the forenoon with Dr. G.E. Anderson and Mr. Selzer instructors in Geology and Chemistry respectively in the Imperial Mining College at Wuchang. They described in great detail the workings of the school and the peculiarities of their relation to it which need not here be recorded in full. They teach in English but the preparation of their students is so poor in this language that they have thus far spent a large part of their time in teaching English. The appointments of the school are, as yet, limited and a large part of the resources goes to maintain the excessive staff of officials, there being 15 or more of these as against about 6 full time teachers. There is a lack of appreciation of scientific work and even of the readiness and desire of these instructors to undertake it both with the students and individually for the increase of knowledge relative to the mineral resources of the region. The school has recently been removed without warning from better to poorer quarters by order of an official in authority at Peking. Such changes and such lack of appreciation of scientific work together with the surplusage of officials and the diversion of funds through them together with the characteristic changeableness of Chinese policy constitute the chief dangers to the institution and they are certainly rather serious.

Dr. Anderson gave the best information thus far obtainable relative to the iron ore deposit that supplies the Han Yang iron plant. He describes it as an irregular deposit occupying the summits, in the main of three hills which are chiefly formed otherwise of limestone and granite or syenite which seems to be intrusive. It is Dr. Anderson's opinion and that of the German Engineer in charge of the mining that the ore is a contact deposit inserted chiefly in the limestone area which probably is displaced. Dr. Anderson has never been able to secure chemical analyses but understands that there is some phosphorus. The Bessemer process is said to have been tried and abandoned for the Siemens basic process. The best of the ore is being sold to the Japanese and is being culled out to the ulterior damaging of the mine. Inferior grades are said to be used at the Han yang works. It is said that operations do not now pay although there is a large margin between the cost of running and the price paid by the Japanese. The loss is probably therefore at the Han yang works which belong to the same company. If the ore deposits is really a contact deposit whether it is segregated from the igneous rock or precipitated from the solution the prospect of a very large and enduring supply is relatively poor. If this is true the sale of culled ore to the Japanese is a grave imprudence. The mine is located near the Yangtze about 90 miles S.E. of Hankow and 60 miles from Kin Kiang at a point known as Ta ji. Dr. Anderson does not have any reliable information of any other considerable ore body in central China. There are however some ore deposits reported from the vicinity of Po yang lake. In the light of this scantiness of information and the present indifference to exploitation and scientific study the future of the Han yang iron industry is in serious doubt and with it a part of the future of the Wu Han distinct and Hankow in particular.

Incidentally Messrs Anderson and Selzer gave considerable information regarding missionary work - Boone College in particular – the later being of a favorable mature. One item of importance relative to the Mining school should have been added above. The students being largely sons or relatives of officials rule the school rendering effective discipline as well as good work impracticable. It also leads to vitiation of markings and other degeneration. The Boone College and other missionary schools are said to have and to exercise close discipline and this is the chief distinction between the two classes.

The afternoon was consumed in a reconnaissance of the possibly available ground for a university along the river front east of the foreign concessions. East of the Japanese concession there is a frontage of about 500 yards with a depth of about the same dimensions. Next beyond this is the Belgian concession which has a retaining wall but no buildings of about the same dimensions. East of this the river front is occupied by the side tracks of the railway and by the Asiatic Petroleum Co. for about two miles (45 minute walk at estimated rate of 3 miles per hour.) In this stretch the railway is also much nearer the river than farther west or farther east. Beyond the petroleum works there is a considerable stretch of unoccupied frontage with a depth at the west somewhat less than 500 yards increasing eastward to more than that amount by rough estimate. This ground is too far away from the city at present to be regarded as a city location. Photographs taken will show details of situation.

Saturday May 8th. 1909

The whole forenoon was taken up in a conference with Bishop Roots at his request to go over in detail the memorandum drawn up after our first conference with Lord Cecil to which he agreed and a copy of which had been placed in his hands, also in going over a copy of our preliminary Ms. on the type and scope of education commended for colleges and universities in China. A copy of this to be returned after 10 days with the agreement that it shall not be copied, was left in Bishop Root's hands. Incidentally in this conference the scheme for an international university in the Wu Han district was discussed with many incidental matters pertaining thereto. It was understood that Bishop Roots and Mr. Sparhan who requested the statements above named would present these and our views in detail to the local university committee in the course of the next 10 days.

Sunday May 9th. 1909

Got ready to start in the early morning on the trip north into Honan. In the evening took dinner with Bishop and Mrs. Roots. In the course of the conversation of the evening Bishop Roots called attention to a new work on China as quite inaccurate and cited as examples the assigned populations of Hankow, Han yang, and Wu chang. The Bishop gave as approximately correct estimates Hankow 200 000 Han Yang 100,000 and Wu chang perhaps 300,000 or altogether 500,000-600,000 He gave as the foreign population about 1,000.

Monday May 10th. 1909

Left Hankow station on the train at 7.45 A.M. The flat flood plain extended as far as Niekow where we arrived at 8.20. Then came low swells and long sloughs. Swells of very red clayey material; fields & lowlands buff. Deeper cuts show red loam above; river gravels below. Houses have mud walls and tile roofs and look neat and tidy. Country appears very dry. At 8.48 a cut 30 ft deep showed gravel and some subangular stuff together with clayey beds which look as if they might belong to the Tertiary. At 9.10 AM long cut through ridge before crossing small stream. This stream has a valley about a mile across. 9.15-9.20 more cuts some showing deep reddish colored beds mingled with some whitish layers. The reddish beds resembled the Permo-Triassit red beds except that they were much softer, possessed that peculiar irregular, ill-assorted mottled appearance which we associate with the Tertiary or Quaternary.

Chiao Kan Sien. Houses and walls of unburned brick. At 10.10 the country becomes nearly a flat plain. At 10.36 sand dunes appear & the hills in the distance have a sandy appearance. The sand waste area is very local. At 10.43 we are alongside of a stream with broad sandy bottom lands. The dunes apparently came from this sand. Cuts show a rock which looks like a metamorphic schist. At 11.20 we are going up a broad, flat bottomed valley. Higher hills seen in the distance to the west. 10.30. Wang kia tien. Just back of the town to the east are bluffs of coarse purplish gray to purplish red sandstone, some 300-400 ft. high. Beds not far from horizontal. 11.50 beds of reddish sandstone dipping about 15º to the S.E. This is a comparatively hard sandstone. In a few minutes a cut showed what appeared to be a light colored schist with cleavage at a high angle.

Soon reached Yang Kia tchai (12.01) Found here pebbles and fragments of a bright mica schist which is chiefly quartz and mica. It is apparently a metamorphic rock. Hills to the west of Yang are 150-200 ft high. We are soon abreast (to the west) of hills as high as 600 ft. Though the slopes are gentle these hills are nearly bare of trees and appear to be entirely uncultivated. Comparatively gentle slopes near the villages are also only partially cultivated. The soil does not appear very good. Little terracing of the slopes. At 12.20 hills to the west rise abruptly as a ridge of peaks. Railroad cuts show mica schists.

At 12.30 stopped for 15 minutes at Konang choei during which time we ate lunch. Beyond Tong Honang tien we climb into the hills. At 1.15 P.M. we passed through deep cuts in metamorphic rocks. Thick views of quartz are very numerous. These highly siliceous rocks produce but very poor soil. Also furnish sand for the sandy stream beds seen this morning. The north facing sides of valleys and ravines are much more thickly clothed with vegetation than the south facing slopes. Inference: The vegetation needs protection from the drying influence of the sun. At 1.30 P.M. we emerged from the tunnel and reached the divide which is also the boundary between Hupeh and Honan. Topography of hills – the typical erosion forms found in a region of hard rock. Some of the hills may be as much as 1500 ft. above Hankow.

Li kia tsai at 1.55 P.M. Reached Sin Yang at 2.45 after passing through a region of metamorphic formations. Left at 3.10. At 3.25 P.M. we are in an open rolling hilly country. The erosion appears much less advanced than in the region seen this morning. General aspect about that of the middle Quaternary. Much available land uncultivated. Hwai Ho crossed at 3.40 P.M. This river is in the middle of a very broad flat whose southern edge is bordered by well-defined bluffs 40-50 ft high. Ming Kiang reached at 4.15. The region between the Hwai Ho and Min Kiang is partly flat and partly a gently undulating plain whose topography could not be improved for agricultural purposes. But the soil does not appear to be particularly fertile. The fields become larger. The region is not very densely populated. The plain continues until at Sin Guang tien (reached at 4.40) a prominent ridge appears somewhat less than a mile ahead. The hills are several hundred feet high. This appears to be a mountain spur running east and west. We cross this through a wide gap beyond which the plain continues as flat as before.

At 5.15 we are on the plain still but to the west are groups of hills. These hills generally rise abruptly from the plain which appears to be one of the sedimentation. The plain has been filled in plumb against the hills. The whole aspect of the country has changed and more closely resembles an American landscape. The fields are much larger than before and are without the dividing ridges; trees dot the landscape pretty generally and not only around houses. Cattle more numerous. Roads show two tracks apparently made by carts. Train stopped for night at Tchu ma tien at 6 P.M.

Tuesday May 11th. 1909

Last night was spent on the train to avoid the bother of moving all our possessions to an inn. The railroad company makes no provision for passenger's baggage. The baggage car door remained open all night but Mr. Chang had baggage in the car and so kept one of his soldiers on guard. We woke up early, returned our small pieces of luggage to the baggage car and after a long delay in obtaining tickets got started. The train left Tchu ma tien at 6.15 A.M.

Sui ping was reached at 6.47. The country is a smooth flat plain, almost entirely devoted to the raising of wheat at the present time. The fields are large and the landscape is quite American in appearance. It looks as if it should be a very productive region but it is said to be poor. I assign dryness as the reason. The villages suggest sights seen in the arid western states of the U.S. Train left Si ping sien station at 7.40 A.M. The walled city is about a mile to the west. Our map is all wrong here. We have not had a glimpse of even a low hill yet this morning. 7.50 As perfect a plain as can be found anywhere. Great open prairie Reached Yen techeng sien at 8.15. Country still a perfect plain with the exception of one or two stream trenches which we have passed. The streams are in steep banked trenches in the general plain just beyond the city of Yen the train crossed the Scha Ho whose trench is perhaps 200 yards across and possibly 30 ft deep. There were many boats upon the river.

The plain continues 9 AM. Several patches of poppy. The dryness and overutilization for wheat probably account for the poor crops. Rotation of crop necessary to keep up the productiveness of the soil. Chu tcheon at 10 o'clock; left at 10.20. At this village I took several photos of the native life. At 11.05 AM we are opposite hills (several miles to the west) which are probably the end of a mountain spur. Passed a typical arroyo cut in the plain.

At 11.12 came the first break in the perfect plain which we have followed since starting this morning from Tchu ma tien. There are low undulations for a few hundred yards and then we crossed the Ying Ho whose outer bank is cut so that on the bend it stands as a nearly perpendicular bank 25-30 ft. high. The swells now would seem to have been loess - like accumulations blown up from the river. Beyond the river are gentle swells.

11.20 Sin Tsien Sien a dry dusty town where I took two photos. Large orchards which continue for several miles. Apples or pears? The soldiers on the train said plums or apricots. Many houses with thatched roofs. Wall all of dried brick mostly unburned but with an occasional burned brick. 11.42 Sand dunes or at least dunes of a material which looks like sand but which may have been loess like. The dune area increased until Tsen techeon was reached at 12.30. The dunes are covered rather generally with trees, many of which are of the fruit bearing variety. This suggests that the material may not be ordinary sand but a loess - like deposit. At Tsen tcheon we changed cars for Honan fu but on account of the inefficiency of the railway baggage system and the extreme unreliability of the information obtainable two of our trunks and the provision box were carried on towards Peking the train starting before they could be removed from the baggage car.

The plain continues to the west but it was soon noted that the cart roads were becoming sunken. They were sunken to the extent of 3-15 ft below the level of the plain. This has been produced obviously by the wear of the cart wheels which loosens the dust so that the wind may blow it away. The walls stand like typical loess walls. This appears to be the beginning of the great loess area which is continuous as far as Mongolia. Some arroyos. Ying yang Sien at 1.50 P.M. Gravel road bed. Dull greenish and reddish pebbles. Perhaps from the Hoang Ho? The arroyos and ravines become deeper and deeper and the erosion forms & cliffs more and more picturesque until the ravines are canyons more than 100 ft. in depth and the R.R. cuts are 40-50 ft deep with steep smooth faces. The slopes have only a few trees here and there upon them, but they are pretty well terraced. At 3.10 I saw a layer of stratified gravels 8-10 ft thick, in the midst of a loess bank. There were about 20 ft of loess above the gravel. This loess bank was really the river (Lo Ho) bank though the stream was about a mile away. Off to the South, perhaps 5 miles away are hills which are probably those which are so badly represented on the map.

Yen she Sien at 4.20 P.M. Hills to the north 400-500 ft high. A few terraces upon their lower slopes but they are completely bare of trees. Brown and bare as a desert. The train gradually leaves the picturesque loess area and gets out into the plain of the Lo Ho. On this plain are many mounds up to 30 ft in height which appear to be large graves and call to mind the pyramids of Egypt. We reached Honan fu station at 5.20 and went to the inn near the station.

One of the remarkable features of the afternoon's journey was the fact that for a long distance at least, after we entered the true loess area the upper surface was a flat plain into which arroyos and ravines has been cut exposing nothing but loess to depths up to 50 ft or more. If this loess be an aeolian deposit low account for the surface plain? The top surface should be irregular and dune like it would seem under the eolian hypothesis. When we were in the midst of the loess area the railroad line passed through a succession of deep cuts so that the character of the surface could not be so well seen. I am inclined however to think that the surface was more or less uneven so as to be not inconsistent with the wind hypothesis. The main loess may be eolian and the plain due to local cooperating causes. Water and wind together. In the midst of the true loess area the cuts and canyons show at least 100 feet of loess. These are true loess canyons. This is by far the finest display of the loess formation which I have ever seen.

A prominent feature of the morning's journey on the Peking bound train and even more conspicuous all day yesterday was the military salute given our train at each of the principal cites along the route. It happened that a younger son of Chang Chi Tung the Prime Minister was aboard the train with a small retinue. When the train came into each important station a squad of khaki clad soldiers came to attention while the officer in charge saluted and the bugle call was given. While the train was halted at the station these soldiers who numbers 30-50 marched past and stationed themselves near the track in front of the train and then repeated the salute to the Prime Minister's son as the train started on.

Wednesday May 12th. 1909

At Honan fu. Our inn was located near the R.R. station half a mile outside of the nearest corner of the city wall and still further from the gate. The intermediate ground is cut up by many sunken roads between which are poor wheat fields and is excessively dry and dusty. The wall of Honan fu is constructed of burned bricks. Outside of it is a broad platform or terrace which is surrounded by a trench or moat. The moat was entirely dry. The streets of Honan fu are considerably wider than those of the cities thus far visited in the other provinces of China. Narrowness of streets has no object since they are not paved and hence there is no economy of material. Carts are common in the streets and hence ruts are frequent. The streets are very dusty but there seems to be less filth than in many of the cities of paved streets. In this respect this province appears cleaner than those previously visited.

Our inn was very clean. The stores and shops and the city as a whole gave the general impression of decadence. The inhabitants did not seem to be very busy. The people are somewhat larger and more robust than those farther south. There are two distinct types of faces – one a round, full face, and the other a pronouncedly angular face, full of character and generally accompanied with sharp, penetrating but not unpleasant eyes. The effeminate type is also present here but is less common than further south. The people in the city do not appear to have seen many foreigners. The women folks in many cases go into the houses on our approach. The city of Honan fu was said to have about 20,000 inhabitants. This figure seems about right for the walls are only about ¾ of a mile on a side and the city is not densely built up.

After strolling about the streets to get an idea of the city we mounted the wall for a general view and left the city by the west gate. To the N.W. of the city as well as the north is a long even crested ridge with gentle slopes. Toward this we made our way. The wheat fields were not producing a good crop owning to the dryness the farmers said. They said that last year they had a good crop. Water is what is needed here. We followed sunken roads which became deeper as we neared the higher land. At one point the road was as much as 25 ft deep. (See photo of T.C.C gathering roots at the bottom) This shows that the roots penetrate deeply in this material for these were modern roots.

At the lower ends of the fields on the gentle slopes were low retaining walls built to hold back the water and soil. These walls were about a foot high on the inner side (or even less) and often 6-8 ft above the ground outside. The result is a series of terraces. The terrace flats are so extensive that it hardly seems likely that they have been graded in artificially. It seems rather as if the retaining walls had been built to hold back the water and the soil and that with the heavier rains there was some washing of the soil down the slopes toward the retaining wall so that in time the ground was gradually brought up toward the height of the wall which was then from time to time probably built up anew.

This production of terracing by utilizing the slope wash throws much light upon the hillside problem and furnishes a concrete example of how the question may be solved. It was very suggestive and instructive. It is well worthy of consideration for some of the hilly regions in the U.S.

We followed a road up the slopes some distance and then turned to the East in the general direction of the R.R. station and our inn. The deep cuts enabled us to get a good idea of the character of the material. At one point near the bottom of the cut we saw the limestone formation. Above it were broken fragments of the rock together with a very red residual clay resulting from the dissolving away of the more soluble parts of the limestone. In many other places there was much residual clay without the limestone being actually seen and in fact nearly the whole formation on these slopes contained a considerable element of residuary material. With this was mixed loessial material.

Apparently there has been washed down the slopes a steady deposit of residuary soil from higher up and that at the same time the deposit of loess has contained. This mixture of residuary material and loess while it contains occasional stones behaves in many ways like the true loess. It stands in steep cliffs like the loess and in fact grades almost imperceptibly into the loess. On the way back to the inn we had to cross one ravine whose flat bottom was at least 60 ft below the general surface.

Thursday May 13th. 1909

The train started from Honan fu at 7.00 A.M. by our time. The gentle rain which fell last night cleared the atmosphere so that we can see longer distances than on the trip up. We reached I tsing pon at 7.26. The flat valley floor at this point is perhaps 4 miles in width. To the north are gently sloping hills while to the South they are more mountainous and rugged. The valley floor is very flat and made up of alluvium derived from the residual material and the loess. It has a brownish red color. At 7.40 we passed the largest of the pyramidal graves noted on the up trip. Some of them are as much as 25 ft. high and 75 ft on a side. Some have been eroded so as to have cliff like sides and a few have been terraced and are growing wheat. We soon reach the hill area on our left. The slopes are very strongly terraced. The trees on this valley flat are flourishing and look exceedingly well. Many large splendid trees. This means that the soil is rich. As observed yesterday roots penetrate to great depths in this porous material. The deep roots of the trees doubtless reach water which appears to be all that is needed in connection with the excellent soil to produce the best of results. This region probably could be made a first class fruit growing district if there were the demand for fruit which we have at home. As we rise into the lower hills the reddish brown alluvial material grades slowly into the buff colored loess. There is no sharp dividing line. At 8.20 limestone comes into sight in some of the cuts. Just above the limestone is a very red residual clay.

Just before reaching Kiang Sien we got a good view of the river gravels below the loess. The section now appears to be solid rock loose angular rock, residual clay mixed with loessial material, river gravels followed by true loess. In the deep cuts further on there were exposed many different ferrotto zones one above another, which are very instructive in giving a clue to the formation of these deposits. In many places belts of concretions and nodules were noted 3-5 ft below the ferrotto zones. These represent the belt of concentration when the surface was at the ferretto horizon. Looking north along some of the deep ravines we caught glimpses of the Hoang Ho which appeared at a considerably lower level than the bottoms of the ravines. The possibility of using water from the Hoang Ho for irrigation of this region is greatly reduced because the water level is so much lower than that of the neighboring country here.

At 10.20 we rose up onto the broad plain which extends all the way to the junction with the Peking line. The hills to the South are perhaps 5 miles away and look as if formed of beds dipping to the east but this may be the pitching of the fold at its eastern extremity. We followed the plain down to Tsen tcheon where we arrived at 11.35. The plain is very broad and slopes steadily toward the east. The sign at the station spells this town "Tcheng tcheon." We had to wait for the train from the South and had plenty of time to change over our baggage.

We left Tcheng tcheon at 12.26 P.M. and followed the plain which descends to the Hoang Ho. At 12.36 set the aneroid at 500 ft. At 1.08 P.M the train stopped just before reaching the Hoang Ho bridge to allow another train to cross. The aneroid read 450 ft. showing that the Hoang Ho is at least 50 ft below the plain at Tcheng tcheon. The right bank of the Hoang Ho in this vicinity is a steep cliff of loess probably as much as 150 ft. high. The river runs against this bank. There are no cliffs on the left or northern bank. The Hoang Ho is cutting the South bank like the Yangtze. The Hoang Ho bridge rest on 102 sets of steel piles. The distance between each set of piles was nearly 100 feet so that the river must be 1 ½ - 1 ¾ of a mile across. It is very shallow. Probably a man could wade across it. There were a few junks upon it but most of these were aground with men standing around in water up to their knees. The water is exceedingly yellow – practically the same color as the loess. The air was so full of dust that from the waters edge on the north side the 150 ft cliffs on the South side could only just be made out at the nearest point. Only the sky line could be traced; no details of the land whatever. And from a point ¼ of a mile inland beyond the water's edge no trace of even the sky line could be detected. There is much anastomosing of the river. The region immediately north of the Hoang Ho is a nearly perfect plain which is very dusty. The aneroid rose to 470 ft, but at 2.05 P.M. had fallen to 455 ft. 2.15 P.M. Kan Soun Y. Aneroid read 430 ft. There is now a strong wind from the north. The dust storm becomes worse. 2.43 P.M. Aneroid at 400 ft. Soon crossed a railroad running E. & W. which runs from Tan kou to Tcheng Hwa. 2.50 P.M. Hsing Hsiang (Sin Siang Sien). Left at 3.17 Aneroid read 400 ft. 3.30 P.M. The soil is getting much more reddish.

We reached Wei Hui fou at 3.50 P.M. and went to the new run near the station. There was now a strong wind from the north which blew clouds of dust before it making it very uncomfortable to be out. The north China dust storm has not been exaggerated. A little later in the afternoon we went over to the city which is about 5 li from the station. The dust storm made this little excursion very uncomfortable particularly in the open country before we reached the city gate. They city wall was of brick. For a short distance inside the wall the main street was paved with slabs of stone but beyond that only a dirt road lead across the city. The streets were wide like those of other Honan cities but the shops generally had an air of poverty about them. There was little that was attractive offered for sale. Running through the city was the Wei Ho which reaches the sea near Tientsin. The return to the inn was less dusty for the wind had subsided somewhat.

Friday May 14th. 1909

Started out on foot at 7.25 A.M. to make a short excursion to the foot hills to the west of Wei Hui. The plain is followed to the very base of the hills which rise out of it with almost no intermediate slope. We were able to get a fairly good idea of the character of the material which makes up this plain from frequent exposures along sunken roads and occasional stream courses. In general the material is wash from the hills. The upper portion which appears at the surface everywhere is a brownish loam probably a composite of residual material and loess. In the lower portion of this deposit in many places are calcareous concretions. They are generally larger and much harder than the typical "loess kindchen." In some places they are exceedingly numerous. Some of the cuts exposed coarse gravels beneath the loam, or layers of gravel in the midst of the loam. Limestone pebbles predominate. All of the material above is very calcareous.

We reached the foot hills at 9.50 A.M. These we estimate to be about 6 miles from the railroad station, and possibly 3-4 miles in front of the main range though this is purely an estimate without having traversed the distance. The foothill which we climbed was just 400 ft above the level of the plain. The adjoining hill was perhaps 100 ft higher while other hills a little to the south were several hundred feet higher still. The range in the background was very much higher. The material of this foothill was largely a black limestone though on the crest some fragments of fine grained sandstone were found lying loose. The beds dipped 14° - direction S 56° E. Everything looks like a fold here but both to the north and the South the mountain front ends rather abruptly with strata essentially horizontal coming out to the cliff like front. Appearances here suggest fault face but may be that it is a fold with the outer limb eroded away. The question must be left open for the present.

We returned to Wei Hui and inspected a mound ½ - ¾ of a mile N.E. of the R.R. station. Was perhaps 40-50 ft high. The surface was everywhere strewn with calcareous concreteous and fragments of limestone but we saw no limestone in place. We left Wei Hui fu on the train at

3.57 P.M. Khe Sien: 4:30 P.M. We are now at the point nearest to the mountains which are about 3 miles distant. The mountains have an abrupt east face and the strata are generally not far from horizontal. At this point we observed a sharp hogback standing in front of the mountain face though pretty close to it. The beds of this hogback appeared to be dipping to the S.E. at high angles. This hogback was quite a striking feature sketched at 4.55 P.M. The true relation of the hogback to the hills behind is more apparent. Off to the east are low mounds rising above the plain. The front of the mountains turns away from the R.R and runs more nearly N. & S. 5.22 Tang Yin Sin Several large pyramidal graves. At the station saw several more of the fat, round faced type of men we have observed that the wheat rows and boundaries of the fields run N. & S. with the compass and that the train which is running N.E. cuts diagonally across these lines. The natives use rectangular fields set at the points of the compass.

We reached Tchang te fou at 5.55 P.M. The city however is much further from the mountains than represented on Stieler's map. Wang and I visited the city to photograph the peculiar type of pagoda which we could see from the train. We found that they city compared very favorably with either Wei Hui or Honan fu. There seemed to be more activity than in either of these other Honan cities.

Saturday May 15th. 1909

Slept on the train last night. Train started from Tchang te fou at 7.12 A.M. and five minutes later we crossed a small river. At 7.46 crossed the Tchang Ho from Honan into the province of Chi-li. On the east is a plain with occasional large pyramidal grave. A mile away to the west long low ridge. Mountains in the distance. 8.03 AM. Tze tcheon. The fields in this neighborhood are watered by irrigation and the crops look much finer than those back in Honan. 8.15 Mountains 8-10 miles to the west. The beds along the front appear to dip to the E.N.E. at angles of 20°-30°. The people of this region water their fields by drawing up buckets of water from wells by means of rope and windlass and pouring the water into ditches which supply the fields. 9.05 AM. The mountains to the west appear to be made up of beds dipping toward the plain at angles of perhaps as much as 30°. Everything looks like a fold here 9.18 Ling Ming Koan. West of this village the foothills stand out a long distance in front of the main range and the foothills themselves display much irregularity both in height and in distribution. There has clearly been much erosion in this vicinity. The main ridge in the distance appears to be generally uniform. The beds in the most prominent of the foothills dip away from the plain (toward the west) at low angles. May be simply the west limb of an anticline whose eastern half has been swept away by erosion. 9.40 we are crossing and old river bed which is a mile or more in width and is now a sandy waste. On the border are sand dunes.

10.25 left chum te fu. This city has a fine appearing wall. A spur or range of lower foothills running generally parallel to the main range is made up of beds which dip gently down to the plain. Several miles further back the strata in the main range appeared to be not far from horizontal or only slightly inclined. The foothills are unquestionably the result of a fold and it would seem as if the main range were a part of this fold as suggested in the diagram. Looking back from further on it is clearly seen that the essence of the structure of the mountain front here is folding. This mountain front together with the extensive plain in front of it suggests the front Range of Colorado and the Colo-Kansas plain. It would seem as if this plain here were analogous to the Colorado plain in the manner of its formation rather than limited to the work of the Hoang Ho. 11.20 AM. The country is very dry and somewhat barren. 12.20 Yuen She Sien. At this station there were quite a number of coal miners standing about. The range of foothills continues several miles in front of the main range. So persistent a feature must be significant. The beds generally dip toward the plain which would seem to imply a fold rather than a fault.

We reached Chen Kia tchonang at 1.05 P.M. There being no train to Tai yuen fu before morning we were obliged to go to the inn and spend the night here. Starting out at 3 P.M. I strolled off toward the mountains. The fields in region looked splendidly. A fine crop of wheat was to be seen. This was due largely to the industrious irrigation practised. The water is obtained from wells, sometimes drawn up bucket by bucket by hand pumping and sometimes by a pump worked by a donkey or pair of donkeys. The water is poured into the main irrigation ditch from which there are various branches which carry the water to the different portions of the fields. Some good barley also growing. The material of this plain wherever seen in cuts & sunken roads was close to loess in general character though somewhat darker in color. It was without pebbles for the most part. I saw no gravels but it is true that the number of exposures seen was limited. Went to a mound about 6 miles from the town in a straight line and perhaps 1.5-2 miles from the mountains. This mound was 75 feet high and made up largely of residual material. Its crest and slopes were covered with a great many fragments of vein quartz. Did not see any loess upon it. From this mound as excellent view of the mountain front showed that to the south there were low foothills or outliers a long distance in front of the mountain face and that the beds of these outliers rose up out of the plain and if projected would pass over the tops of the mountains. Fold here no fault or at least no fault of great importance.

Sunday May 16th. 1909

Started from Chen kia tchonang at 7.25 AM by our time (7.00 AM Shansi RR time). At 7.45 foothills to the north of the road are made up of beds dipping gently to the west. Hou lou hien. At this city there was a battle between the foreign troops and the Chinese troops at the time of the flight of the Empress Dowager into Shansi in 1900. The front cliff of the mountains back of this town is not noticeably steeper than that of the second set of hills. The strata in the front hills are generally nearly horizontal but some isolated hills display quite marked dips in quite marked dips in quite irregular fashion. 8.20. The valley which we are following is nearly a mile wide at this point. The valley bottom has been filled with wash and alluvium and is now extensively terraced. These mountains give the impression of greater age than the Wasatch range in the U.S. The valley continues broad. 8.30 Pe Wang tchonang. A great deal of accumulation in the valley which means a long period of filling while the hills were being rounded. 9.00 AM. Reached and followed along a small river. 9.08 Nan Houng keon 9.40. Tsing Hing Hien a walled city with a large pagoda of the yellow colored Honan type on the hill opposite.

For the last half hour we have been coming through a low rounded hilly country with thick deposits of residuary clay and loess. The mountains are some 3 miles to the north. Cannot say how far the mountains are to the south for the view is cut off by the nearby hills. The general aspect of the topography suggests that the arching up of the region took place at least as early as the Miocene. 9.50 AM. The valley closes in and we cross the river at a point where its trench is canyon like. 9.55 Pe yao. Black limestones. A great deal of river gravel exposed in cuts along the hill sides. Further on are banks of nearly pure loess. Some banks show one or more layers of gravel in the midst of the loess bank – deposit of loess, then gravel, then loess etc. 11.30: Hia pau chen. River gravels high up above the present stream and at the same time resting upon loess. The valley must have been cut & then filled with the loess material, followed by deposition of the gravel and the subsequent cutting. Yang tsinen = ping ting. Arrival at 12.30; left at 12.55 this is the half way point. We soon saw coal seams in the hillside on our left. The coal outcrops along the slopes for several miles but it is only being mined on a small scale. The hard rock associated with the coal is a buff sandstone.

Sai yu at 1.12 P.M. At the station is a cliff of solid coal about 15 ft thick. Above the cliff is some talus which appears to conceal still more coal. Higher up the hillside is another seam of coal. The coal appears to be a high grade of bituminous. The country is steadily becoming more arid and desolate. There are very few trees on the hills. 2 PM. Dark purplish shales with sandstone layers. Beds dip generally toward the west at low angles so that we are rising in the geologic series. Kin tsinen at 2.10 PM. The houses in this part of Shansi at least are built of stone and are of a quite different style of architecture from any we have seen in other parts of China. The rock formations are becoming more and more reddish and at the same time the loess – like material near the rock partakes of this tint to a greater or less degree. 2.27 P.M. Cheou yang Hien. The country is no longer mountainous. Round hills instead. The stream which we are following has cut down perhaps 150 ft below the higher hilltops and the hills themselves are mostly formed of the loess like material. Reddish sandstone appears. Chang Hou at 3.10 P.M. Beds dipping to the west at low angles. 4.30 P.M. We leave the hills and come out into a plain which appears to be of considerable extent. 4.40: Yu tsen Hien. A large walled city to the South. The train followed the plain to Tai yuen fu where it arrived at 5.30 P.M according to our time.

Monday May 17th. 1909

At Tai yuan fu. Our inn close to the station was by far the best inn at which we have stopped in China. I therefore made a plan of the establishment to give an idea of the size and character of the inn. We occupied the quarters at the further end just as we have done at all the other inns in the country. The usual open courts had to be crossed. Adjoining these are the 2nd class quarters and quarters for servants. While this inn was much more pretentious and better built than the others at which we stopped it may be taken as an illustration of the general plan upon which Chinese inns are constructed. From the entrance one

[Hand drawn pen sketch diagram on page 66]

passes through one or more open courts and keeps right on in a straight line until the 1st class quarters (in name only for the most part) are reached. These are always at the end of the inn farthest removed from the entrance. The kitchen and servants quarters line the open courts. In this inn our reception and dining room was very large (ft possibly) and furnished with several tables and plenty of chairs. The walls were covered with paper scrolls covered with Chinese inscriptions and characters. The floor was of brick. The brick floor is unusual. Generally the floor in this part of the country is the natural dirt. In Szechuan it was generally wood. In the poorer class of inns in Szechuan there were generally no scrolls or decorations on the walls but the inns in North China are better and scrolls with characters are the rule. In the bed rooms there is a platform generally of brick but sometimes of wood which is 2 + ft above the floor. Upon this the Chinese beds are spread see photo No 7 inch) The charges per person per night vary greatly. One night in Szechuan the party paid 40 cash = $.04 Mex each. At Tai yuan fu we were charged $.75 Mex. a piece.

While T.C.C. visited the Imperial University of Shansi I strolled out of the South gate to photograph the leading features of the loess hills & plain and the extra mural life. The sunken roads and erosion channels showed that while there was a great deal of loessial material there was also considerable sand and gravel in layers scattered among the finer material. The loess prevails generally at the surface. The deposit appears to be due to different agencies working sometimes simultaneously, sometimes alternately. There has been stream action, there has been slope wash and there has been deposition of wind borne dust. Some of the dust carried along by the wind has been deposited directly where it is found today but clearly a great deal of it is secondary, being dust which lodged somewhere on the hill slopes and like the sand and gravel has been washed down the slopes. Much of this material may have been worked over and over again. The whole is a composite deposit. The hills east of Tai yuan fu at the time of our visit were very dry and bare and appeared to be of little value for agricultural purposes. However I am told during the rainy season in July and August their appearance is much improved. We are seeing the region practically at its worst.

In the afternoon went about the city with Wang. The streets of Tai yuan fu are wide and some of the principal ones have been macadamized. A very wide macadamized street runs to the South gate and affords excellent conditions for walking. This is now a busy street; formerly we are told it was nearly deserted. This and other streets were actually being sprinkled by watering carts. From what we can learn the city has improved considerably during the last few years and at the present time is showing signs of fairly rapid growth. We visited the middle school of the city and secured its catalogue. There are about 80 students and the buildings appeared good. There were two small rooms containing apparatus – one devoted to physics and the other to chemistry. The material however did not appear to be used very often. The instructor in these subjects is a graduate of Shansi University. We also visited the Chinese section of Shansi Imperial University but the time before dinner was so short that we could only look around. There are two nearly parallel instructions here – the western and the Chinese divisions – which have separate sets of instructors and are quite separate. There is a very extensive set of Dormitories and individual study rooms. After reaching the inn Pres. Soothill of the Imperial University called on his way home from escorting T.C.C out to the foothills. He appears to be an able man.

Tuesday May 18th. 1909

The train left Tai yuan fu on the return journey at 7.40 AM (our time) 8.40. Cliff 25-30 ft high. Lower part typical loess, then 10 ft. of finely laminated material of the same color, followed by typical loess above 9.05 AM. Men are quarrying the limestone for building purposes. Looks like good building stone. Then come the red beds. 2 P.M. Have been noticing for a half hour back that the loess like material only extends up to a certain height in the valley and that the higher rock hills are bare of loess in the upper parts. Though the loess may be 100 ft thick toward the bottom of the valley the upper slopes of the hills may be nearly bare rock. This striking feature seems to indicate that the deposit is alluvium and that so far as it is loess it is secondary loess which has been brought down the valley from the head where there appears to be true eolian loess. In the midst of this valley loess were numerous layers of gravel and laminated material. It is a wash deposit. The loess on the hills near Tai yuan fu was apparently of eolian origin. It is not a great distance from Tai yuan to the Ordos desert. Entirely in accord with the observation & interpretation that the valley loess is a wash deposit is the observation made near the foothills west of Chen kia tchoang that while sunken roads showed that the material of the plain was scarcely to be distinguished from eolian loess the low mound which I climbed was entirely devoid of loess. There were unknown thicknesses of loess on the plain but not enough on the mound a few feet above the plain level to cover up the fragments of angular vein quartz which were strewn everywhere about. We reached Chen kia tchoang about 6 P.M.

Wednesday May 19th. 1909

The train for Peking left Chen kia tchoang at 6.30 A.M. The region traversed was a flat plain. After about an hour's run we observed that the tombstones along the railroad were made of white marble. The quarry from which the marble is obtained is said to be no great distance away. This means that we are in a region of metamorphic rocks. The hills are 8-10 miles to the west of the railroad. On the train met Mr. A.W. Staub of the Oberlin who is interested in starting a school at Tai ku which is backed by alumni of Oberlin. This school will be an academy with the freshman year of college work added next year. Mr Staub says that there is considerable iron in the mountain's S.W of Tai yuan fu which is being mined at the present time. There is also water which could be obtained by dorms and controlling works. Also some timber back in the hills. He thinks the region possesses possibilities of becoming a manufacturing district. He says that the valley bottom of the Tai yuan plain is often so covered with water in the rainy season as to be partially impassable.

9. AM. Wang tu Hsien. Beyond Wang tu the mountains to the west become serrate, especially the peaks back in the distance 9.30 Yu kia tchoang. Ridge of aiguilles beyond the foothills to the west. The mountains further on appear to show dips of the older period of deformation. Beds dipping to the north. The train followed the plain until the outer wall of Peking was reached when it passed into the Chinese city and reached the station just outside the Manchu city at 2.05 P.M.

Thursday May 20th. 1909

At Peking. Spent the morning in our rooms in the Wagons Lite Hotel completing past reports etc. Called upon Dr Tenney and Mr W.W. Rockhill at the American legation in the afternoon. Took a rapid stroll into the imperial city late in the afternoon.

Friday May 21st. 1909

Visited the Temple of Heaven with Li San. The temple comprises a large estate located ½ mile or more outside the South gate of the Manchu city after entering the first gate one passes along a lane amid fine trees to another walled enclosure inside of which are extensive grounds within there grounds are various buildings scattered about which are themselves surrounded by walls. The Temple of Heaven itself is a circular platform with steps leading up to it where the emperor offers a prayer three times a year – Chinese New Years, in the late spring for rain and in the fall for exoneration from responsibility for the execution of criminals etc. At the time of our visit, workmen were setting up the canopy for the intended visit of the Emperor within a few days. The whole platform and steps are made of white marble. To open each gate cost 10 cents and the gates were so numerous that the whole coast of the visit was $ 1.20. Took tiffin with Dr Tenney at the American legation. Got much general information about the Chinese. In the afternoon made arrangements for the Kalgan trip.

Saturday May 22nd. 1909

Left the hotel des Wagons Lits at 7.45 to cross the city to the Hsichihmen Station outside the N.W. gate which is the best starting point for the railway journey to Kalgan. In this rickshaw ride across the Manchu and part of the imperial city we had a good opportunity to see the internals of life in Peking. Streets generally broad and showing evidence of recent improvement (since 1900). People appear active and enterprising. The Hsichihmen station on the Peking – Kalgan RR is just outside the N.W gate of Peking and the sight of smoking locomotives on the track in the foreground and the tall massive gates of the ancient regime in the background presented a strange contrast which was deemed worthy of a photo.

The train left Hsichihmen station at 10.03 A.M. The country outside Peking to the N.W is a flat plain just as that to the S.W. Across this plain we caught a distant view of the summer palace of the Emperor which is built upon the top of one of the foothills to the west. The foothills at this point are about 2 ½ miles to the west of the railroad. Shaho at 11.05 crossed the Yu Ho. Saw some fields back near Chingho where corn & black beans were grown together in alternate rows. 11.20 The foothills to the N.E. consist of beds dipping to the S.E. or toward the plain. We are advancing toward a corner in the mountains.

From Nankow the range which we have been following runs to the south. the same time another range of peaking hills or mountains runs to the east. To the east of Nankow the beds dip to the S.E. and appear to rise out of the plain as an ordinary fold. But in the high mountains back of Nankow (to the North) what appear to be strata are nearly horizontal. These however may be lava flows. The gravel in the reentrant angle between the mountain ranges becomes coarser and coarser until boulders appear and the engine puffs hard on account of the increased gradient. 12.20. We are entering the range by a narrow valley. The first beds dip to the S.E at angles of about 40º. This dip continues for about a quarter of a mile and then eases off until the beds become approximately horizontal in the higher peaks. 1 P.M. Beyond the high peaks the beds dip to the N.W. The rocks are considerably metamorphosed. Further on they are highly metamorphosed. Pinkish rocks which at first are too fined grained to detect their nature from the moving train. They form sharp peaks. At 1.20 P.M. coarse pink granite which weathers in the characteristic botryoidal forms. The hills soon become lower and round domes replaced the pointed peaks. The fine grained pinkish rocks may have been a phase of this granite. This may mean an intrusive – coarse granite in the core, finer grained near the contacts.

The inner branch of the great wall was seen at Ching lung chiao. The train soon traverses the mountain ridge by a long tunnel and emerges out a broad valley plain which is bordered by steep faced hills and mountains. 3 P.M. Huailai. Large walled city in the middle of the plain. Rugged mountains to the N.W. The city is built upon isolated hills of sedimentary rocks dipping about 70º to the N.W. These hills are 100 – 200 ft in height. Shortly before reaching our destination the train passed along the foot of a jagged peak on the western edge of the valley plain. In the lower slopes of this peak there are numerous shafts sunk for coal. Many dump piles. There is said to be one mine having a shaft 300 ft deep with a drift 700 ft in. The coal is a good grade of bituminous. The upper part of this peak like the tops of the adjacent hills (one of which I climbed later) consists of igneous rock – probably lava flows.

The train arrived at Hsia Hua yuan about 5.40 P.M. I climbed the hill located to the west of the village and found that it was made up of a brownish or purplish brown porphyry with feldspar phenocrysts. The prominent hill west of the station shows a series of distinct layers which I think may safely be interpreted as successive lava flows. As there is no good inn at this village we spent the night on the train. The afternoon had been cloudy and almost threatened rain but while we were eating dinner the western sky cleared near the horizon and the last rays of the sun which was obscured from our vision by the next hill were cast against our coal bearing mountain tinting it in a most unexpected manner. The sunset was exceedingly grand and somewhat different from what is usually seen elsewhere. The blue tints were especially fine. Towards the horizon & fringing the distant peaks was thin ethereal blue; balancing this in the other direction was mystical greenish blue, heavy, dense and thick. Separating these were the salmon stained clouds half on fire. About this time a caravan of 72 camels passed along the ancient route to Kalgan, Mongolia and Lake Bankal region.

Sunday May 23rd. 1909

The Peking – Kalgan R.R. is not yet finished and tickets are at the present time issued only to Hsia Hua Yuan. But we were fortunate in catching a construction train which left at 6 AM and carried us some 20 miles to Hsuen Hwa which is the end of the present tracking. Sitting upon the ties on the open cars we enjoyed fine views of the scenery which in the early morning light was exceedingly pleasing to my mountain tastes. Soon after starting we followed the stream thru the prominent range which is called Hwang yang shan on our map. The lower beds near the RR level are metamorphosed sedimentaries while the higher parts are apparently lava flows. Saw some greenish specks on the rocks which strongly suggested copper to me – perhaps malachite. Beyond the mountains is an open undulatory basin. Wash material shown in the cuts. The northern face of the mountains is abrupt and splendid in the early light. On the slopes low down were dunes sharpened to knife edge arêtes in a fashion which I have not seen anywhere else.

Reached Hsuen Hwa, the end of the track, at about 8 o'clock. This is a large walled city. We stopped for breakfast at the inn there and engaged carts for the next three day's journeying. We started for Kalgan with three mule carts at about 9.30. Hsuen Hwa was an important city 2000 years ago and has broad streets and massive gates. The large trees in the side streets made it an attractive city with picturesque vistas. The gates at the west ends of the separate cities were different from what we had seen before and showed more ornamentation than usual.

From Hsuen Hwa we proceeded in a northwesterly direction along a broad flat valley bottom. After a time we reached the S.W. slopes of a ridge of hills which paralleled our course on the right. Later after following an uneven hilly course we crossed the line of hills and entered a similar plain on the N.E. side of the hills. Tea was had at a tiny hamlet in the hills. Shortly after tiffin and we had descended to the plain beyond a strong wind sprang up from the N.W. and blew great quantities of dust in our faces. This dust storm continued with little abatement until we reached Kalgan. The going was so exceedingly uncomfortable that little note could be taken of the surrounding country except that the way to Kalgan.

Kalgan 5 P.M. At Kalgan we were told at the first six or eight inns to which we applied that they were either full or else they did not take foreigners. We were afterwards told that they latter reason was the real one at all the inns. The trouble was caused by missionaries who have insisted upon paying a certain price (lower than the Chinese pay) and the innkeeper has had no redress. The innkeepers say they cannot tell who are missionaries and who are not & so take no foreigners. We finally located at a Mohammedan horse bazaar establishment & fared well.

Monday May 24th. 1909

Our mule cart caravan left the inn at Kalgan for Mongolia at 7.40. When we passed through the north gate of the city we were practically in Mongolia since the Great Wall of China comes down the hillside to this gate and outside of the gate is beyond the Great Wall into what used to be regarded as Mongolia. After riding up the valley road to the west for a short distance. I left the road and climbed the hillside to the Great Wall which runs along the crest of the hills. This is the true ancient wall which was built 200 B.C. The inner wall at Nankou Pass which is a larger wall was built only about 600 years ago. It is to the more recent wall at Nankou that the tourists go. The ancient wall which runs over the hills at Kalgan is built of blocks (irregular) of stone and boulders which do not fit in together as well as they might and so do not produce a very good wall. The wall at Nankou is of brick. The Kalgan wall is about 15ft. high and perhaps 6 ft wide at the top. Instead of being a vertical wall the outer face is a slope of only about 70°. It appeared to be an easy matter to clamber over it at almost any point.

From the wall a splendid survey of the dissected topography of the border of the Mongolian plateau was obtained. To the S.E was the broad basin like type of valley by which we had come to Kalgan. To the North as far as could be seen were hills and mountains without any definite arrangement determined by structure. They are the dissected border of the plateau. The hilltops to the north rose higher than the hill upon which I stood and hence I got no impression from this point of the table land which lay beyond Our caravan passed rapidly up the valley toward the N.W. The Mongolian General Han rode by with a long train of cavalry following. Several caravans of camels. Many donkeys, mules & horses. The Mongolians are great horse dealers and horsemen and many of their horses are fine animals. These are raised on the grassed plains of the tableland. The Mongolians are larger physically than the Chinese, not only taller but apparently much heavier of build. They are a sturdy but somewhat stolid people. They are very swarthy-much darker than the Chinese with occasionally a reddish cast which is somewhat suggestive of the North American Indian.

Following up the valley to the N.W. we passed varied type of igneous and pyroclastic rocks. There were some reddish conglomerates which resemble volcanic agglomerates in places. These suggest surface lavas. But the greater masses in the peaks looked more like intrusives. We followed the rather monotonous valley until 12.15 when we came to steep slopes and the road zigzagged up the hill front. This was the most abrupt rise of the plateau face. We attained the brink and shortly after reached the small village of Totai, 60 li from Kalgan and the point at which caravans bound for usually stop for the first night. We arrived at Totai at 1 P.M. Had tiffin here. After tiffin the ameroid read 5 ft. At the inn at Kalgan in the morning it had read 2770 ft. We climbed the hill of lava just west of Totai upon the top of which the aneroid read 5600 ft. or 2830 ft above the inn in Kalgan.

From the top of this hill we could see the comparatively flat plain of Mongolia to the N.W. We were on approximately the same level as the table land plain for we could just see its surface at points back from the edge. According to Li San the plain which begins here extends for long distances into Mongolia. He says that in many places it is covered with tall grass. It is here that the horses are raised. The plain is apparently a basic lava flow laid upon a peneplained surface. The lakes represented on the map are probably depressions in the lava surface which have become filled with water. The front of the plateau is not an abrupt wall like face but instead there is a region of perhaps 15 miles width between the valley plain and the higher plateau plain which is extensively dissected by erosion. In places it resembles the Bad Land topography of the western U.S. Photos were taken of it in spite of the high wind and snow storms to show the highly dissected character of the rise to the plateau. The total rise is about 3000 ft from the valley floor to the tableland. See photos The steepest portion of the rise to the plateau is the last few hundred feet just before reaching the flat top. This is apparently caused by the lava cap (see photo No) The rocks beneath the lava capping are less resistant to erosion. On the top of the lava hill which we climbed we found fragments of scoriaceous lava which showed conclusively that this is a lava flow.

We were very short of time and could spend but a few minutes in observing the fine view which our hill afforded of the front of the plateau and the photographic work was greatly hindered by a piercing, cold north wind which shook the tripod and brought intermittent bursts of snowflakes which obscured the landscape. We were entirely unprepared to meet a snow storm toward the end of May in this latitude. But the climate of Mongolia appears to be bleak and cold. Many of the Mongolians whom we saw riding into Kalgan were wearing fur lined garments. It must be remembered that the plateau is nearly 3000 ft above Kalgan.

We had ascended so gradually that we had not appreciated the difference in altitude which is such an important factor in climate.

We returned to Kalgan by a different road which bore off to the east and descended another valley which lead to Kalgan from the N.E. while our other road enters the city from the N.W. At first we descended rapidly through a peculiar conglomerate formation made up largely of light colored igneous rocks. This conglomerate in general appearance resembled the early Tertiary deposits in the U.S. Its relation to the igneous rocks of the region could not be determined from so superficial an inspection of it. It must be some 300-400 ft thick. Further down the valley the rocks were largely igneous rocks which looked rather more like intrusives than lava flows. There were some reddish prophyries with feldspars phenocrysts and some fine grained rocks not unlike a rhyolite in composition. The hills were scarred and gullied by erosion in lines which stood out sharply before the slanting rays of the sun. In places steep cliffs of the Hwang tu formation occurred up to certain heights above the valley bottom while the rocky hills were entirely bare of loess.

Further down the valley the stream appears coming out of the sandy bottom. At places here and there the water largely disappears to reappear further downstream. This helps explain the extensive aggradation of these valleys. The water only flows along on the surface for short distances and then sinks into the porous material leaving behind whatever material it is carrying in suspension. The higher gradients at the borders of the valley allow the water to flow swiftly and carry a load which is dropped later on the flat valley floor. In this way the valleys are widened and the valley bottom kept as a flat plain of aggradation. Operating in conjunction with this is the principle suggested by T.C.C. that there is greater precipitation on the hills bordering the valleys than in the valleys themselves. This should widen the valleys and cause the aggradation of the valley bottoms. There can be no doubt that this principle of greater precipitation on the hills is sound. The only hesitation which I have is that whether there exists sufficient differentiation over limited areas to produce the results. With the valley several miles in width the principle would seem to apply. This appears at the present moment to be a very important contribution to the explanation of wide aggraded valleys which are so general in arid regions. Follow this matter further. Shortly before reaching Kalgan we passed some steep rock cliffs at the base of which were some enormous talus piles. In this land of frost talus piles become very large and conspicuous. In South China where there is little frost talus was very scanty We reached Kalgan shortly before 7 P.M. in tune to get through the gate before sundown.

Tuesday May 25th. 1909

Our caravan of mule carts left the inn at Kalgan at about 7.30 A.M. and moved slowly through the streets of the city toward the new railway station which is being built at the S.E. extremity. The appearance of the city which is not just like the other cities which we have seen can best be judged from the hasty snap shots taken on the march. As we marched along on the return journey the N.W. wind increased steadily in force until it was sweeping before it large quantities of dust which made the going most uncomfortable. Before Hsuen Hua was reached at 1 o'clock (west gate) a full-fledged dust storm was raging so that little note was taken of the surroundings.

We had tiffin at the same inn as on the journey up and shortly before 4 o'clock went over to the railway station and got permission to return to Hsia Hua yuan on the open gravel train. Had to wait half an hour alongside the track during which time the dust storm raged at its worst and a bitter wind chilled us through and through. The dust was so thick that the neighboring hills were completely obscured. The dust was not only near the ground but filled the air so that it became quite dark. As the train went almost exactly with the wind we got along fairly well as long as it was in motion but fared very badly when it stopped at several stations on the way. Upon arrival as Hsia hua we saw the station master and secured permission to spend the night on the Peking train. We occupied the 1st class compartments while the boys scattered our outfit all over the 2nd class seats at the other end of the car. The wind went down before dusk and the air cleared up so that we could see the blue sky. We slept soundly on the railway seats after the trails of cold dust storm.

Wednesday May 26th. 1909

The train left Hsia Hua yuan for Peking at 6.00 AM just as we were starting to dress. A clear beautiful morning affording fine views of the distant hills. These bear the erosion lines which are so generally seen in semi-arid regions. These lines were brought out to good advantage by the long shadows of the early morning. The granite at Nankou Pass seems to be pretty clearly as intrusive mass. Between the pass and the town of Nankou a large number of separate dikes and intrusions, mostly of granite but some of dark basic rock, were seen to cut the metamorphosed sedimentaries. The structure at the mountain front appears to be a fold with apparently some fracturing and local faulting which has been cut by numerous dikes and intrusions of igneous rock. This anticlinal fold appears to be general along the face of the mountains not only of the range running N&S, but also of that which trends off to the east from Nankou. A short journey over the plains brought us to Peking (N. W. gates station) about 1.30 P.M. One of the notable features of the day's ride was the fact that the country seemed unusually green to us, due to doubt to the great contrast which it presented to the desert of Mongolia.

Thursday May 27th. 1909

Paid off Chang our cook. Bishop J.W. Bashford spent nearly the whole morning in conference with T.C.C. In the afternoon rode about Peking with Li San and visited some of the bazaars. Later developed pictures.

Friday May 28th. 1909

Visited the Imperial University of Peking. Called first upon the Director accompanied by Mr. Far T. Sung & Wang. Nothing of importance developed during the interview. The Director was glad to meet us and asked some questions about starting a department of geology. Also inquired about Dr. Oskar Eckstein whom they are trying to get here. We saw several classes in English and one in German just before the time came for the classes to be dismissed for tiffin which was about 11 o'clock. The zoological preparation laboratory showed that it had been used for some time since the desks were stained with chemicals and indicated wear. This is the first time I have seen evidence of much use of a laboratory in China. The chemical laboratory however has not yet been used. One general chemistry laboratory with desks for 50-60 students. Adjoining this is a smaller laboratory room for 15-20 students. At the other end of the General chemistry lab is an instructor's private room. In another building nearby is a laboratory for advanced students which will accommodate about 60. In addition to these there are two storerooms well stocked with chemicals and apparatus. The reagent bottles are out on the desks but they have never been used. Mr Sung at the present time is teaching English as preparation to the courses in chemistry. There is a laboratory for physics which is much smaller than that for chemistry and a physics lecture room. We went through the usual dormitories and student's rooms such as form a part of every Chinese University. There were also reading and resting rooms for the instructors.

The University as a whole is about on a par with the imperial universities at Cheng tu and Tai yuan fu though perhaps not quite so much progress has been made here as in the provincial institutions. But there are signs of larger plans for the near future. What is now the University will become the Imperial College. On top of this they are planning to plant and develop a university. The expansion is to begin with the opening of the next term for this purpose they are engaging foreign instructors and paying young men large salaries. In the afternoon developed pictures and at 6 P.M. were taken by Bishop Bashford in a carriage to the Methodist University where we dined as the guests of Bishop Bashford and Dr. Lowry, head of the institution.

Saturday May 29th. 1909

Were conducted about the city for a couple of hours by Li San. Went first to the observatory located on the east wall. Here there are a splendid set of large bronze sun dials, globes etc which date from the Ming dynasty. See photos. From the observatory tower we could view a large part of the city Peking. It does not impress one as such a great city as we had been led to expect. Just outside the wall to the east is the open country while within the wall there are open areas where the houses were burned by the foreign troops in 1900. The city covers a larger area than most Chinese cities, but still not a large area in comparison with American cities, but it is not very densely built in. Richard's Geography of China gives the population as 600,000-800,000 which seems about right. From the Observatory tower we looked down upon the space where the old examination halls were located. These cells have now been torn down so that there was not much to see.

We next went to the Drum tower situated due north of the coal hill in the Forbidden city. From this tower we obtained a splendid view of the northern half of Peking. The several broad streets leading away from the tower show that Peking has the makings of a fine city. It is the most like a European city of any in the Empire largely because of the broad streets and the general way in which it is laid out. The drum tower itself was like nearly every other public building or structure in China in showing evidence of decay and neglect. The state of dilapidation of some Chinese buildings is shocking. When a structure in China is finished it is finished for good. It if begins to fall to pieces at some later time no attempt is made to repair it. Extreme carelessness and indifference to matters of this kind appears to be one of the characteristics of the Chinese people.

Notebook
No. 5

Monday May 31st. 1909

At Peking. In the morning we called at the American and Russian legations to have our passports viewed for the Russian trip. It having rained last night for the first time in many days the dust was laid and the atmosphere very clear. I took advantage of this to get some views of Peking. In the afternoon T.C.C. went to Tung chow while I stayed behind to push the development of the accumulated supply of exposed films.

Tuesday June 1st. 1909

Busy at the Hotel most of the day. Managed to get a few snap shots of some street scenes while taking a little necessary exercise. Pushed the development of exposed films and finished everything up to date.

Wednesday June 2nd. 1909

Spent most of the morning duplicating expensive accounts and the afternoon in getting material in shape for the report. The past few days have been very hot by the thermometer (reading 101-103 as the maximum) but on account of the dryness they have not been at all oppressive. The same temperatures at home and probably also in South and east China, would be very oppressive. The sunlight and the sky entirely free from clouds a large part of the time. I do not think that this light bright as it is nearly so dangerous as the damp hazy sunlight of other parts of China.

Thursday June 3rd. 1909

Spent all day upon report work at the Hotel and did not go out till 7 P.M. when I went over to the station to meet Prof Burton and Reed on their arrival from Shanghai via coasting steamers which stopped at some of the ports in Shautung. Since leaving us in Hankow Prof. Burton has visited Changsha, Nanking, Shanghai, Soochow, Hangchow, Tsintao, and Chefoo. Most of the time was spent at Shanghai and the neighboring cities thus rounding out a district which we had only imperfectly seen.

Friday June 4th. 1909

The day was consumed in rounding up matters making the final arrangements for the Manchurian and Siberian trips and packing up. An east wind during the afternoon caused the sky to cloud over and by 10 P.M. a light rain was falling. An east wind here bringing moisture from the sea and then rising over the hills and mountains to the west of Peking is pretty certain to bring rain at this season of the year.

Saturday June 5th. 1909

The train for Shau hai kuan left Peking at 8.30 S.M. Were seen to the station by Wang and Sung At 9.15 we are running close to the Hun Ho to the S.W. of Peking. Area of sand dunes here. An effort is made to control the sands by breaking up the sandy tract into small rectangular fields with rows of trees as dividing lines. Consider the possibility of covering the ground between rows of wheat, beans etc. with the fragments of stone to prevent evaporation and thus retain the moisture in the soil.

An almost perfect plain lead down to Tieutsin which we reached at 11.25 A.M. We could not see a great deal of the city from the train but what we did see gave the impression that the foreign influence has been very strong here. There were a great many foreign buildings to be seen. The train kept descending toward the sea until Tango was reached near the Taku forts when the course was changed and the sea coast was skirted in the north Easterly direction which leads to Shan Hai Kuan. Saw numerous evaporating basins where the salt water is concentrated by evaporation and the salt obtained.

The land was very flat until the hills were reached at Tong Shau a large city with many foreign buildings and houses. Within the town and not far from the station in a coal mine having a shaft 2000 ft deep. Good looking plant on the surface. Le San who has worked in this mine says that there are 14 miles of entries. He says that the coal is about 40 inches thick at its maximum and lies generally horizontally. At Gu Yie is another large coal mine. The surface works are quite impressive.

Beyond the Sha Ho is a broad valley with some hill remnants and low ridges running parallel to the stream course and clearly divides between different channels of this and the Lan Ho. There seems to have been a vast amount of erosion in this general region for the plains and valleys are broad and the hills interstream remnants. Changli, a large walled city situated at the base of very rugged mountains which are a delight to the eye. About 4-5 miles further on is an unusually sharp ridge of truly alpine aiguilles which are an impressive sight on account of their splendid sculpturing and precipitous sides. They appear to be made up of schistose rocks now standing as the core of a much more extensive mass. Beyond the aiguilles is the broad valley of the yang Ho. This valley was noted for its green grass and general prosperous appearance. With the aiguille range as a background this fertile valley floor with abundant green looked very inviting. The remainder of the journey to Shan hai kuan was amid lower hills and across frequent stream courses which lead down to the sea. According to the map the streams are much larger in the mountains than on the plains near the sea. Apparently much of their water sinks into the loose sand of the great flat valleys.

We reached Shan hai kuan about 6 o'clock and went at once to the Railway Hotel. As soon as possible I strolled out to the wall (Great Wall) which after its long course through North China runs down to the sea at Shan hai kuan. It was nearly 7 P.M. when I got onto the wall so that I hastened to take photos before it got too dark. The wall is about 20+ ft high built of earth on its inner side but well faced with brick on the outer side. It is perhaps 20 ft wide on top. Most of the towers which once adorned it have fallen to pieces and the brick outer facing shows signs of decay but it would still constitute quite a barrier to marauding bands were it not for the gaps in it. Unlike the wall at Kalgan its face is nearly vertical and could be scaled only with difficulty if at all without the help of ladders. Shan hai kuan gave the impression of being a very interesting place to spend the day.

Sunday June 6th. 1909

The train for Mukden left Shan hai kuan at 8.00 A.M. and soon passed through the Great Wall into Manchuria. We follow the plain while the mountains continue on the west. It is a rolling plain with relief up to 50 ft. The material is reddish apparently in considerable part residual with some gravel. Cuts in some of the low swells show crystalline rock apparently granite up to within 5-10 ft of the surface. Between the swells are broad valleys a mile or more across running down to the sea which at points can be seen several miles to the east. The swell surfaces constitute practically a crystalline pen plain. The present broad valleys are not much below it. What filling there has been is all in these valleys. Continental creep toward the sea and filling on the border of the Gulf to offset the advance of the sea. This is becoming more and more of a turf region with less dust. The ground generally did not show evidence of dust storms for there was no lodgment of wind blown material in the lee of obstacles.

At 10.15 A.M. we passed close to some hills of rock rising up to 500 ft. with layers character?) dipping toward the sea at angles of 20-30°. Out in the bay are islands rising several hundred feet above the water. These are remnants and show that while the peneplain is more perfect than the Tertiary peneplain in the Appalacheans it is still imperfect. 10.25 Ning yuin 11.15 Lien shen. To the east of this town a couple of miles is a long range of hills which indicate that the erosion and peneplaination of this general region has taken place since the folding which developed the mountains. In some of the hills some distance back there seemed to be dipping beds of sedimentaries apparently considerably metamorphosed. Veins and igneous dikes in metamorphic rocks are the rule in the shallow railroad cuts. Angular mantle rock. No evidence of any marine deposits or marine submerssion. Frequent glimpses of the sea.

At 11.30 we are quite near to the water. Many ships and boats in sight. The plain slopes down to the tide flats at quite an angle. Abrupt sea cliffs on the headlands and islands. Many salt evaporating basins. By noon the soil has become much darker in color so that the contry resembles the prairies of Minnesota and Dakota. Very few trees except the clusters about small hamlets. The train continued north on the plains graudally drawing away from the mountains until it reached Hsin Min Tun. Just beyond this town the railroad line turns around from a north Easterly course to a south Easterly direction toward Mukden. The country is almost a level plain with considerably grass and trees only sparsely by dotting the landscape. The fields are large and growing a crop of what looks like corn through it is only just above the ground. It is a Minnesota type of country.

After crossing this great plain we reached the Chinese station of Mukden at about 6.30 had to get out and get tickets to the Japanese station about a mile further on since this tiny strip of track is held by the Japanese. The drive from the station to the hotel was very dusty and disagreeable.

Monday June 7th. 1909

At Mukden. We started out with Li San to get a general idea of the city. First went to the wall on the East side of the Manchu city and got a good view of the chief portion of Mukden. For general appearance and details of architecture etc see photos. To the east was a long range of hills of which the main hills were rather more than ten miles distance. Some of the lower foot hills were considerably nearer. The air was very clear permitting good vision of dust and points with the exception of the range of the hills to the east, South east and north East everything was a great plain, the great delta formation of the Liao and neighboring minor rivers.

We were struck in passing through the streets by the very elaborate signs and designs over the doorways to some of the stores and shops along the main E + W. street in walled city of Mukden. There were gaudy figures of dragons, lions and large birds several feet in length which were mounted and perched in front and above the doorways. The stops generally presented an animated business like appearance. The people are more self-reliant and independent and have individual countenances which generally show more characters than those farther South. The women with natural feet walk along and show by their bearing that they are something more than more pieces of furniture. The men are larger and stronger physically and show the effects of the cold bracing winters. They are said to be less acute mentally than the Cantonese. They seem more stolid. The policemen on the streets instead of merely gazing at the street traffic order the rickshaw men and others to keep to the left side of the street, they themselves standing in the middle of the street. They preserve a sort of order and discipline not seen elsewhere. There are more soldiers here than further south China apparently following the lead of Russian and Japan in placing large forces near the frontiers. The soldiers are larger and appear more efficient than those further south. We visited a temple outside of the East gate which consisted of several attractively designed buildings (see photo). There was here a chamber of tortures similar to that at Nanking.

We called upon F.D. Cloud American Consul Generaland had a talk with him on Mukden and Manchuria. Practically no foreign educational work has been doing here. He believed that the Chinese would welcome American educational work here as an offset to the growing Japanese aggression. Would not be received by the Japanese with favor though they would show us hostility openly nor in any way which could be written up by the press for they are greatly afraid of the press. Mr. Cloud spoke highly of the climate of Mukden. Clear weather prevails very generally during the winter and spring. Cold but invigorating. Local dust blown up and disagreeable at times but no great dust storms. Obtaining a pass from Mr. Cloud went out to the tomb of the Manchu emperor which is located about two miles to the N.W. of the city. Before reaching the tomb we passed through some beautiful meadow vegetation. Beyond were stately pine trees. The tomb is reached after passing through several exceedingly imposing gates near which are some striking subsidiary buildings. The whole gives a most imposing impression to the traveler which can best be judged from the photos. The park of pines is very fine.

In the afternoon we called upon Liang Yu Ho. (Mr. M. T. Liang) Acting Senior Chancellor (Lieutenant Governor) to whom we had a letter of introduction from Mr. Tong kai son. Mr. Liang was very friendly and talked just as an American would talk (using fully as good English for he spent many years in the U.S. to which he became much attached.) We did not press questions of governmental attitude toward the introduction of American education into Manchuria but rather got his general view point on the situation in Manchuria. He was very optimistic upon this region and though that there were great possibilities here thinking chiefly of physical development. His friendly attitude would point toward good relations between an American educational enterprise in Manchuria if properly conducted and the government.

Tuesday June 8th. 1909

Bought tickets from Mukden to the limit of the Japanese section of the railway (Chang chun) and changed the excess Chinese money into Russian rubles. Went out of the city to the S.W. to view the battlefield of Mukden. The Japanese are constructing a monument in the form of a rifle cartridge (see photo) to mark the spot where a large number of their troops were killed in storming the Russian trenches. Some rough lines of trenches and rifle pits are still to be seen through the active Chinese have filled up most of them in their agricultural work. They have made way with all the relics of the great battle. The farmers cultivating the fields have no bullets even for sale. However I managed to pick up the steel nose of a bullet which being inside the Russian trenches was probably a Japanese bullet.

The land is one great plain covered, where it is not cultivated, with a fairly thick growth of long grass. In the fields they grow a variety of millet whcih is something like our sorghum. This has a large number of uses - oil, fodder, fuel for burning etc. The long stalks form one of the principal fuels used by the people (see photo). The Japanese are building a Jap town or concession to the S.W. of Mukden in the direction of the monument. Many Japanese shops along the street leading to the R.R. station. Japanese soldiers in evidence. They are smaller than the Chinese but look much sturdier. They appear rouugh and harsh in comparison.

We took tiffin with Consul General Cloud who entertained at the same time a party of Americans. Little new information of importance obtained. Later in the afternoon managed to get in an hour photographing some of the street scenes. Prof Burton and Mr Reed arrived at the hotel at 7.30. After a hurrid consultation with them we started from the hotel at 8 o'Clock to catch the 9.15 train for Harbin via Chang Chun. This is an American built train with standard Pullman cars. Japanese replace the Chinese on this train.

Wednesday June 9th. 1909

Woke up at 4 A.M. in standard Chicago built Pullman car somewhere on the rolling plains of central Manchuria. Splendid land for farming. Black soil quite noticeable. At 5. AM we reached Chang Chun the limit of the Japanese sphere of influence and changed over to the Russian train for Harbin. Transfer and weighing of baggage a slow affair. Russian wide gange begins here. The engine of our train looks heavy though the wheels and driving rods seem very light. Wood used for fuel.

Rolling prarie continues. Houses and people become fewer and fewer as we progress northward. The region is not thickly populated and with the soil superior to that of much of China the wonder is that more Chinese have not move in. The climate may be severe in the winter. This extensive fertile thinly populated region adjoining China may have some bearing upon the question of whether China proper really is overpopulated. If China were really overpopulated there should have been emigration to the more thinly settled but equally fertile areas to the north. The people in this part of Manchuria are rough and hardy. Many of them are as large as the Russian soldiers which abound at every railway station.

The Semgari river is a large stream cutting the South or left bank in its westerly course. The Lalin ho further north has plenty of water in marked contrast to the streams of northern China. This grassy prairie land is much better watered than Chihli. The entire journey from Chang Chum to Harbin was over these rolling plains. Low hills were seen in the distance to the east in the neighborhood of Harbin.

We reached Harbin about 2.30 P.M. on Mukden time or 3.00 P.M. by the Russian Trans-Siberian R.R. time. Got ticket from the agent at the Grand Hotel and had the baggage transferred to the Moscow train. The transfer of the trunks involved a lot of bother and exorbitant charges and squeeze on the part of the porters, interpreter etc. We had no time to see anything of the city but the Russian part of it near the railway appears to be of our western state mushroom type.

Our international train de luxe pulled out of Harbin station at 4.12 P.M. (Russian time), crossed the river and sped in a northwesterly course across the plain. An almost perfect plain continued all the way from Harbin until darkness set in about 9.30 P.M. The plain is covered with an abundant crop of grass except in a few places where there appears to be a little alkali and would correspond to Manitoba on our continent. There are very few houses located upon it - often not a house in sight. It would seem as though this great plain should support a considerable population and develop strongly. The plain appears to be the result of aggradation by the Sungari and its tributaries.

Thursday June 10th. 1909

On Trans-Siberian train in Northern Manchuria. Got up at 5 o'clock to see the Kuigan mountains which constitute the continuation of the border of the Mongolian plateau. But there were no mountains to be seen. The train followed a wide, flat-bottomed valley between hills 200-300 ft in height gradually ascending it makes a complete loop where the valley narrows and the grade increases. A little later it passes through a long tunnel which is the water shed, and emerges into a valley whose stream flows to the N.W. This also becomes a broad flat valley. The descent on this side is much less than on the other. The country is a low tableland after the Kingan hills are passed. These extend for some distance however. Three quarters of an hour after passing through the tunnel the valley which the train follows was about half a mile in width and the hills which border it perhaps as much as 300 ft above the valley floor. These hills [like] those of lower latitudes are generally smooth and little scarred by gully erosion. Their smooth slopes and freedom from gullying appears to be due to the heavy covering of turf. In the lower latitudes the sun is too hot for the grass which it dries up but the less powerful rays of the sun in the more northerly region permit grass to grow thickly and vigorously and to accumulate a strong sod which prevents in a large measure the gullying of the hillsides. The same thing is said to occur in the different latitudes of the U.S. It may be a general principle of wide application. Fitting in with this principle is the observation that the hills in semi arid regions where there is very little grass are excessively scarred by gullies as shown by my photographs.

Further on the train rises up out of the valley onto the tableland plain which it follows for a distance and then takes to the valley floor again at a point where the valley is very broad and the land on either side very low. Broad valleys up to 3 miles across in the midst of an undulatory upland plain is the character of the topography to the town of Maudschuria where the custom house between Manchuria and Siberia is seated. Some dune areas in this strip.

Arriving at Mandschurija shortly before 3 P.M we all had to show our passports and have the luggage examined at the custom house before entering Siberia. Had letter from Russian Legation in Peking to customs officials which facilitated matters. The officials were polite and made little trouble for any of the passengers. Our first glimpse of far famed Siberia was of a moderately rolling treeless plain in no way different from much of north western Manchuria. Large number of prairie dogs though the region in less dry and much better grassed than that in which the prairie dog live in the U.S.

Our "Carte Geologique de la Trambaikalie Meridiovak" represents the rolling plain as formed near the frontier or basalt, followed in turn as we go N.W. by granite, more basalt, rhyolite and then diabase up to the quaternary deposits in the basin of the Borzia rivers where we arrived about twilight. This map shows considerable areas of Achean a little further on so that apparently the region is an old pen plain upon which there have been some more recent lava flows together with coarser intrusives. Throughout the whole region between Manchuria and Lake Baikal according to the geological map there are but very limited areas of sedimentary rocks and these are of rather doubtful age. It is a great region of crystalline rocks.

II 钱伯林中国考察笔记

Oriental Educational Investigation
Synopsis of Notes on South China

By T. C. Chamberlin and R. T. Chamberlin

We spent three days at Hong Kong (Feb. 13-15); went thence 300 miles to the northwest to Wuchow in Kwangsi province; spend one day there; went 200 miles eastward to Canton, the capital of Kwangtung; spent 2.5 days there; thence 100 miles southeastward to Hong Kong, where an additional day was spent, the trip terminating Feb. 23rd, making ten days in all.

Our chief endeavor was to note the fundamental characters of the people, the significant features of the topography and the climatic conditions of the region, the natural resources utilized and particularly the possible resources not utilized, especially lands not adequately cultivated. The bearing of these on the educational problem and on suitable sites for educational institutions were foremost considerations.

The topography was found to embrace two prevalent factors, the one, well defined, rather steep hills and mountains, irregularly dispersed over the surface, ranging in height from 3000 feet downwards, with the average below 500 feet; the other, an aggradation plain occupying the valleys and forming the apparent base from which the eminences rise but, in reality, constituting a progressive filling of the valleys which separate the eminences.

The whole gives the impression that it has stood higher in recent geological times, when the main carving by erosion took place, and that it has been slowly sinking (perhaps by continental creep) while the wash from the hills and the alluvium of the rivers has been gradually building up the valleys. On the coast border, the depression has exceeded the filling, giving rise to numerous inlets and islands; while inland the building up has exceeded the depression, and alluvial plains have been formed. Economically considered, there has been a change from high slope to low slope, with agricultural advantage to this extent, but some loss of territory on the coast borders.

So far as we can judge, these general impression are applicable to the whole southeastern border of China.

Wherever it was possible to make close examination, disintegration of rock was found to be a dominant feature. The hills and even minor mountains were mantled, rather deeply, it would appear, with disintegrated or semi-disintegrated rock material, in other words, the basis of soil. This radically affects the question of soil maintenance, which in turn lies at the basis of permanent fertility. Extremely little hard-rock surface was seen, through surfaces bare of vegetation were abundant. Soil-material appears therefore notably more persistent on the slopes than vegetation.

The present cultivation is chiefly confined to the alluvial bottoms and to the very low slopes. The hills are practically uncultivated. Speaking generally, they are but scantily covered with trees, through considerable areas are occupied with scattering pines of small growth. This smallness of growth seems to be due to youth and not to dwarfing agencies; in other words, to adverse human and not to adverse natural agencies. There was found very little shrubbery or underbrush, perhaps because rooted up for fuel. Aside from the scanty pine growth, the surfaces were generally clothed with a coarse reedy grass which is cut and burned as fuel. It appeared to be poorly adapted to grazing or use as fodder, and all information gained from inquiry supported this view.

It is difficult to estimate, even approximately, from our limited observations, the ratio of slope surface to flat surface. In the great delta region surrounding the head of Canton Bay, the alluvial plains preponderate, but even there hills protrude at such close intervals that they are rarely out of sight. In the back country, the hill-surface greatly preponderates, and this is probably the fact for the whole of South China if the maps that best show topographic feature can be trusted. The problem of the utilization of the hill surfaces seems therefore to be the dominant physical problem of South China.

It appears further that this is a problem which permits a favorable and not difficult solution, since adequate soil material still remains; is rapidly reproduced by disintegration below; the rainfall is adequate, and vegetation occupies most of the surface in spite of adverse human agencies.

The distribution of inhabitants is profoundly affected by the preceding conditions. The people are almost wholly located on the alluvial flats and the low slopes. The hills are almost uninhabited (an exception to this is found in Hong Kong and similar locations where European ideas and methods prevail). On the plains, the people are densely clustered in cities, for commercial reasons, and in villages, for protection. Robbers and tigers are assigned as the chief threatening agencies. We were naturally astonished at the assignment of tigers as an agency affecting human distribution in an ancient land of this kind, but testimony as to the presence and terrifying affect of these animals was given by various parties. It is even said that the destruction of the hill forests was prompted as a means of protection against both robbers and tigers. There is abundant testimony as to the influence of the robbers, who are chiefly called "pirates" because they largely use boats on the streams in attack and retreat. It is said that the distribution of the people is wider in districts back from the waterways, and our observations may need to be discounted because of this. In both the cities and villages, the crowding is intense; the streets are reduced to a few feet, usually less than ten, in breadth; the houses are generally windowless and even the door small, all of which affects the higher development of the people, and is anti-educational. The problem of the redistribution of the people is therefore a radical one, first in securing more ample food supplies and better economic condition generally, and second in developing greater individuality and independence of action, with better home conditions, and through these, both the possibilities and the enjoyment of education. The robbers and the tigers are easily disposed of. The problem of effectively cultivating and utilizing the higher slopes is a more far-reaching and difficult one, but apparently altogether soluble.

Owing to our prepossession as to the extreme density of the population, we were astonished at its apparent sparseness in much of the region traversed. This appearance is doubtless misleading because of the extreme density of the villages and cities, but we still retain the impression that the country is not really overpopulated when its possible productiveness is considered. We entertain the impression that the population may be very considerably increased and yet be well supported even on a less frugal basis than now prevails. The conditions of a comfortable life in this warm climate are relatively inexpensive while the productiveness of the land due to double or multiple crops, is relatively high.

We have taken such individual testimony as to climatic conditions and their physiological effects as was practicable, but this is necessarily defective and needs to be supplemented by systematic and prolonged observations. Consul General Amos p. Wilder has offered to aid in procuring such statements as are available. We endeavored particularly to get testimony bearing on the scantiness of vegetation on the hills. The most common reason assigned is human action. The dry season of the fall, October to December, is also assigned; also the relatively cold, dry winter, which kills tropical plants, and the hot, wet summer, which kill temperate plants. The subject needs much more study.

Apparently a proper handling of the vegetation so as to furnish its owner protection and protection of tis soil, would solve the difficulty. The British have reclothed large portions of Hong Kong hills with a large variety of shrubs and trees, while slopes not so treated in the immediate vicinity and similarly exposed are relatively bare or scantily clothed.

The universal testimony is that the summer months, by their high temperature and humidity, are very trying physiologically. This appears to be a matter of serious consideration from the educational point of view. We have sought for highlands adjacent to centers of population that might furnish sites for institutions where these adverse conditions would be mitigated. We ascended Wuchow peak, about 1200 feet, the White Cloud hills near Canton, about equally high, and Hong Kong peak, somewhat higher. Our notes in detail will show some serious difficulties connected with the two first named heights. There are greater heights farther in the interior that should be considered. The conditions at Hong Kong are mitigated by the sea and are, on the whole, much more favorable than the inland points unless we go much farther inland than we are able. Sea-border conditions as favorable as those of Hong Kong can doubtless be found at various other points along the coast.

Such observations as we could make and such testimony as we could gather concur in indicating that the Cantonese are exceptionally active and industrious for so low a latitude, that they are extremely frugal, are in a qualified sense, ingenious, adapting ways to means with facility, suit themselves to new conditions reasonably well, are physiologically strong with special powers of endurance, have a considerable measure of acuteness, and are fairly honest in business. There is little evidence of the deeper moral convictions or of intellectual penetration. There are evidences of certain trickiness, and the fleecing of strangers by various forms of "squeeze" seems to be a well-developed art. The testimony as to their success as students places them on a par with foreign youth but rather in the direction of mental acquisition than of investigative insight. They appear to be less stable and more given to excitement than the more northerly Chinese. We gather the impression that they are better adapted to form an efficient factor in the development of a higher grade of tropical civilization than most tropical peoples. Perhaps they are the best adapted to this of all oriental races. We have made inquiries industriously relative to the Chinese in the more tropical latitudes. The concurrent testimony places them in advance of the other races in industry, frugality and competency.

The question has therefore arisen whether the Cantonese are not an element which may well be educated not only in respect to their development in South China but also with reference to their playing a part in the great problem of evolving a tropical civilization is one of the greatest problems yet before mankind. No doubt various elements of the civilizations of higher latitudes must contribute toward it. May the Cantonese not contribute one of these of large moment? At any rate, if they are developed into an active civilization of a higher order in South China, will they not almost inevitably become a great factor in the Oriental tropics?

When this element of the educational problem is joined to the local elements in South China, it appears to us that Hong Kong is a strategic point of the higher order, for there the Cantonese may come immediately into contact with occidental civilization in its commercial and material aspects, at least, and at the same time come under control of English political institutions, and if there were superadded to these the strong intellectual and moral influences of the best modern education and a cultured society, they would be prepared, in transit as it were, for radiation into the tropical latitudes, and for reflex influence in their own country. No doubt this is Britain's opportunity in a peculiar sense, but it is noe the less a part of the oriental educational problem.

Oriental Educational Investigation Synopsis of Studies in Central China

February 27th to May 3rd, 1909

By T. C. Chamberlin and R. T. Chamberlin

1. Itinerary

We reached Shanghai on our return from South China, February 27th, and started from Hankow by steamer on the Yangtze, February 28th. Brief stops were made at Ching-Kiang, Nan-King, Wu-Hu and Kiu-Kiang. Hankow was reached at midday March 3rd and Mr. Burton joined us from Peking that afternoon. A day was given to the educational adaptions of the local geography, and to the mission schools; and a day to the government schools at Wuchang, opposite Hankow. On March 5th, we started for Inchang, at the mouth of the Gorges, but owing to delays from low water, only reached it on the evening of March 11th. Visits were made at Ichang to the mission schools on the 12th and in the evening of that date a house boat was taken for the trip thru the Gorges to Wan Hsien. This up-stream voyage of reputed perils was completed with a minimum of the arduous in seven days, only a little more than the record time. The usual assignment is nine to fourteen days. Starting westward from Wan Hsien overland by chairs on March 13th, we reached Chentu, the capital of Szechuan fourteen days later, precisely the estimated time. After three days given to local educational matters, our section of the party made a five-day' excursion across the Chentu plain and into the high mountains beyond, to the basal crystalline series. After three additional days given, on our return, to the special educational problems of Chentu, the whole party started (April 14th) on the return journey, travelling one and a half days by chairs, to a navigable point on the Min river, whence we took boat down the Min to the Yangtze at Sui Fu, and thence, by the same boat, we journeyed down the great river to Ichang, stopping one day at Chung King and more briefly at other points. The excursion into the upper Yangtze rigion was thus ended April 30th, just seven weeks from the day of starting. May 1st was spent by our section of the party in physiographic studies in the country back of Inchang, while Mr. Burton's section was engaged in conference in the city. Hankow was again reached May 3rd, most of the time of the voyage being given to consultations with Lord William Gascoyne Cecil relative to a proposed international university in China.

As much of our time as could be spared from the physical studies while on the return trip form Chentu, was given to a preliminary organization of our matter, with a view to an early report on our chief conclusions when we reach America.

Our studies of the schools on the trip into the west province were made jointly with Mr. Burton and are covered, in a general way, in his journal. The following synopsis will therefore relate chiefly to the physical features that seem to us to bear, directly or indirectly, on educational problems, the purely scientific aspects being here neglected. The lower and upper Yangtze valleys will be treated separately, as they differ markedly from one another.

2. The Lower Yangtze Valley

As the delta of the Yangtze is the sits of Shanghai, its physiographic aspects passes special educational interest. It is an extensive flat plain rising but little above the extreme flood stages of the great river, but yet it is relieve here and there by isolated hills that rise through the enveloping sheet of silt. Off the southern mouth of the Yangtze east and southeast of Shanghai, are islands which are the sites of hills that in the future may, in a similar way, rise from the alluvial plain that shall them have grown outwards 50-100 miles. The immediate vicinity of Shanghai is level. The city lies 15 miles from the Yangtze on a tributary, navigable for all but vessels of deepest draft and easily susceptible of deepening to accommodate these. This distance from the Yangtze, however, does not seem to be important, for the lighter system prevails generally in the East and is well adapted to local distribution.

The Shanghai plain is traversed by small distributaries which afford easy drainage lines and give availability to the tract, with only limited danger of damage from extreme high floods, against which protected on is comparatively easy and inexpensive.

Climatically Shanghai, its latitude is low, has the advantage of land-and-sea breezes which mitigate the excesses of temperature and give a rhythmical relief. The air is rather damp in summer and chilly, though not very cold, in winter. Relative to the inland points on the Yangtze plain, the climate is stimulating, though it is not to be regarded as stimulating when compared with places in higher latitudes.

The immediate delta plain of the Yangtze may be said to be limited by the Grand Canal which runs near its western border, cutting off some hills that border the plain on its west side, and leaving some stretches of delta plain protruding into the hills on that side. The great bend which the Yangtze makes to the north as it approaches its delta, and which reaches its climax east of Nanking, is caused by this tract of hills coming up from the semi-mountainous region lying to the southwest and extending in scattered hills some distance north of the river. From this bend to Ichang, which may be taken as the upper limit of the lower Yangtze valley, there is a sharp division of the whole tract into two components—the alluvial plain and the hilly uplands. The best picture of the whole is perhaps built upon on conception of its origin. At a remote stage, the whole region stood at a higher elevation relative to the sea, and the drainage system sculptured it into hills and valleys, the deeper trenches of which lay below the bottoms of the chief present rivers. At a later stage, lodgment of silt took the place of erosion, and the greater valleys were silted up widely, forming broad alluvial plains reaching far back among the hills, and wrapping about them; often isolating them from one another and causing them to seem to rise directly and often steeply out of the alluvial plain. There are therefore two very distinct elements, --the plains that are formed of silt, and the hills that have rock nuclei and are mantled by soils and semi-decayed rock derived from the nuclei by their own weathering.

These two elements enter in a strangely contrasted way into the economic life of the people, and through that into the problem of their education. Roughly speaking, the population of the Lower Yangtze valley is crowed upon the plains, which are tilled intensively, while the hills are largely unoccupied, save by the graves of the dead. In our notes on South China, we called attention to the similar conditions there, but we were then somewhat disposed to give a degree of credence to special causes alleged to affect only tracts adjacent to the rivers and the sea; but in the Yangtze valley we found a similar contrast between the high utilization of the plains and the conspicuously low utilization of the hills. It is, perhaps, unsafe to extend this generalization over the great hill tract that lies between the Yangtze and the southern and southeastern coast. It is a matter of regret to us that limitations of time, intensified by the difficulties and the slowness of travel in this great hill tract, left the problem of this contrasted utilization indeterminate for want of personal observation. Testimony on such matters in China is peculiarly unreliable. Such as we have been able to gather, that seems worthy of any appreciable weight, supports, in the main, the view that this great hill tract is utilized only in an inferior way, but some of the testimony favors a utilization of portions in a manner similar to that which will be described later as prevalent in the Szechuan province. It seems safe, therefore, to infer that, in addition to the tracts actually observed by us, there are still more extensive tracts where high utilization of the plains is contrasted with low utilization of the hills. [Added later] We found this true in the trip north from Hankow.

The Plains:--In addition to what has already been said regarding the immediate delta plain of the Yangtze, it may be remarked that its aspect is very generally diversified by trees clustered about the houses, or scattered along the dividing dikes or paths where they least interfere with cultivation. These trees are sufficiently numerous to limit vision across the plains even when bare of leaves, to some such distance as a mile, on the average, giving the impression of a thinly wooded country. This is the best expression of artificial forestation we have thus far seen in China. On the plains west of Nanking, forestation of this class grows progressively thinner, in a general way, until it becomes a decidedly minor factor and openness dominates.

The houses of the country people on the plains generally bear a poor and unattractive aspect. The roofs are often only thatched and the walls made of unburned brick or earth and sometimes of more temporary material. Brick houses with tiled roofs are present and seem even to outnumber the thatched houses in the better portions, but the home conditions of the mass of the people sadly need improvement.

The Hill Tracts:--We scrutinized the hills with glasses constantly to detect their precise condition, so far as determinable under the conditions of our voyage up the Yangtze. Practically everywhere they were bare of trees, but generally covered with grass. There is much less of bare rock surface than we had been led to suppose from the descriptions of writers. "Bare hills" is to be interpreted as treeless hills,--not soilless hills. A mantle of soil covered with grass is general and seems to imply possibilities of utilization with fairly remunerative results. The grass, so far as we could ascertain, is mainly of the same order as that of South China, viz. coarse and little serviceable for pasture or for fodder. It is chiefly gathered for fuel. Men, women and children, bearing bundles of grass, shrubs, roots and other vegetal matter stripped from the hills, were frequent sights, and the heavy blue haze which hangs so generally over this region is, perhaps, attributable to the wide use of grassy and trashy fuel. This searching and relentless gathering of fuel by the people is said to be the chief barrier to the starting and preservation of forest on the hills. Strangely enough, however, it does not seem to lead to as great denudation of the soil mantle of the hills by wash, at least in this region, as we had anticipated.

The Sites of Leading Towns:--We tried to gather such data in passing as might bear on the eligibility of the chief towns as seats of educational institutions. Of Shanghai we have already spoken. Of Nanking, it may be said that it lies some distance back from the Yangtze on a plain surrounded by hills, a few of which are even within the walls of the city. The topographic setting is thus rather attractive and might be made mere so by forestation of the hills and better treatment of some small lakes that lie outside the walls. The weather at the time of our three-day visit and at the time of our passing up the river was delightful, and the city bears a good reputation, relatively, in respect to its climate. The present city falls far short of filling the walled space, and abundant and fairly elegant grounds within the walls are available. The adjacent hills, while sometimes high, are perhaps scarcely eligible for summer schools.

Wu-Hu is located on a fragment of the plain backed by hills of moderate elevation which are somewhat occupied by foreign residences and establishments. Topographically it is not ineligible, nor, on the other hand, is it specially attractive. The city itself does not appear to present advantage of note.

Kiu Kiang is seated on a terrace with a rock nucleus rising somewhat above the usual flood-plain and thereby presents some eligible features. A few miles back rises the mountain group on which Kuling is situated. Kuling is at present the chief summer resort of central China and is said to be satisfactory climatically and attractive scenically. About one thousand foreigners are now accommodated there, but the limits of the available area are said to be nearly reached, as also the capacity of the water supply. Probably both of these, however, could be notably extended by proper expenditures. So far as our studies have thus far gone, this seems the most eligible site for a summer school suited to the needs of the foreign constituency. It has merit in the fact that the missionaries and others gather here largely for two to three months in the most heated season. Suitable work through them might reach indirectly a large constituency.

Hankow, Wuchang and Hanyang:--These three cities are located at the junction of the Han river with the Yangtze and constitute a single center of population conveniently known as the Wu Han district. They lie chiefly on the alluvial plain, and are subject to occasional inundation at high water. The Bund of Hankow is from 4-7 feet above the natural surface and yet is occasionally flooded at stages of very high water. Probably 7-8 feet of filling would be a protection against all but the rarest floods. The sites of Han Yang and Wuchang are relieved by a few hills rising to a maximum of 900 feet, but the summits of these offer only limited areas and are scarcely available for the site of an institution of learning of the larger order. The most available site is in the foreign concession facing the Yangtze where an area roughly 1500 feet square is unoccupied by permanent buildings of value. The climate of Hankow is not altogether propitious. Winds are not prevalent and it is spoken of in common parlance as a "dead air" region. It has the reputation of being one of the hottest places in China. The temperature during both of our stays was not, however, high for the season, but rather the opposite. During our stay in early May the air, though not oppressive, was not stimulating. Populations are always uncertain in China, but what seemed the best estimate given us, places Hankow at 200,000, Hanyang at 100,000, and Wuchang from 500,00 to 600,000.

3 The Gorges of the Yangtze

The geologic and scenic features of these famous gorges must be passed lightly by. They are formed by the cutting of the Yangtze across three folds of ancient strata. They are a part of the system of folding that characterizes the Upper Yangtze region. Their scenic merits are great, the extravagant and awesome descriptions of most writers obscure the finer truths. Their educational value is great and is an asset yet awaiting its main realization.

As a means of communication between the Upper and Lower Yangtze valleys, the rapids of this reach of the river seemed to us much more susceptible of improvement at moderate cost than we had been led to suppose form existing descriptions, the we have no claims to expertness in these matters. Only two of the rapids were so bad as to make it seem prudent for us to leave our boat in coming down the river, the water stage was low and the rapids near their maximum height. The worst feature of these would yield appreciably with a moderate amount of blasting. At very high states the eddies are said to be strong and dangerous for boats not under complete control.

The difficulties of the constructing a railway through the gorges is also less than the emphasis laid on sheer walls in current descriptions would seem to imply. Except for comparatively short stretches, the side-walls are slopes retreating at angles rarely exceeding 55° to 60°, and averaging much lower. Hundreds of cultivated patches lie on the slopes within the stretches that are usually designated the Ichang and the Wushan gorges, the two greatest gorges. At the same time, a railroad through the gorges would be very expensive because it must be carried a hundred feet or more up on the side slopes to escape the high floods and this would involve many bridges and tunnels. Lovers of native scenery will regret the possibility of ever seeing the beautiful slopes of the gorges marred by the mutilations incident to railway construction. We were informed by an official at Chengtu that a more practicable route can be found some distance north of the gorges. There are also topographic suggestions of another available route some distance south of the gorges. It is much to be hoped that the river through the gorges may be so improved as to give relatively safe water navigation and that railroads may find more economical routes elsewhere.

The gorge walls concentrate the wind and perhaps also to some degree generate breezes by their own thermal action and are said to be cool and inviting in summer. The adjacent heights range from 4000 feet downward and give elevations of comfortably low temperatures. The only serious difficulty to their occupancy as stations for summer schools and private studios seems to be an inadequate water supply, but this is probably not beyond remedy. The lowest or Ichang Gorge—about 14 miles long—is quite accessible by boat form Ichang, which lies only 5 miles below its mouth. The gorge has a multitude of picturesque situations at various heights above the water level up to 2000 feet or more. On some of these suitable sites for summer schools and summer retreats for the staffs of institutions forced to leave the plains in summer, could probably be found. In these low latitudes, provision for the summer months is an important factor of the higher educational problem. The inherent interest of this region makes it one of the places worthy of further study in this regard.

4. The Middle Yangtze

The stretch of the river between the Gorges and the foot of the high ranges of mountains that border the Tibetan plateau, tho usually classed as a part of the Upper Yangtze, may better be regarded as a middle portion, since the uppermost portion in the high mountains and on the Tibetan plateau has quite different economic and human relationships. The Middle Yangtze is even now a great avenue of commerce and is susceptible of much more effective use by the introduction of specially adapted steam vessels, and experiment in which is soon to be tried. This long stretch of the river has many semi-rapids, but they are not formidable even at low water and disappear at high water, which, however, has its strong swirls and eddies in constricted portions that must be mastered without seriously taxing the large margin of safety which security in navigation here requires.

5. The Province of Szechuan

Our overland trip from Wan Hsien, beyond the Gorges, to the border of the high ranges fronting the Tibetan plateau, gave us an exceptional opportunity of seeing, in a passing way, the interior of this great province along liens not much frequented by foreigners and almost absolutely uninfluenced by them.

As we ascended the last stretches of the Lower Yangtze and approached Ichang at the outer border of the mountains through which the Gorges are cut, the cultural aspect of the country improved. Within the Gorges the terracing of the hillsides and even of the steep mountain slopes awakened surprise after our observations of the neglected hills of the Lower Yangtze region and of South China. In the tracts along the river just beyond the Gorges, beautifully terraced slopes and charming home-sites hidden in clusters of trees, and orchards in blossom became common. Along the whole land-route from Wan Hsien to the western mountains, a marvelously complete system of terracing of hills and even of mountains prevailed. The neatness of the culture and the beauty of the general effect on the landscape were a constant source of pleasure. This can be appreciated better from the photographs taken than from any description, with this added advantage, that the photographs do not put in any colored rhetoric, the unfortunately they leave out the native tints that from an element in the scenic charm. The region is chiefly occupied by the red shale and sandstones of the late Paleozoic and early Mesozoic ages, which not only lend themselves felicitously to terracing, but give prevailing red soils whose tints harmonize with the deep red-brown and gray-brown ledges and are relieved here and there by lighter and darker colors, all of which combine to form an effective background for the deep greens of the crops and the trees and for the various hues of the flowers and colored crops.

The terracing is largely for the sake of forming rice-paddies to be flooded in summer. This leads to the division of the slopes into curving strips conforming to the configuration of the slopes. These are partially concentric with one another, but vary in form to fit one another and the slope and this element of natural control yields results of high artistic value. If the work were done slovenly, this would be marred, but usually the retention walls and the bounding dikes are built on smoothly curving lines and are kept in admirable repair. Often they are set with plants at regular intervals to get the most that is possible from the land and this adds to the artistic effect. Whether this neatness and beauty of form are given for artistic effect as well as utility seems uncertain. It is hard to believe it purely an incident of utilitarianism. But on the other hand, it is strangely in contrast with the shabby, ragged and often dirty clothing of the farmers, and still more with the slovenly, evil-smelling homes that are as constant features all through this region as are the beautiful terraces themselves. These homes, set often in charming situations, among the terraces and the trees and the hills, are a striking anomaly. A couplet of the old Missionary hymn kept coming into mind constantly, "Where every prospect pleases and only man is vile". But this beauty of prospect was in no small degree man's product and the couplet failed to fit the case with exactness. As this puzzling contrast between field and home was traversed day after day, the apparent solution at length flashed upon us with startling force. The field is the domain of the man; the home is the domain of the woman. The man is a healthy, phenomenally industrious being; the women is a self-mutilated cripple, stunted by suffering as a child, and incapacitated as an adult for the duties of a housewife. The victim of feet-worship, she neglects the home and the raiment to which as a healthy, action-loving being, she might otherwise give as much willing labor and skill as the man gives to the fields. There may be fallacy in this, but once it came over us, it never left us. It remained a most forceful plea for the emancipation and education of women of China. Fortunately the binding of feet is now largely abandoned, but the education is yet to come.

One other feature makes Szechuan notable, --its paved roads, mountain stairs and stone bridges. From Wan Hsien to the Chentu plain, perhaps 350 miles, we trod a paved road, with the most trivial exceptions, even though we were not always on the chief line of travel. The paved width varied from 3 feet to 15 feet. Some portions were made of well-cut, well-fitted slabs, others were flags split and roughly fitted, and some only unshaped blocks, while occasionally cobbles were used. For the larger part, the road was in fair repair, in some places excellent, in others neglected.

The steeper ascents and descents were made by stone steps, not infrequently out from the rock in place. To climb mountains on stones stairs in the back country of a "heathen" land is an instructive experience for an American.

The stone bridges which spanned every stream and streamlet except the large rivers, which had free ferries, were surprises. The simpler forms consisted of two or three well-hewn blocks, 18 inches, and sometimes even 2 or 2 and half feet square in cross-section, commonly

12 to 15 feet, and occasionally 18 feet long, laid side by side across substantial pieces of similar blocks, with corresponding end-buttresses and retention walls on either side. The more elaborate forms were arched and were both substantial and artistic. Some had stone balustrades, sometimes ornamented with carved figures. The arching and fitting were usually admirable. The photographs will best speak of these.

There is extremely little waste land in all the Szechuan region traversed by us. It is difficult to see how the land products can be much increased except by the use of more productive plants, if this be possible, and by more effective manuring, if this be practicable. Manuring is now carried to great lengths. TH e prevalent retention and use of human excrement for this purpose is the source of noisome odors from houses, wayside receptacles, buckets in transit, and from the fields themselves, when freshly treated, and to western sensibilities is the supremely trying feature of a land almost superlatively attractive in most other respects.

By reason of the mild climate the Szechuanese are able to raise two or more crops annually. We saw the winter crops, chiefly wheat, barley, beans, peas, etc. Mustard is largely raised for its oil. Rice is the dominant summer crop. Although this is a region of tea and silk raising, we saw relatively little of either. The raising of the food staples is the preponderant industry. This province has been famous for its poppies, but they have been greatly limited by the recent vigorous action of the authorities. If this is persisted in, the opium evil will essentially disappear. Incidentally, it may here be said that while we saw no little of the curse of opium, we did not see an alcoholically drunk man in Szechuan in the six weeks of our travels by land and by boat.

A multitude of details concerning farming in Szechuan are instructive both as items in soil-management and crop-handling, on the one side, and in the industry and character of the country people, on the other, but these must be reserved. One seems suggestive enough for a place here. We noted many cases of mixed crops, usually wheat and beans, wheat and peas, etc., planted in alternate rows or hills, for the larger part a cereal and a legume, but this was not always the case. In response to inquiries as to the reason of this, it was claimed that they raised more of both members of the combination. The increase of the cereal by the nitrifying bacteria of the legume is in accord with recent western sciences, but the reciprocal benefit to the legume is, we believe, new if it be true. As we have recently urged trials in the line of imitating nature's "plant societies" (conservation paper), these observations on Chinese practice in this remarkable province have a personal interest.

Forestation in Szechuan is in a better state than in the hill-lands of the Lower Yangtze region and in south China, but it has its striking variations. The first mountain ranges crossed by us were largely stripped of their native trees, though not left so bare as in the eastern and southern regions, but later we crossed ranges normally clothed with trees and shrubs. These ranges also bore coal deposits in their flanks, and the concurrence of coal mines and clothed mountains soon suggested a mutual and rational relationship. The generalization which arose from it, viz: that where there was a sufficient supply of coal to relieve the stress for fuel, the mountains were permitted to produce their natural crop, was fairly well sustained by all subsequent observation. It points to the remedy for the serious deforestation that prevails over so large a part of China. A reasonable measure of utilization of the coal deposits scattered with singular breadth over China, which would be practicable with cheap transportation, would permit a much higher utilization of the hill country, to say nothing of incidental benefits to climate, scenery, home sites and other interests.

In our westward journey, we crossed four folds which bring up the coal measures. Some of the folds had active mines on both flanks. The coal beds are relatively thin but are worked with very little removal of waste rock. On the return voyage down the river, a large number of coal mines were seen, and all, so far as our information goes, of the same thin-bedded type. The two lines were 100 miles apart at their greater separation and the folds were in part identical and may be assumed to be essentially continuous between the two lines. How far they extend beyond, in either direction, is indeterminate, but probably a considerable distance. They are probably not productive at all points for these distances, but all may be assumed to be so in general. In the gorges, also, several other folds carry coal beds. This wide distribution of the coal beds and their relative thinness carry the suggestion that the coal is adapted to local distributive use in moderate quantities for house fuel and small factories, but is not well suited for very extensive manufacturing or for mining for distant shipment on a large scale. It fits in with other features of the region in implying that it is adapted to a multitude of small industries, rather than a few large ones. These conditions also raise the question whether electric trolleys, rather than standard railways, are not best suited to the region. Transportation in the inland parts of the province is largely carried on at present by porters in the hill regions and by wheelbarrows and porters on the Chengtu plain. This can be made to feed the lighter railway system easier than the heavier, while a network of trolley lines would better serve the country than a few standard roads, except in the matter of distant transportation to the outer provinces, which is so self-sustaining and independent a province as Szechuan is not likely to be heavy for some time to come.

This adaptability of electric lines suggests a use for the very large amount of unused water power which Szechuan and the adjacent provinces possess. Electric power is so obvious a resource of this region of great reliefs and excellent rainfall that it need not be dwelt upon at length here.

One of the notable resources of Szechuan is its salt wells which are distributed over a considerable area near the middle of the province. Natural gas is found in some of the same localities and is said to come from strata below the brine-basin beds. We frequently saw gypsum in market but not in place, and did not succeed in locating it from the vague and unreliable answers to questions. Both salt and gypsum are common products of the corresponding red series of Europe and America are to be expected here.

Many of the geological features of Szechuan are technically very interesting and some of the special features are connected in suggestive ways with the development of the people, but to state them with adequate fullness would unduly burden this synopsis.

The people seem to be among the best we have seen, and our relations with them were pleasant and kindly. Returning from the high mountains at the extreme limit of our trip on the road over which we had gone out a few days before, this kindly spirit was expressed by the salute of honor and good will of the common people of the region, and the setting off of a quick-firing bunch of their specially resonant fire-crackers, which drove away the evil spirits and ensured us good luck.

Oriental Educational Investigation Synopsis of the Observations of the Messrs. Chamberlin

North of the Yangtze River

May 10th. 1909

Our trip from Hankow northward made possible observations on the north border of the Yangtze basis and we have reason to think that these observations are applicable to a considerable area on the east and west similarly related to the basin, and therefore supplement the general conception of the Yangtze plain was formed by an alluvial deposit spread out widely along the axis of the valley, wrapping around and penetrating laterally among the higher hills within the tract and along its border. This conception remains true, but the deposit is not wholly of recent alluvium and the plain is not subject to as wide overflow, with its attendant enrichment and damage, as might perhaps be inferred from our previous notes and the general literatures on the subject. We found that the present flood plain, near Hankow, even in the highest water stages, extended but a few miles north of the city, and that this flooded portion was succeeded by a gently undulatory surface carved by long erosion at low levels. This gently undulating portion of the plain north of Hankow is about seven times as wide as the smoother and lower portion subject to occasional overflow. Beyond this undulatory plain, to the north, hills of ancient rock come in with increasing frequency until they largely displace the older alluvial plain. These are replaced in turn by the Hwai Yang Mountains, a low range that separates the Yangtze basis from that of the Hwang Ho and its associates. In our trip up the lower Yangtze, we noted terraces at intervals in the country back from the river and sometimes coming out to it. Similar terraces, eroded gently in a like manner, were seen as far east as the region between Nanking and Shanghai. Putting these with the later observations just given, it seems probable that only a minor portion of the great Yangtze plain, belongs to the present flood-plain, and that the larger portion is safer and more salubrious for homes than the better known river border. In the region north of Hankow we noted more substantial houses than we had usually observed near the Yangtze Kiang. The apparent productiveness of the higher portion was not generally better, and perhaps on the average not so high, as the tract near the river. The irrigation is imperfect so far as it goes, and is incomplete in extent, and appears to be solely dependent on local streams from the hills and mountains lying to the north. There seemed to be no general system fed by the Yangtze or by the Han River which could be controlled for this purpose.

The houses of this tract are clustered in hamlets or small villages, with rather wide open spaces between. The inclosing walls and trees of the villages make it difficult to estimate the number of dwellings in them, ---much more the number of people. While the population is dense, it did not give us the impression of being excessive. Patches of waste land were not uncommon, aside from the amount given to graves, which is large relatively. A more economical as well as a more fitting mode of paying respect to the dead and preserving their memory is one of the problems of China, for which a solution may be found without involving the objectionable features of cremation, if laudable sentiments can be made to take the place of inherited ones; but this is not the place to discuss the subject.

The absence of a very severe stress for land seemed to be as pointedly indicated by the ground mutilated in the construction of the railway as in any single feature observed. In so plain a country it would have been easy to get the earth needed for grading from comparatively narrow trenches on either hand and these might have served irrigation and drainage purposes. Quite as wide a strip was dug over or mutilated by trenches as is common on American plains where special economy is not observed, and no very general effort at recovery seems to have been made.

In the hill tract, north of the plain, are sand dunes, derived from the river bottoms. Neither these duns nor the rivers whose sandy flats give origin to them are under control. The river beds are relatively wide and the water flow relatively small. We saw them, of course, toward the close of the relatively dry winter and spring season, before the southern and eastern monsoon set in, but their condition implied that the waters were not put under control farther up either for irrigation, or power, or both. Proper control would make narrower channels sufficient, would save land and would reduce the sand flats which breed the dunes. The absence of such control is substantiated by observation on the streams above, and generally elsewhere in China.

We had opportunity to make further observations on the utilization of the hills of various sizes and slopes up to the mountain type. We found the utilization very low, much as we had previously found it almost everywhere in the lower Yangtze valley and in South China, in contrast to the very high utilization of Szechuan. Some terracing and some slope cultivation is present, but the hills generally bear nothing but inferior grass, which is of slight use as pasture. Not a few of the hills were seemed and scored by erosion.

On the mountains shrubs and trees were more abundant, but they were far short of a normal clothing. Bushes were more abundant on the north than on the south slopes, implying that there is a climatic factor in the case, but this may have more to do with the starting of young plants than the growth of those once established and with the perpetuation of these when they are able to protect their young by their own shadows.

We have endeavored to be merciful respecting matters of merely technical interest to the geologist, but we may here venture to the Hwai Yang mountains are formed of highly metamorphosed rock. The ranges out by the famous Gorges and those crossed by us in Szechuan, were not greatly altered by the agencies which folded them. North of these ranges, however, in the Han basin and on its south border, Willis found highly metamorphosed ranges. It is inferred, therefore, that it is this metamorphosed tract that is extended eastward and forms the Hwai Yang Mountains, and not the ranges cut by the gorges. This implies that these ranges either die down or continue to curve more and more easterly as they are extended in that direction, and have disappeared by erosion, while the harder altered series still stand up as low, much worn ranges. This, while a remote and weak substitute for knowledge gained by actually traversing the ground, is favorable to a practicable railway route north of the Gorges, by following valleys between the folds. The view is not in accord with existing maps of the ranges in the region in question.

At one time, we had planned to stop a day on the Hwai Yang Mountains to study their availability as a site for a summer school as an alternative to Mt. Kuling, near Kiukiang on the Yangtze, the present favorite summer resort for central China, but information gathered at Hankow seemed to give Mt. Kuling so much superiority in accessibility, in height, and in established reputation, as to make it unimportant to seek and an alternative at present. These mountains seemed to have some possibilities in this direction that may deserve consideration when Mt. Kuling becomes over-crowded, as is quite possible in the future.

Oriental Educational Investigation Synopsis of the Observations of the Messrs. Chamberlin in the Province of Honan

May 11th to 15th, 1909

The province of Honan straddles the Great Yellow River, the Hwang Ho, where it debouches from the mountains upon the great plain of northern China. The valley of the Hwang Ho is held to have been the gateway of the most important immigrations form the west into the fertile plains of eastern China, including that of the original Chinese themselves. It is the natural highway of commerce between east China and the vast western tracts of the Empire. It seemed therefore to be a strategic tract and we gave it much preliminary study. It was a matter of great regret that we could not so shape our plans as to penetrate as far as Hsingan os Sinnan Fu, the capital of Shensi, a place of historic interest. We were unable, however to learn that the region now presents anything in the educational line of special strategic importance. We traversed the province from south to north by day stages, made an effort to Honan Fu, the ancient capital of the province and in the line of ancient migration, and stopped a day at Wei Hwei, on the plain north of the Hwang Ho, abreast the notable curve in the Tai Hang mountains whose foothills we visited. The present capital, Kai Fong, lies on the Hwang Ho plain, at a level lower than the river itself, and has heretofore suffered destruction by inundation, a fact which excludes it from serious consideration as an educational center and it was not therefore visited.

1. From the Hwai Yang Mountains to the Hwang Ho

The Hankow-Peking Railway, after crossing the Hwai Yang Mountains north of Hankow, keeps near the junction of the great plain and the western mountain tract, running most of the time on the plain, but occasionally cutting across lines of isolated hills which represent the dying out mountain ranges from the west, and thereby gives glimpses of both upland and plain.

The north side of the Hwai Yang Mountains in somewhat more clothed with bushes and occasional trees than the south side and so are the hills north of the range, but the clothing is still very scant and erosion has done much destructive work. The population seems appreciably less dense than south of the mountains, and in some parts not markedly more so than would many parts of the plains of America if land cultivation were reduced to hand methods and apportioned to farmers on that basis. The region of rice culture is essentially passed and the curvilinear paddies are replaced by rectilinear fields laid out by compass. The open stretches between villages become wider, ranging up to two or three miles, and the village are more completely buried in groves of larger trees of aspects more familiar to a northerner. For some distance north of the mountains old plains of mantle rock-residuary soils and accumulated wash-prevail more largely than smooth flat plains but farther north the latter predominate. On these, between the scattered village-graves, almost uninterrupted fields of wheat in fair-sized rectangles, interspersed with peas and a few other crops, prevail. Roads with two-wheel tracks, an almost forgotten land mark, appear and awaken a comfortable home feeling, and cattle gradually become more common. Two-wheeled carts soon become common, with a horse or mule in the shafts and one, two or three attached abreast well in front by long ropes, a novel combination. The typical Chinese here are appreciably larger than those of the Yangtze valley and of South China, have more masculine, stronger features, and move more briskly as a rule, though the Chinese are nowhere sluggish as a people.

Incidentally it may be stated here that a son of the Prince Regent was on the train and that at numerous points from Hankow to the Hwang Ho, the local troops were drawn up at the stations and saluted the royal traveler. The troops seemed to be well armed and well drilled. Dressed in neat Kaki uniforms of European type, they put up a very creditable appearance. The companies were never large, but the number of points at which they presented themselves was notable.

Apparently the country here has suffered from lack of rainfall and the crops are inferior, in some tracts not more than half a crop. There is some irrigation, but it is not general. The streams coming from the hills and mountains to the west carry some water even in this driest time of the year. They could not doubt easily be dammed in the hills and the smoothness and eastward slope of the plains would make distribution easy and effective. In this latitude it is probable that two crops, both better than the present one, could be raised if there were an adequate water supply always at command to force the crop. It seems to be a region that invites a higher order of agriculture.

There were signs of progressive lessening of the annual rainfall as we went north. Adobe houses with tiled or other roofs, adobe walls about the compounds and adobe walls of defense for the cities became common, which seemed to be scarcely compatible with prevalent humidity. As we neared the Hwang Ho, dunes began to appear, not clean quartz-sand dunes, but dunes of loess-like silt with loess deposits on the adjacent territory. With the appearance of the dunes came orchards in abundance, pear orchards in the main, but others also, a feature rather rarely observed before. Some of these were on the duns and other trees had been set to hold the drifting silt. These features continued to the immediately vicinity of the Hwang Ho. It was clear that we had entered on the south margin of the great tract of wind deposits that characterize north China and still more the great arid tracts of Mongolia, Tibet, and Turkestan.

2 The Immediate Hwang Ho Valley

A railway now runs from Kai Feng, lying well out on the great plain, parallel to the Hwang Ho and some miles south of it to Honan Fu, the old capital, on a tributary of the Hwang Ho, but in the main valley which beyond Honan Fu narrows to a confined pass between two high ranges of mountains.

Soon after leaving the junction with the Hankow-Peking railway, the Honan Fu line begins to cross that tell-tale phenomenon of a semi-arid region of deep soils, sunken roads, caused by the blowing away of the dust stirred up by wheels and feet. The depth of these rapidly increased and soon gave place to the vertically faced terraces, walls, cliffs, monuments of a typical loess region. This extended most of the remaining way to Honan Fu. The erosion features reach above 100 feet in vertical relief and the dissection has reached a marked development. While the accumulation of this loess is clearly due in large part to wind action, it was equally clear that local wash from higher lands had also played its part.

The loess tract, even in its highly dissected portions, is cultivated and villages and even walled towns nestle in its unique valleys.

Great as was the interest attaching to this strong expression of the loess formation in this valley between the mountains and far from the well-known arid lands beyond the mountains, its appearance in such strength here was not wholly welcome, for it set a serious barrier to the diversion of the waters of the Hwang Ho on its south side well up in the pass between the mountain ranges, and the carrying of these along the south side as such a height that when the valley widened out on the great plain they could be carried out upon it to the southward and supplement the scant supply of water on the great southeastern wing of this plain, the western border of which we had been traversing. Apparently the practicability of carrying out an analogous scheme on the north side of the Hwang Ho is greater, but on this we have very little personal information. The Lo Ho valley, in which Honan Fu is located, is open, pleasant and fertile with wide plane bottom, well suited to culture and irrigation. Hand pumps, power pumps usually operated by a mule and the diversion of natural flow, are all used, but reservoir storage and wind power seem to be absent. Stieler's map of the tract adjacent to the Hwang Ho on the south from the Peking-Hankow Railway westward to Honan Fu and beyond so far as we could see, exaggerates the mountainous aspect. Real mountains are merely in sight on the south and these interruptedly. Farther west, near the elbow of the Hwang Ho, stout ranges approach the river on both the north and south and really from a gateway from the vast arid west to the great eastern plain.

3 The Plain North of the Hwang Ho

The Hwang Ho is an ugly, muddy river, broad and full of bars, an exaggerated Missouri River. Loess cliffs reaching up to 100+feet lie on the south bank just above the railway crossing, but below this and on the north side, both above and below the crossing, the banks are low. The rivers overflows on the north for some distance and the rise of the plains in that direction is scarcely perceptible. Our aneroid indicated a rise of 20 feet and then a decline to points below the Hwang Ho level, but as a dust storm had set in these readings cannot be trusted.

At Hsing Hsiang an east-west railway crosses the Peking-Hankow line and runs short distances only in both directions. Its immediate purpose is said to be to develop the coal and iron resources of the mountains on the west. It may be an important factor in the future development of the region, for the future of this region seems yet to be quite indeterminate.

We spent one day at Wei Hwei as one of the more promising points of this region educationally and otherwise, but were disappointed in finding an unattractive city without special educational or other promise. Perhaps this should be discounted a little as we saw it in a dust storm for which we may not have made due correction. The country about is good and the villages, in which adobe plays a large constructive part, are interesting. We also stopped for the night at Chang Tu, near the north edge of the province, which is a more attractive place than Wei Hwei.

The border of the great plain traversed throughout its whole north-south range by us is, on the whole, quite attractive and its problems awakened much interest. They are not different from those of the whole great plain, in the main, and are worthy of serious consideration as this plain is one of the greatest and most populous of the globe, yielding perhaps only to the Ganges plain, if indeed to that. There seem to us to be two factors of the problem that lead the others industrially and underlie the supreme problem of intellectual and moral development. These are: (1) an enhancement of the productiveness and reliability of the agriculture, and (2) the development of collateral industries from the coal, iron and other mineral resources of the adjacent mountains. The iron ores have not yet been exploited sufficiently to determine their extent or value, but the coal appears to be exceptionally abundant and in very thick beds in easily workable situations. The juxtaposition of coal-bearing mountains and fertile plains is exceptionally close. The soils of the plain are not only naturally fertile, in the main, but are subject to enrichment by wind-borne dust from the arid tracts which contain an element of undecomposed minerals bearing potash and lime, and by stream distribution, if these are controlled, or, on the other hand, are subject to wastage by both wind and wash. Permanent fertility may be maintained or lost by the control or lack of control of the exceptional natural agencies of the region. Provisions for the lodgment of dust and the prevention of wind erosion are gained chiefly in vegetation, proper crops and protective hedges and trees. The control of the wash calls for a well-organized system of saving and distributing the rainfall of the region and the inflows from the great condensers, the mountains. The Chinese have gone further than most peoples in doing this and their surfaces have been better prepared for a completed system of water handling than probably those of any other great people. But there are obvious short-comings which might apparently be greatly reduced. They divert stream and distribute them over the plain tracts near the streams to considerable extents and to the most obvious benefit. It seemed altogether safe to estimate the crop-prospect of the irrigated fields as at least twice that of the non-irrigated fields adjoining, with contingencies yet to be met. They also pump water from beneath the soil and spread it upon the surface. Perhaps this was in wider use than stream diversion. But the two combined do not irrigate half the area and swells of 20 or 30 feet height were very unproductive, sometimes almost barren. Pumping these is laborious and stream diversion is only applicable through an extensive system of irrigation. Our suggestion are of two classes: (1) local and individual, and (2) general and co-operative, perhaps governmental.

(1) In a region notable for its winds, it seemed to us strange that wind-mills were nowhere seen. Pumps operated by mules and almost as ingenious as a wind mill were common. Why then do they not add wind mills, and now that transportation can supply cheap coal, steam power?

(2) There are abundant opportunities for damming the streams in the mountains and storing the rainfall for use as needed. There are two incidental advantages in this. The water is needed in the mountain valleys for manufacturing purposes. Protection from floods is needed on the plains. A percentage of the great famines of the plains is due to devastating floods. An extensive system of canals and controlling works is needed to carry this plan into effect and there is where the Chinese are weakest—large enterprises under honest and efficient control—and this weakness has its head center in the government.

The educational suggestion which grew out of this was the establishment of missionary farm villages or country hamlets in which the whole of an improved type of country life should be exemplified. Country village life is the leading form of Chinese life and the villages of this great plain are an unnumbered multitude. It is held that the missionary physician is quite as effective as the evangelical missionary. Might not the missionary farmer be the equal of either and might not home life and home education of the simpler types—all the better suited to propagation because simple—go with this and round out its value in a most vital way? We have some thought to details, but they are yet crude and this is not the place to state them, if they were worth it at all. Those more competent in these lines should take up the matter if the suggestion has real value.

Oriental Educational investigation
Synopsis of the Observations of the Messrs.
Chamberlin in the Province of Shanxi

May 16th to 18th, 1909

Our observations in Shansi were limited to three days occupied in a railway trip from the Peking-Hankow line to Tai Yuan Fu, the capital of the province at which one day was spent. Scanty as this time was, it is fairly proportionate to the nature of the educational problem presented by Shansi, for that is simple, viewed from the physical point of view. The province occupies a mountainous plateau of moderate elevation, so much dissected that it has come to consist of an irregular assemblage of mountains and valleys. The reliefs are mostly below 4000 feet, largely below 3000 feet. The tract is rich in coal and perhaps in iron, but this has not yet been exploited sufficiently to warrant a positive statement as to its extent and value. These furnish the foundation for prospective industries of a large order. At present they are local and limited.

The province lies on the border of the great arid tract of central Asia and participates in its conditions. It may be said to be on the fighting line between inhospitable conditions and those that give reasonably reliable returns to soil management. Its climate is dry for eight or nine months of the year, but considerable rain falls in July and August and the country is said to be attractive at that time. Cereal and other suitable vegetation then grows vigorously. For the rest of the year little rain falls and the country is bare, sear and dusty. Shortage in the July-August rain brings much disaster to the crops in spite of irrigation which, in the forms previously described in Honan, is widely practiced. As there, much relief is no doubt possible by a storage system and by increased pumping from wells. The scantiness of the water-supply also conditions such manufacturing as requires much water. It has even been feared that it might seriously restrict the reduction of iron within the region when coal and ore are close together, because of the water required to keep the furnace tuyeres cool, but this seems to us unnecessarily pessimistic, for the mountain valleys and canyons are admirably suited to effective damming.

These conditions sharply define the great problem of the people and the special forms of education they need to meet the special issues of their circumstances. It centers in the battle with aridity and takes the two forms of localized agriculture and manufacturing. The mountains and its situation on the borders of the arid tract debar the province from becoming a therefore of commerce. If it develops strongly, it may ship out large quantities of coal and iron and their products, and ship in the supplies of fabrics and food stuffs requisite to supplement its own agricultural products, but this will be about the limit of its commerce. Engineering and agriculture are therefore the special lines of education which should supplement the standard lines required by all peoples.

So far as aridity is concerned, we saw the province at about its worst, and it cannot be said to have been inviting. The main rivers were low and the small streams generally dry, and the general aspect was arid. Irrigated fields gave grateful relief. Non-irrigated fields were uninviting. The trees, so far as there were any, were generally green and healthy, implying that they had made good their means of resistance.

This may be made a text for indicating the chief lines which we think research should take in this and analogous situations, viz: the search for and the selective development of plants that have notable powers of adaptation and resistance to aridity and which yet give reasonable returns in some form. The arid region of Asia does not seem to have done as much as some other regions in the line of natural selection and development to meet its own conditions. There is probably a geological reason for this, but that is immaterial here. The process of evolution can probably be helped on by intelligent aid. Besides this, the result of natural adaption in other arid regions may be imported and tried with a reasonable presumption that some of them would prove to have value, not impossibly a value they do not possess in their native lands. We believes this to be one of the great line of effort of the future—in which mutual exchange and co-operate effort between workers in all arid lands shall be a vital feature. An experimental station in Shansi might be a source of benefit to other lands more or less irrespective of its value at home.

Mr. Chamberlin, Senior, gave the day at Tai Yuan Fu to the Western Department of the Imperial University of Shansi, and Mr. Chamberlin Junior, to the fields, erosion phenomena, and loess deposits of the vicinity and to the city itself, his best notes being his photographs which, as has been his habit from the first, were developed as soon as practicable, to secure them from deterioration and accident and to guide in later manipulations.

The Western Department of the Shansi University arose from the refusal of the missions to accept monetary compensation for the 157 lives lost in the Boxer trouble in 1900 and from the substitution therefore, on the recommendation of Dr. Richard, of a tax of taels 50,000 per year for ten years to establish a college for instruction in Western learning. The administration was placed in the hands of Dr. Richard for ten years, after which its control will be in the hands of the Provincial Government. Subsequently a university with a Chinese College and a Western College was established, the former in the hands of a Chinese Director and the latter in those of Dr. Richard. The two have grounds and buildings adjoining, but are conducted separately. It was planned at first that the Chinese College should follow Chinese lines of education, but it has gradually undertaken most of the Western subjects of the Western College. In the judgement of the western faculty this work is poorly done. The western Department has a serviceable plant of fair buildings, pleasant grounds, and practical apparatus. Its chemical laboratory and some other features are the best we have seen in China. On the whole, the work in scientific lines seems to be the most advanced and probably the best in China. The courses and the attendance are as follows:

Civil Engineering	13 students
Mining Engineering,	23 students
Chemical Engineering,	15 students
Law,	28 students
Total Advanced,	79
Preliminary Course,	120
Total,	199

Under the old Chinese regime the students were selected from Provincial graduates of the first and second degrees. Since the suspension of the old system the students are received from Chinese High Schools, subject to passing their equisite entrance examination. They then spend three years in the Preliminary Course, after which they are admitted to the four professional courses named above. All students take English as a subject but the instructional work in other subjects is in Chinese.

The staff consists of six foreign professors at the head of the leading sections, and ten Chinese assistant professors. The professors seemed to be good men. Principal Soothill appeared to be well qualified for his position.

The ten-year period has yet two years to run. Whether the present staff and the general line of the effort and of standards will be retained is a vital question which is already receiving quiet and solicitous attention. The time has been too short to raise up competent Chinese graduates to take up the work and if the management goes into the hands of Chinese officials a serious decline in efficiency is likely to follow.

It was our good fortune to fall in with Mr. A. W. Staub, who is connected with the Oberlin movement in Shansi, and to get from his both personal and documentary information regarding this, which is, we think, the only other important western effort in this province. The Oberlin movement is also a memorial. Prvious to the Boxer outbreak of 1900, Oberlin men had made some progress in Missionary work at Tai Ku and Fen Cho Fu, important towns in the central valley south of Tai Yuan Fu. Fourteen of the Mission people, all then on the ground, lost their lives at the hands of the Boxers. This has stimulated the formation of the Shansi Memorial Association, among whose purposes the educational element has a large place. The present effort is to build up a central school at Tai Ku and maintain day schools in several neighboring towns. The central school now has 43 pupils of Academy and Grammar grades, with 6 teachers, and the other schools have together 123 pupils and 10 teachers. The development of a college either at Tai Ku or at Fen Cho Fu is contemplated.

Oriental Educational Investigation Synopsis of the Observations of the Messrs. Chamberlin in the Province of Chili

May 15th to June 5th, 1909

Our observations on the plains of the province of Chili are of the same tenor as those made on Honan lying next south and need not to be repeated. The climate of Chili is somewhat colder and more arid, and the region is more subject to dust storms from Mongolia and related phenomena. These intensify, in an appreciable degree, the importance of a more complete control of the water supplies of this region. For Chili and Shantung we have recent German charts which map the villages and illustrate roughly their importance relative to the cities. This is also indicated by statistics given in Richard's comprehensive Geography of the Chinese Empire (1908) in which the population of Chili is given as 20,930,000, while that of the six chief cities sums only 1,605,000. The population of Shantung is given as 38,247,900, while these are not complete date and probably are lacking in accuracy, they appear to represent the radical fact that the Chinese people is overwhelmingly rural. This impresses upon our minds more than ever the importance of considering special means by which the village life of the Chinese may be reached. The rural population on this great northeastern plain, and in most of China, is mostly gathered into villages, and this furnishes a more definite integer to work with than we have in rural America. Further reflection leads as to think that if it is practicable to teach better farming and household management by example in these villages, it may prove a line of approach to these very practical Chinese, more effective than those yet attempted. No doubt we ought to acknowledge that the seed of this idea of missionary villages comes from the monumental work of the General Education Board in the Southern States, though it seemed to come spontaneously from the village and the village graves scattered over the open fields of Honan. An attempt in this line ought not to be made, however, without duly considering whether American science can successfully compete with Chinese frugality.

We spent five days in a trip to Kalgan to see something of the mountainous border of Chili on the northwest and its relations to the Mongolian Plateau and the Mongols, who form a subordinate factor in the educational problem of North China.

As in Shansi we have here a phase of the arid problem. In the minds of some the desert is steadily advancing, partly by reason of the tendency of sand to migrate and partly because of the notion that the world is drying up. Nothing but a protracted series of very careful observations or a very circumspect interpretation of historic records, buried ruins and similar data, can throw much light on the secular problem, but the immediate problem is more tractable. We were blessed with a sharp touch of the problem in the concrete. Throughout the afternoon of the second day we faced a dust-storm of moderate vigor and throughout most of the fourth day we had a storm of the higher order of vigor at our backs. Taken with the dust-storm at Wei Hwei we have had, as we are advised, rather more than our average portion of this unpleasant evidence of the nearness of North China to the Great Desert of Central Asia. We had some hint, however, that it is possible to overestimate the significance of dust-storms on the borders of the plains and in the bordering mountains. When on the edge of the Mongolian Plateau, we noted that the wind, though strong, was not greatly dust-laden, while that in basins of North Chili, upon which we could look down, was dense with the fine yellow earth of the loess-formation. The Mongolian plain had apparently been swept already and was clothed with grass whose turf held its soil, while the dust lodged in the lower basin exposed by cultivation and pulverized by carts and hoofs in the roadways, furnished material which only needed a strong wind to give a very demonstrative phenomenon. It is, in some measure, a marginal phenomenon. It would be an error to suppose that it increases in intensity all the way back to the heart of the desert. It is this mobile element of the marginal tract that gives rise to the immediate problem of control. The control of the waters and the use of permanent plants on the ground not controlled with water are the two leading lines suggested in previous notes. Forestation is one phase of this, but not so near a sovereign remedy as its strenuous advocacy might seem to imply, for the dust storms of this region do not gather their material chiefly from the tree-less hills, but from the roads and cultivated fields. Stone treatment of the great roadways would remove the worst features and for this there is abundant material in the basins bordered by mountains where the storms are worst. The Kalgan road in the basins that lie between the Mongolian plateau and the Chili plain cuts to depths of 10 to 20 feet for an average breadth of 6 or 8 rods, throughout much of its course. It is the source of much the largest part of the dust of the more common storms. The roads of the plains and the streets of the cities are the other chief feeding grounds.

This point has been dwelt upon at some length because the dustiness of North China is one of its most unpropitious climate features.

We found all the broader valleys of northern Chili which we crossed notably filled with lodgment material. The basins surrounded by mountains were very markedly so. This has usually been assigned to ancient lakes and to depression of the region. It seemed to us, however, to be a normal development in the systematic history of basins eroded in plateaus or mountains. The reasons for this opinion would be inappropriate and tedious here, but it has this bearing on the current reasoning that because these basins were formerly occupied by lakes and have dried up and become dust breeders, the country is seriously drying up, the encroachment of the desert is inevitable and the future gloomy. We have thus far seen no large basis in China that seemed to us to bear any evidence of having once been a great lake and since dried up. The large lakes adjacent to the Yangtze are probably made by the ponding of tributaries by the building up the Yangtze bottoms, rather than the remnants of great lakes approaching disappearance. We do not question the former existence of lakes in the warped basins of the great plateaus, nor the drying up of some basins, and our opinion is still unformed relative to the secular progress of aridity. We merely make not of our conviction that a certain class of evidence that has played some large part in current pessimistic opinion is untrustworthy.

All our studies point insistently to the conclusion, that China needs preeminently investigation in a multitude of lines, that this must be searching, patient and restrained by scientific caution and that if education can give her this and with it the spirit and moral effects of genuine inquiry it will be a boon of inestimable value.

Oriental Educational Investigation
Synopsis of the Observations of
the Messrs. Chamberlin on the Borderland
of the Gulf of Chili Between Peking
and Mukden

June 5th and 6th, 1909

Two subjects were uppermost in our observations between Peking and Mukden: (1) the best available location for summer work in North China, and (2) the practicability of occupying such a location all the year around, this last embracing as one of its factors a location suitable for a portion of the more advanced scholarly work thought to be essential in developing and organizing fundamental matter and in inspiring and giving direction to the whole movement, for which the best working conditions are desirable.

(1) One of the thoughts that has grown upon us during the last weeks of our inquiry is the importance of educational work upon the teaching forces during their summer vacation. One of the gravest defects of work in the new lines in China for the next two or three decades will necessarily be the weakness of the teaching and directing force. Most of the missionaries went to China with other than educational work in mind, at least primarily and they are not specifically prepared for teaching. More than this, in so far as they may seem to be prepared, it is not often in the lines which the now situation demands and they are likely to need instruction and inspiration in these lines quite as much as if they had no preparation at all. There is need also for the education, incidentally, of the non-teaching portion of the foreign population as well as of those specifically engaged in teaching, for the sympathy and co-operation of the evangelical workers, the missionary physicians, the wives, the business men, and others is highly important. Nearly all these people find it necessary to their health to spend two or three months, more or less, at some resort where climatic conditions permit recuperation, while they avoid the excesses of heat and moisture and the dangers of disease at their various stations. Such resort is almost imperative in Central and South China, and is only somewhat less urgent in Middle and north China, for the summers are very hot in the inland portions. This necessity has already led to the establishment of resorts at which assemblages of various kinds are commonly held, and even summer schools of a limited sort started. The chief of these resorts are Mt. Kuling, near Kiu Kiang, on the Yangtze, as previously noticed, convenient for those stationed in Central China, and Peitaiho on Rocky Point on the west side of Chili Gulf, the chief resort of those stationed in North China. As early as the first of June this year, missionary people were already going to Peitaiho from the vicinity of Peking and special transportation to Peitaiho on Friday evening and back from there on Sunday evenings was already provided. These provisions and what they imply in a measure answer the question of the most available point for summer work in North China, for this is the verdict of local opinion expressed in the concrete form of action. There can be little doubt that for immediate summer-school work and similar lines of effort of established types, Peitaiho is the most available point. It is located on a broad irregular ridge or range of hills that projects some at into the gulf and catches the full force of the sea breezes. Ample ground rising from the beach on tenable slopes is said to be available. We regret that it was

impracticable to find a day between imperative engagements to stop at this point and make personal examination of the details of the situation.

But however much Peitaiho may seem to be a predetermined locality for a certain class of work at the outset, at least, if attempted at all, there are two other phases of the problem that seem to us to require attention.

The weakest point in Chinese education today is the unpreparedness of the native teachers employed in the government schools to give the new education. Obviously they cannot impart that which they themselves do not understand. The transformation or production de novo of an adequate body of teachers for so vast a population is something stupendous. The question therefore arises whether a summer school for the Chinese teachers of the government schools is a practicable mode of doing something toward this. If so, it might (or it might not) require a location apart from that of the school for missionary and other foreign teachers and yet it would need much the same physical condition and accessibility. This made it seem worthwhile to study the availabilities of the whole western border of the Gulf.

There is still a third element. If the whole educational system of China is to be transformed on the best lines which we can now frame, a large amount of intellectual work of the highest order must be done; for the subject-matter must in some large part be evolved and organized on Chinese lines; direction and inspiration must be given to even the best present workers, native and foreign alike; suitable language for the new matter must be devised; the crass errors of previous and present efforts must be mitigated and in time displaced, and so on. This work of the first order seems to us crucial, if the best returns in proportion to the expenditures are to be secured. The place and the conditions for this work, if attempted at all, are important elements.

We incline, at present, to the opinion that this work may have to be more or less distributed in location, because it is likely to be connected in various ways with other work and it may itself require various conditions, but some special concentrations of some of it might to advisable at the outset. In central and south China there are climatic difficulties that, with some constitutions, seriously impair efficiency. In north China, taking Peking as a type, the heat of summer and the high winds and dust storms of the long dry season compromise what would otherwise be an excellent climate. The problem in this northern region, therefore, is to find a location protected against the strong winds and dust storms of the dry winter and spring and at the same time tempered by the see-breezes of summer. Peitaiho, immediately on the Gulf shore, is cool and bracing in summer, but bleak in winter. Experience near Lake Michigan, however, suggests that this bleakness may be much mitigated at points only a few miles back from the shore, without entirely losing the summer effects of the gulf.

Reference to Stieler's or other maps which represent the physical features, shows that between the Gulf and the plateau of Mongolia there is an exceptionally broad belt of mountains. On our Kalgan trip we found that the Plateau itself was not especially a breeder of dust in this latitude. It appeared therefore possible that in the lee of this broad mountain tract and a little back from the immediate shore of the Gulf conditions of measurable freedom from severe dusty interior winds, on the one hand, and from excessively bleak winter winds from the icy Gulf, on the other, might be found, while participating somewhat in the coolness of mountains and Gulf in summer---somewhat of a medius in res.

It may seem that too much stress is being laid on the element of dust, a confessed annoyance in what is regarded, on the whole, as a very fair climate; but if a pronounced scientific trend is to be given Chinese education—and we deem this the key to the situation—it must be led and inspired by some measure of work of the highest order in the several fundamental lines. It would be difficult, if not impossible, to conduct some of the more delicate researches in chemistry and physics, and perhaps in bacteriology, micro-biology and other lines, in an atmosphere raining down dust at frequent intervals during nine months of the year, to an extent that makes the dust-accumulation a recognizable geologic factor in the surface formation of the region. We found the dust of North China the most trying of all obstacles to our work experienced in China, though otherwise the climatic conditions were grateful. While our experience may have been, in some measure, exceptional, we think the dust element is not to be ignored.

From Peking to Tientsin and from Tientsin to a point beyond Yungping, on the Twan River, dust lodgments were observable on the surface and left no doubt as to the prevailing atmospheric conditions. After passing the nose of the mountains, where they come down within a few miles of the Gulf, the evidences of prevailing dust accumulations disappeared and from this point northeasterly to Kinchow, apposite the head of the Gulf, dust drift was essentially unobserved. Some dunes on the immediate Gulf shore are mapped, but these are local features. Several localities in this long, narrow tract between the mountains and the sea seemed to be eligible for the purpose indicated above. Fortunately we have very detailed maps of this tract up to the border of Manchuria, on the basis of which details can be discussed and further studied. It is obvious that other considerations enter into the problem, but our purpose here is only to report the direction of our observations.

Supplement:

The Gulf Border and Mukden

1 I studied the Gulf Border with two thought in mind, (a) a possible summer school for

teachers and (b) a research school

In addition to the thought outlined on my report on summer work which I hand you herewith I have had in mind the possible continuance of some part of the research work thought the winter at the same location. Some of the men employed to direct the research of the summer research school might continue research through the year, at the summer location and thus use the property, etc. This may not be practicable for two reasons, (1) the summer location may not be suitable for winter occupancy. (2) It may not be practicable to employ men for the summer instruction alone and leave them free for research all the rest of the year, and (3) it this were practicable, their fields might lie mainly elsewhere. Still, I have kept the matter in mind so far as to see if I could find a location suitable for summer and winter work alike. The heat of south and central China are stubborn features in those latitudes and the dust of the north is more serious in some lines than might at first be supposed. Refined instrumental and chemical work would be much embarrassed by the severe dust storms. Close fittings would be liable to be clogged, smooth surface scratched and chemical solutions contaminated or the balance vitiated by the dust. I have speculated whether the Gulf Border in the lee of a wide range of mountains might not be relatively free of dust and be sufficiently cooled in summer to furnish better conditions that Peking and the great plain. A location on the immediate shore of the Gulf is likely to be bleak in winter, but a few miles back this might not be the case and yet the sea breezes be sufficient to mitigate the summer heat. I think these qualities are possessed by some of the location between the Gulf and the mountains, but a single trip is insufficient for determining this. I looked for evidence of wind drift in the lodgment deposits and these seemed to be essentially absent from some stretches. I will talk about this in detail when we meet in Chicago. I merely want to report progress here and open the matter for further conference.

2 Mukden

On yesterday afternoon we entered upon the great plain of Southern Manchuria, the wind rose almost to a gale and whenever we crossed one of the larger streams that had sandy bottoms exposed by the low stage of water, much dust was raised and dunes were evidence of similar action at other times. Away from these river tracts, the air was much cleaner. The streets of Mukden were comparable to dry river channels, and I went to bed with my heart lying hard on my diaphragm for you know I have had dreams of Mukden. Today things have looked much better, and this is, I think, more nearly two normal condition. There are local dusts of an annoying kind where dusty streets and dusty roads are left without mitigating care as is inevitable in every city of moderate humidity and active air circulation as we know in Chicago, but I am told they never have true dust storms here as they do in Peking and the loess country generally, and our visit to the country today measurably supports this, for this is not a loess country. You will no doubt have noted the grassing of the "right of way", the tree rows, etc. much as in our own country. This spontaneous grassing began on the Gulf Border and increased northwardly. We rode out to the tombs north of the city today and seemed to be in a new country very like our own. The turfed surface which we have not seen before since we left the Mississippi Valley was peculiarly grateful. I think the climatic conditions here are much better than those south of here for a vigorous constitution adapted to the higher latitudes.

As to the people, I have been much struck by the individualization of their countenances. Large features are common and generally large faces, but sometimes large crania and small faces. At any rate, everyone seems to have a face of his own. How much this may mean in character and talen, I do not know, but I like it, as distinguished from a standard type which all seem to copy. I think you will be struck by the larger sizes of the majority. Am sure also that you will be pleased to see so many of the women moving about with an easy step and showing a good physique. I do not know that I have seen a handsome women yet, but they look more healthy and capable than the mincing cripples of the south. The foolish habit of painting which seems even more prevalent here than in the south stands over against their normal feet and graceful bearing.

We have had a very pleasant interviews with Consul Cloud and Vice-Governor Liang. The latter speak English very well indeed and seems to take a very intelligent view of things.

I am quite of the opinion that his is an important field and it is practically open so far as foreign educational work is concerned.

At present I incline to a plan that shall start on the school of education idea as the nucleus and grow thence into a university as fast as practicable. By this I mean, establish schools of all grades as models or as experimental schools and through those train up schools for the university these schools taking the place of preparatory schools as such. Through these schools and teachers' classes, train up teacher for the grades below college and thus extend the preparatory work to other schools and thus at length develop the colleges and the university. In this way it would perhaps be possible to build up the colleges and university sooner than by the usual preparatory system and at the same time develop the school system on broader lines than is usually done on the preparatory system with the college and university more narrowly in mind.

I give my present impressions thus freely with the presumption that they may be modified on several points with profit.

Oriental Educational Investigation Synopsis of the Observations of the Messrs. Chamberlin on Manchuria

June 6th-10th, 1909

Manchuria, taken as a whole, stands in strong contrast in certain respects, to all the regions previously visited by us. These latter are pronouncedly old countries, densely inhabited and bearing everywhere the impress of a remarkable people. Compared with these, Manchuria bears the aspect of a new country waiting to receive the impress of such a people as may be destined to subdue it. The few large cities are obviously not new, and there are said to be old ruins concealed in the forests, implying perhaps a larger former population, but under the scant population of recent centuries nature has largely resumed control and the country has renewed its youth. In southern Manchuria we could easily imagine ourselves on the plains of Minnesota and Dakota and, farther north, on those of Manitoba and Saskatchewan. The plains are broader, more level, and more unbroken by ranges of hills, than might be gathered from current descriptions and from the physiographic maps. The reliefs in the bordering hill-country are more moderate, more openly disposed and more tractable. Even the "Great Kingan" mountain range on the west of the plains is a softly rounded, tree-clothed belt running along the brow of the broad swell of land by which the Manchurian plains rise into the Mongolian plateau. Even the plateau between the Kingan range and the Siberian border, at least along the line we traversed, is rather an upland pasture than a rocky waste or a sandy desert. Near some of the rivers there were, indeed, considerable tracts of dunes blown up from the river sands and shifted back from the bluffs for some distance upon the uplands by progressive driftings, but these seemed to be minor rather than major features of even this portion. No doubt selection entered into the location of the railway line to which our observations were confined, but across the plateau the river valleys seem to have been the chief factors in this, and the rivers seemed to be the chief breeders of dunes.

From various signs, rather than positive date, one gathers that along the western border of the main Manchurian plain, at the foot of the rise to the Kingan range and the Mongolia plateau, there is a less well-watered tract, and if the normal west-easterly movement of the atmosphere which prevails with us in these latitudes, also prevails here—and we were led to suspect this from all we saw in Manchuria and Siberia and from the meteorological predictions and weather maps we saw at Shanghai—it would be but natural that a relatively dry belt should lie at the east foot of the Kingan range and a correspondingly humid belt on the east side of the main Manchurian plain where it rises into the ranges that have their culmination in the White or Snow mountains of East Manchuria. At any rate, the eastern hilly or mountainous tract is described as clothed with heavy timber. This is practically the only notable timber resource left in the Chinese Empire, except that of the high mountains of West China and a few special localities.

The soils of the Manchuria plain are generally a dark prairie loam of light arable type. Where uncultivated they spontaneously take on turf. This again puts Manchuria in contrast with North China, where turf is practically absent and where it is even difficult to induce it to form on lawns by cultivation. The transition between the turfing and non-turfing tracts takes place on the narrow Gulf border tract described in the last installment of our report and is one of the grateful signs of progress from one set of climatic conditions to another. At the time of our visit, the channels of the eastern Manchuria streams were full of water, in contrast with the scant threads of water on the broad sand and gravel bottoms of the rivers of North China. This implies a sufficiency of spring rains, at least this year. There was a soaking rain the second morning of our stop in Mukden, June 8th. There had been no considerable rain in the Peking region up to the date of our leaving, June 5th.

Testimony as to the fertility of the Manchurian plains is wholly favorable and often takes on an extravagant tone. Especially emphasis is laid on the great crops of the larger "millet", a variety of the sorghum family, raised for the grain, not the sap; but the season was too early for us to see more than a favorable start of the crops. The country seemed adapted to about the same range of crops as Minnesota and Manitoba, and to the same modes of culture, of harvesting and of subsequent handling and use. While the land seems to be cultivated in small rectangles, which are usually narrow and long, there are no physical barriers to the wholesale methods of our own northwest. There are no fences or dikes and the house groups are wide apart, leaving broad open fields. In introducing the larger methods, probably conjoint action might have to take the place of the single large proprietor, to a considerable extent, for a time at least, but the manifest advantage of these methods should be sufficient inducement to such combined action and ultimately replace it by larger proprietorships. There is much uncultivated land.

Manchuria seemed to us a fine filed for commercial missionary work on the part of the manufactures of agricultural appliance of various kinds. The relatively little that has been done in this line, we are told, had not been well enough done to secure its best results. If a group of manufactures of farm and related machinery, so constituted as to cover the field of improved appliances, were to establish some of our suggested missionary farms on really sound, broad, philanthropic lines, and were to thus educate the Manchurians in a true altruistic way, we venture to think it might ultimately give good financial returns and demonstrates the utopian proposition that in a sufficiently large view altruism and selfishness are identical qualities.

At any rate, Manchuria seemed to us an inviting field of our own sort. We did not indeed hear a Macedonian cry in the human tongue, but it seemed to be trumpeted by the natural condition of things. The human element, however reserved in expression is, we think, on the whole, propitious.

At Mukden we had instructive interviews with Consul General Prout (and on the following day took tiffin with him and met several other guests who skirmished, in the way such an occasion permits, over interesting ground); and with Acting Senior Chancellor Liang Yu Ho (M. T. Liang), who was educated in America, and who received us very cordially and the next day returned our call in person; also with Mr. Robertson, at the head of the Scotch and Irish educational work, and incidentally with some others. Without going into details, we may sum up the impressions we gained as follows:

1 What the government is making a genuine endeavor to introduce the new education in the grades ranging from the Normal School downward, but not at present in the grades above.

2 That the effort is limited by the present state of things in Manchuria and that it has made much less progress than in Chili and many of the provinces farther south.

3 That the government under the viceroy who has just retired was very hospitable to the missionary education effort, and offered to furnish a site for the missionary college and urged those in charge to hasten their plans so as to realize this before he retired, but the slowness of action by the home board prevented this.

4 That though the attitude of the new viceroy is yet to develop, there is ground for believing that the government would go farther in encouraging, aiding, and co-operating with an American effort here just now than in China proper, for diplomatic and self-protective reasons.

5 That the Japanese might not really welcome such a movement but would not openly oppose it.

6 That the missionary effort has not gone far enough in educational lines to offer any serious embarrassments by preoccupancy of ground, etc.

7 That, on the whole, the situation is open and inviting. In some respects it seems to us especially promising.

In our interviews, we purposely avoided traversing the special ground we presumed Professor Burton would desire to inquire into on the next day or two, by specific educational questioning. We sought rather to gain impressions from the non-technical phases of commercial and political affairs, and from those physical elements of the situation whose bearings are significant, though not always obviously so. Professor Burton will no doubt be able to report more specifically and more trustworthily on some or all of these points, but as supplemental to them in an effective way. It seemed to us quite possible that here is the diplomatic point to initiate co-operation with the government.

The situation in Manchuria seems to call for the establishment of a complete educational system on the most advanced modern lines, ranging in grade form the bottom up and having for its central line of effort, at present, the production of teachers and workers in pure and applied science. The conditions will be of the pioneer order for a time, and the higher and broader work must naturally come later, so far as it is not imported, but we think these later results are likely to be stranger and freer from inherited bondages than those of the older regions. The Chinese here are relatively recent immigrants, many of them quite recent. Some are, indeed, but transients, and new immigrants are coming each year. Immigration is said to have the stronger encouragement of the government.

There are here also two aggressive foreign element, the Japanese and the Russian. There is here also a tripartite military influence, ---a Chinese, a Japanese, and a Russian. This has several bearings on the situation, in part diverting and disturbing, and in part stimulating and virile.

All these elements will be likely to render the first decades of educational work, if undertaken, uneven in results and formative and prophetic in character, rather than uniform, finished and mature, but strength should ultimately come of it.

The physiques of the Manchurian Chinese seemed to us to be in accord with this view of their educational adaptabilities. They are appreciably larger, on the average, than the Chinese of the southern sections. They are notably more individualized in form and features. Everyone seemed to have a face of his own, though usually a rather homely one from our point of view. On the whole, they seemed somewhat more stolid than the southern Chinese, but more independent and self-directed, a cruder but a stranger people.

Historically the Manchus have shown marked qualities for conquest and for permanent government of the conquered. This has come in recent time to take on a form not far removed from parasitism and this has adversely affected the original Manchurian race. The chief people at present are immigrant Chinese, of earlier or later date, and the products of Manchu-Chinese mixture. We entertain the view that these are growing into a new Manchurian race under the free and stimulating conditions of Manchuria, and that this new race will have many of the virile qualities of the former Manchus. Some significant expressions of this are to be seen. The policeman of Mukden stands rigidly in the middle of the street and waves teamster, rickshaw-man and others, high and low, foreigners and natives, to the lawful side of the street, and they unhesitatingly obey. The southern Chinese policeman is more likely to stand on the curb and look apologetic. The northern Chinese soldier looks as though he would shoot; the southern soldier looks as though he might perhaps, but it is not quite certain. How much of this difference of bearing is due to contact with Japanese and Russian examples, and how much to native strength, may be uncertain, but the result is declared, and we think significant of educational possibilities in other lines.

The contact, if not the conflict, of nationalities in Manchuria, is an element of the situation that will, we think, on the whole, tend to strength of educational development if peace prevails. If the country is to be torn by strife or by wars, the forecast is gloomy, but the need of education is perhaps not less indicated as a remedial agent.

In another communication we propose to summarize our observations on the belligerent phases of education in progress in the empire generally, though its climax is in Manchuria.

Ⅲ 附录

Thomas C. Chamberlin's letter to the President of the University of Chicago regarding Chinese Expedition, 1901

May 15, 1901

My Dear President:

 With little doubt, the greatest geological field not now under active cultivation is the Chinese Empire. It embraces the greatest plateaus on the face of the earth, and probably also the greatest canyons and the most magnificent exposures of the strata. Its exceptionally arid climate has no doubt given to it, in an intensified degree, all the advantages of vegetal and soil nudity possessed by our western plateau. Reconnaissance has shown that its geological series ranges from the earliest to the latest, and it must be especially rich in its record of events from the Paleozoic on, and is thus specially supplementary to our own field. There is certainly no province on the face of the earth where the great dynamic problems involved in the formation of mountains and plateaus have so intense and stupendous a development. Appreciating this, I have naturally turned again and again during the past few years to the question whether it would not be possible for the University to reach out and occupy this great field, so soon as our own development should reach the proper point and favorable circumstances should concur. Several recent circumstances have led me to think that this coincidence of preparation and circumstance is now near at hand. The gratifying information which you conveyed to us at the close of the Senate meeting on Friday has brought up the whole subject again with a new phase, and I therefore venture to lay a sketch of the matter, as it lies in my mind, before you.

 It now seems probable that a temporary settlement of the difficulty between the Chinese and the Western nations will be reached at early day, and that the settlement will involve the placing of China under the burden of an indemnity that will seriously tax her financial resources. There seems ground for the suspicion that this indemnity will be made so onerous that her future as an independent nation will be put in jeopardy. It is not unlikely that the purpose of European nations is to secure a financial control over the Celestial Empire which will eventuate in a series of protectorates merging into permanent possessions, much as Egypt, at first put under such control, is now, to all intents and purposes, a British colony. The salvation of China as an independent empire may therefore hang upon the astuteness with which she recognizes the source of danger and the way of escape. The one great source of hope, as I see it, is in the development of her natural resources. There is little reason to doubt that there is a potential wealth lying beneath the surface of the Chinese Empire, as yet unrecognized and unutilized, that would more than offset the proposed indemnity, if properly disclosed and wisely developed. From my point of view, therefore, the future of China may in some large measure hang upon her astuteness and to bring them promptly into productiveness.

We seem to stand in a position to help China affectively at this critical moment.

In the first place, the attitude of our nation to China during the recent troubles should and, I think, does command the confidence of the Chinese people.

In the second place, we are just now giving a most marvelous illustration of what may be done in financial achievement by utilizing intelligently and skillfully our natural resources.

In the third place, while we cannot know beforehand that the resources of China are comparable to those of this country, there is reason to hope that they may prove to be so. Sufficient is known to make it certain that there are at least large resources that may be utilized.

In the fourth place, we exemplify the right method in that we are spending more means and effort in the scientific study of our resources and our natural formations that any other nation on the globe.

In the fifth place, the unusual ability and skill of the Chinese Minister has contributed to a congenial feeling between our people and the Chinese.

In the sixth place, the courtesies and honors that the University and the Chinese Minister have mutually exchanged have opened a direct line of initiation for a University effort such as is suggested below.

In the seventh place, the foreshadowed alliance gives a new ground for interest (museumistic) in the word contemplated.

The proposition in outline is as follows:

In view of the considerations set forth, let a mutual exchange of good offices between the University and the Chinese Government be sought, by which the latter will be aided in the development of her intellectual and material resources at this critical epoch, while the former will be given an opportunity of enriching her collections, broadening her scientific studies, and extending her educational influence in acceptable lines. It might be confidently hoped that the modes of mutual helpfulness would widen as time went on, but at first it might be wise to limit them to material subjects related to financial problem, so as to avoid as completely as possible those sources of friction that have rendered foreigners obnoxious to the Chinese. To this end the effort should be shaped toward helping the Chinese to solve their own problems, rather than an effort to do their work for them, except in certain higher scientific phases for which they have no present aspirations.

In more detail, assuming mutual concurrence, let the Chinese Government select a suitable body of young Chinese of the highest order of ability and, so far as consistent with this, of the highest social and political standing, who shall have received the best training which Chinese institutions of learning can give, and send these to the University for special study and training in preparation for undertaking a survey of the natural resources of the Chinese Empire. It would doubtless be wise to clearly define at the outset that the line of effort was to develop a survey essentially by the Chinese themselves and not a survey by foreigners, and that the effort of the University was to aid in putting China upon her own feet and not to occupy China in our own interest, except as this should come about consistently with and advantageous to Chinese development. Some supervision and personal assistance on our part would doubtless be required for a period at least, but the work should be concluded as largely as practicable by young Chinese trained for the purpose. Let it be understood that the economic results, however and by whomsoever obtained, shall remain exclusively in the possession of the Chinese Government, except so far as it may see fit to give them to the general public, while the scientific results, which are not at present a matter of special interest to the Chinese people, come to us as the chief compensation for our efforts. I do not mean by this that there should not be financial compensation for whatever work is done, in the modest, partial way in which compensation is made for scientific work. I merely mean that our great incentive would lie in scientific lines, while the great incentive to the Chinese would like in industrial development and in extrication from the dangers of their great financial burden. Let the arrangement be such that the staff of the Geological Department of the University shall direct the work for a period and shall give such personal aid as may be consistent and desirable, for some oversight on the ground would be indispensable if the work is to be made effective as promptly as practicable, and the political conditions are such as to render promptness highly important.

The method of procedure in further detail might be somewhat like this: After the selected body of young Chinese (whose number should be such as could effectively be handled as a distinct class, and as a distinct field party, if need be) had continued their studies here long enough to gain an advanced stage of preparation in geology and tributary sciences, let them be put into the field in China under supervision for a period until they shall have gathered at once experience and material in large quantity. Let them return with that material to the University and work upon it until they develop a higher order of efficiency based upon this practical experience.

If there should be objection to this, so far as the economic material is concerned, provision might be made for the elaboration of this on Chinese soil. So also, if there should be objection to the precise phase which this has been given, the entire work could perhaps be done in China; but this would be at great disadvantage, because the young Chinese should be brought into effective contact with the methods and the resources of America, in order to obtain the moral as well as the intellectual equipment which comes from actual participation in the scientific and industrial spirit of our country.

From the museumistic point of view, the great consideration is this: We have now a great lead, so far as the early portion of the geological record in the heart of America is concerned, and with this start, aided by our situation, we may hope to hold the leadership. If to this we can add material from the same formation on the eastern border of Asia, it will give us an immense advantage in the extension of our purview. But more particularly, if we can bring to our museums a systematic series of collections from the great series of the later ages that are so amply displayed in the Chinese Empire, it will give us an advantage wholly unequalled by that of any museum of which I have present knowledge.

It would seem, therefore, that here is possibly an opportunity for leaping almost at once into the forefront; and this has the further advantage of proposing a method which should be fully self-sustaining from the financial point of view. It would not be unreasonable to ask such a compensation for the services rendered as should constituted a real contribution to the support of the departments involved, and would make possible their amplification.

The chief difficulty which I see is the greatness of the labor involved in carrying the proposition into effect. It is not in the precise line of my personal aspiration, although in the end it would greatly contribute to them. My one dominant desire is to recast the doctrines of geology on the basis of a new set of fundamental postulates, which, I believe with growing confidence, are required by the progress of science in its several cognate departments. This is in itself a larger work than perhaps I can reasonably hope to accomplish in any event; and the assumption of responsibility for an effort whose preliminaries must involve much diversion from the immediate end sought is not wholly welcome. But that is a minor consideration, if the great end contemplated can be attained.

I recognize the possibility of complete failure at many points, because the suggestion involves the cooperation of a people whose attitude toward such an enterprise has not been at all promising in the past. The hope for the scheme lies in the desperate situation in which the Chinese people will probably find themselves at the close of the negotiations now pending.

Very truly yours,

(Signed) T. C. CHAMBERLIN

President William R. Harper,
The University of Chicago.

The Chinese Expedition of
1909. Recollections by
Rolling T.Chamerlin, March 28th, 1929

THE CHINESE EXPEDITION OF 1909

Recollections by Rolling T. Chamberlin, March 28, 1929

The idea of these notes is primarily to give a general outline of the main features of the trip to China in 1909. There is no attempt to check up on the minor details.

Father had presided at the meeting of the American Association for Advancement of Science in Baltimore during the Christmas holidays of 1908. As soon as it was possible for him to leave Baltimore, he returned to Chicago, arriving here about noon of January 3 or 4, 1909. I had packed his trunk and most of his belongings already, and in the three or four hours after his arrival he completed the packing and we left on the overland Limited at 6:30 that evening. Mother accompanied us to San Francisco, and while we were in China she stayed with my uncle, Rev. James A. Chamberlin at Berkeley, with whom we had visited before sailing.

We sailed from San Francisco on the S. S. "Siberia," January 9, arriving in about six days at Honolulu. The beauty of this so-called Paradise of the Pacific impressed us tremendously, particularly as we were in the hands of friends who showed us about, as much as could be done in one day.

The trip from Honolulu to Yokohama was exceptionally stormy, but even during these unfavorable days my father gave much attention and thought to the Chinese problem. In Japan a visit was made to Tokyo and calls made upon Mr. O' Brien, the American minister to Japan, and to various other officials in addition to a visit to the University.

After two or three days in Yokohama and Tokyo we took the day train to Kyoto, where Col. Davis, a classmate of father's, met us at the station and conveyed us by rickshaw late at night through some two miles of winding, narrow thoroughfares to the Doshisha College, whose success is largely the result of Col. Davis's efforts. We visited several other institutions of learning in Kyoto, paying official calls. We regarded all of this as an introduction to Oriental education which would prove useful in the work in China.

At Kobe we caught our old steamer, the "Siberia," and sailed through the beautiful inland sea and across to Shanghai.

At Shanghai we met Dr. Ernest D. Burton and his secretary, Mr. Horace G. Reed, who had been there several weeks. Here about a week of long and intense conference took place, after which the entire party went to Nanking to interview the Viceroy, Tuan Fang. This seemed to us to be one of the most critical parts of the undertaking, since it was very important to have the cordial cooperation of the Chinese authorities and to give them a thorough and accurate understanding of our purpose without committing ourselves further than was advisable so early in the enterprise.

When we approached Nanking we came over marshes and waste land that had been depopulated in the Taiping rebellion. It was a very weird sight in the moonlight. We arrived in Nanking long after dark, were met at the station by the official carriage of state of the Viceroy and taken to the Yamen or official palace. Even though the hour was very late, an exceedingly elaborate state dinner was staged about an hour after our arrival. The dinner was a most extraordinarily interesting occasion. The Viceroy's title was Emperor of the Southern Ocean, and he had powers of life and death over nearly 70,000,000 people.

The next morning His Excellency granted us an interview lasting rather more than an hour. As his interpreters he had his two Taotai or lieutenant-governors, one of whom at least spoke perfect English. The negotiations were carried on with extreme care, primarily by Dr. Burton, but with considerable participation by my father. Both sides felt rather uneasy. His Excellency almost at the outset produced his native pipe, which would hold only enough tobacco for about four or five puffs. This he filled, lighted, emptied, and refilled forty times during the hours' interview by actual count. But the upshot of the whole interview was that he realized the essentially altruistic purpose of our mission and the great benefit which was likely to come to China if our projects were carried out, and in consequence he assumed a very cordial spirit of co-operation. The mission to Nanking was a decided success, establishing the fact that our efforts would be welcomed by the Chinese officials.

The following days being the day on which he had to perform his yearly oath of allegiance to the Emperor in Peking, all the available troops in the vicinity were lined up in the neighborhood of the Yamen and at the appropriate moment a silk pillow was placed upon the pavement in the courtyard. The Viceroy prostrated himself, and as a subordinate official called out "Kow tow," he bowed his forehead to the pavement facing Peking. This was done in rhythmic order twenty seven times. His Excellency had invited us to witness the scene from behind a screen about fifteen feet distant, so that we witness what probably very few foreigners have ever seen.

The Vice-Roy gave us a great farewell luncheon, with many hundreds present. We had to catch a train to take us to the Trans-Pacific steamer which was being held up. Father and Dr. Burton were seated up with Tuan Fang; I was quite a way down the table. The Viceroy escorted them out to the door and then bade them goodbye, which was a mark of unusual attention.

We returned to Shanghai, where Dr. Burton left the train, while father and I continued on to the Woo Sung forts. Here, under the orders of the Viceroy, a special launch was waiting for us, which conveyed us to the S. S. "China," whose sailing had been delayed several hours under the Viceroy's instructions, to enable us to catch it.

This streamer took us to Hong Kong, where one or two days were spent in that beautiful city, looking into the effects which the contact of British civilization has had upon the Chinese.

We took a steamer up the West River to Woo Chow and afterwards visited Canton on the return. A main purpose of this journey was to get a first-hand view of native life in South China and the general setting of the educational movements in that important part of the Empire. Father was tremendously impressed with the great activity and possibilities of the people, but saw what sad mistakes they had made in deforestation and in the practical application of many of the outgrowth of our western science.

After returning to Shanghai, our entire party sailed up the Yangtze-Kiang to Hankow, often called the Chicago of China. Here there were conferences with Bishop Root and various missionary groups centering about Hankow. At this time also was the first conference with the Right Rev. Lord William Gascoyne Cecil, Bishop of Exeter and son of Lord Salisbury, former Prime Minister of Great Britain. He was representing a somewhat similar mission sent out by the Universities of Oxford and Cambridge. He was a very striking figure, resembling closely the famous Prime Minister.

A Japanese steamer carried us up to I-Chang in six days, during about half of which time our steamer was stuck on various sand-bars in the shallow river. At I-Chang we were met by Rev. Joseph Beech of the West China Methodist Episcopal Mission, which had organized the West China University. He had arranged for one of the best of the native house-boats to take us up through the famous gorges of the Yangtze to Wan Hsien. For nearly 200 miles the Yangtze goes through one of the most remarkable scenery of gorges anywhere on the face of the globe. Not quite so deep as the Grand Canyon of the Colorado, nevertheless the walls are of greater average steepness and the mighty Yangtze is more or less comparable to the Mississippi at St. Louis.

We gave a special bonus for a rapid trip through the gorges, and as the result of a favorable wind for six days in succession we made this trip in the remarkable time of seven days. At several points in the midst of the gorge there are rapids. At the largest of these, the Sin Lung Tan, our own party left the boat below the rapids and walked past them on shore. Meanwhile, some of our crew went ashore with a bamboo rope probably an eighth of a mile in length, drummed up as many volunteers as could be obtained, and with their help dragged our boat up through the rapids. While this was going on, a similar boat tried to shoot the rapids going downstream and disappeared completely form sight, only to reappear several minutes later prow uppermost fully a quarter of a mile down the river. Only one man succeeded in getting ashore; the others were never seen. This, however, did not cause the slightest excitement among the villages, since life was cheap in China.

Form Wan-Hsien we went 400 miles by sedan chair in fourteen days nearly straight across the famous Red Basin of Szechuan. Father walked probably a third of this distance and rode the other two-thirds in the swaying chair carried by four coolies. We were late in getting off the first day, and hence had to continue until about 11 o'clock at night in order to reach our planned destination. During the hours of darkness our caravan, which numbered in all 71 men, was stretched out over about two miles of road. I think that each of the white members of the party, all alone in the hands of four stalwart coolies and entirely unarmed, felt somewhat nervous in this our first experience totally in the hands of the Chinese. Our men all knew that each of us carried more than 50 silver dollars in our pockets, which would have been a very tempting sum to men whose daily wages are but 16 cents. Had it been a week later, however, when we got acquainted with our men, there would not have been the slightest uneasiness.

Szechuan is the largest, most populous, and altogether finest of the eighteen provinces of China, and the Red Basin is the choicest part of the large province. The 400 miles showed us a succession of low, anticlinal mountain ridges rising perhaps 2000 feet above their surroundings, separated by broad, parklike basins perhaps a score of miles in breadth. These basins were cultivated to apparently the extreme limit of intensive cultivation, and with the extremely picturesque and numerous red buttes and the strikingly vividly colored Permian red-beds, made this seem to use one of the most lovely garden spots of the globe.

Father was very strongly impressed with the extreme development of the agriculture, the soundness of principles of rotation of crops, fertilization and other things which were involved, and he predicted then great possibilities for such an industrious people.

This journey of fourteen days, while extremely stimulating to the mind and appealing to the aesthetic nature, was in reality very hard travel. It was in March and early April, the nights were quite cold, and a Chinese inn is nothing more than four walls and a roof where one may camp. Outside, everything is used for cultivation or for graves, and so there is not room to camp. We carried our own bedding, which at times was not adequate for the cold weather, carried our own food, which was cooked by our boys and was not always wholesome, and everything was very irregular. We sometimes started at 7 o'clock in the morning and walked and rode all day till well after dark, and after this our belongings had to be unpacked and the food cooked, which made the meals come at unaccustomed hours. Then hour sleeping bags were set up and we were off again the next morning early, after having packed up all belongings. We did not think of it so much at the time, being filed campaigners by profession, but the effects of this and subsequent similar experience were to exact a heavy toll from father's health.

From Cheng-tu father and I made a very rapid trip of five days of forced marches up into the big mountains which buttress Tibet on the east. After a late start we made more than 35 miles uphill the first day. The next day the coolies went on strike and refused to go farther, but a new set were obtained and the trip carried out as planned. This was a geological reconnaissance, stolen from the time of the expedition. It takes the mail longer to go from Cheng-tu to Shanghai than from Shanghai to Chicago, since it is 2000 miles to the coast. We went down the Min River on a house-boat to its junction with the Yangtze at Sui-fu, and thence down the Yangtze through the gorges again to Hankow. Thirty-nice nights were slept afloat on the Yangtze or its tributaries in the tiny native junks.

At I-chang we met again by appointment Lord Cecil, and the final conferences were held during the several days on the steamer between there and Hankow. These conferences did not result in co-operation with the Oxford-Cambridge enterprises. The general idea of Lord William seemed to be that Chicago was to supply the money and that the educational part would be directed according to Oxford-Cambridge ideas. Father felt very strongly, and Dr. Burton come to agree with him, that the Oxford-Cambridge scheme was essentially the old classical idea which we ourselves had pretty generally outgrown, and that we could put our funds to much better use than to turn them over to the Britishers. However, the most friendly relations prevailed throughout.

Thus ended the investigation of southern and central China. Father and I then went northward by train, visiting certain of the provincial capitals—Honan-fu and Taiyuan-fu. These are in a dryer part of China, where the loess formation affords a thick soil, but which cannot be put to its best use owning to slight rainfall.

One little incident was our stopping at a small village, in the largest house of which we knew that Yuan Shih Kai was in retirement. Before leaving the United States we had been given letters of introduction to Yuan Shik Kai, who was then then all powerful man in China. Before we reached China, however, he had been deposed from power through some act of the Empress Dowager, and had been very lucky indeed not to have his head chopped off. As he was in disgrace, our letter were worse than useless, and we carefully concealed the fact that we were on friendly terms with the party of Yuan.

Professor Burton joined us later at Peking, and there the final filed conference of our expedition were held. Professor Burton's part being rather more laborious than ours, father and I slipped away for a few days to go up on to the borders of the Mongolian plateau on a bit of geological reconnaissance. The first part of the journey was made by train, and the second part in the old fashioned, noisy, Peking carts. One day, while riding northwestward in these carts, one of those terrific dust storms for which this region is famous came upon us. Such an unbelievable quantity of dust was in the air that even though the day was entirely cloudless we could not even see the outlines of the sun to tell us directions. Both of us arrived at Kalgan probably in worse condition than ever before in our field experience. The worst of it was that not a single inn in Kalgan would accept us. The assigned reason was that they thought we were missionaries. Finally our interpreter, Li San, who was an old horse trader and who knew Kalgan intimately, succeeded in persuading a small inn outside the limits of Kalgan, which was frequented by Mongolian horse traders, to take us in for the night. Neither of us, I guess, was ever more thankful than when this news reached us.

From Kalgan we went up on to the borders of the Mongolia plateau to see whether there were any evidences of ancient glaciation on that tableland. The maps of the region show numerous small lakes which are just what one would expect to find in a glaciated region, but when we examined these they turned out to be merely slightly depressed basins in uneven lava flows. There was no evidence of glaciation whatever in the region.

The expedition visited fifteen of the eighteen provinces of China, of which my father saw thirteen, Professor Burton doing the provinces of Hunan and Fukien. We visited a great many of the missionary schools supported from this country and interviewed elaborately the foreigners in China. Many of these interviews with the heads of mission schools already located were rather discouraging, and I recall at one stage father remarked to Dr. Burton: "Why, these missionaries do not believe that God made the world and is now running it!" What he meant was that they were laboring under an older point of view, that science and scientific methods should be regarded with much suspicion, and they seemed to feel that they should be very much on their guard. It was partly because of this attitude that the commission felt that it would not be to the best interests to hook up with the established missionary schools but to start an enterprise entirely independent of them.

We started our long homeward journey by going to Mukden, the capital of Manchuria, where we were able to study hastily the Manchu civilization, just as on the trip to Kalgan we had come in contact with the true Mongols. Ten days on the Trans-Siberian Railroad took us across nearly the whole breadth of the Asiatic continent to Moscow. The strenuous work in China now being over, father was overtaken by a pronounced reaction and was quite ill for a number of days. This was really the beginning of spells of stomach trouble which, however, did not culminate until 1912, when for a number of weeks he was very seriously ill, so that various friends feared that I, who was in South America, would never see him again.

Father spent about a week in Moscow, writing at terrific pace on his report of the Chinese mission; after which we went to St. Petersburg, as it then was, for a few days, thence by steamer to Stockholm, and up through the heart of Sweden to Narvik on the Norwegian coast. Here were had a beautiful excursion of about a week to the North Cape, enjoying three superb nights of midnight sun, and then returned to Trondhjem on our way to Christiania. From Christiania we went to Copenhagen and thence to Berlin, Munich, Lausanne, with three days at Zermatt in the midst of the finest of the Swiss Alps.

We went through the Simplon tunnel to Milan, on to Venice, across the Adriatic to Fiume, and winding in and out amidst the famous Karst topography, went by day to Budapest. Our idea in zigzagging so much of Europe was to get a picture of the various mountain ranges of that continent as a background for major tectonic studies.

From Budapest we crossed the Carpathians by the Iron Gate of the Danube to Bucharest, and then recrossed them again farther east, coming back to Budapest. From Budapest we went to Vienna, from Vienna to Innsbruck, over the Brenner Pass to Verona, and westward to Courmayeur at the south foot of Mont Blanc. From here we crossed the Little St. Bernard Pass to Bourg St. Maurice, went westward across the northern flanks of the Auvergne volcanic region of central France and onward to Bordeaux, thence to Paris and Cherbourg, from which we sailed for New York.

The work was conducted as economically as possible. After returning to Chicago, both Dr. Burton (who had come back by way of San Francisco) and father spent several months in preparing the final report and in making recommendations on the basis of our observations. The general conclusion of this educational commission was that perhaps the best thing which the western civilization and western money could contribute to China was thorough medical education by means of well-equipped medical colleges which would train the Chinese to solve their own sanitary and health problems. This was the gist of the recommendation made.

As a result of this thoroughgoing and incisive report and the recommendations springing from it, a second expedition was later sent to China to lay the groundwork for an elaborate program of medical education. The members of this commission were President Judson, one of the Flexners, and I think a third man. The outcome of the second expedition was the establishment of the various medical schools in China which are financed by the Rockefeller Foundation.

Before this second mission left America, father was called to New York to attend a conference arranged by John D. Rockefeller, Jr.

Frank King, the author of "Farmers of Forty Centuries," tried to see us here in the United States before we left, and also in China, but he missed connections. He was behind us all the way. Many of his observations were very remarkable. Father had recognized King as being a man with possibilities and had brought him to the Agricultural College at Madison. King was tremendously impressed by the efficiency of agriculture in China.

But China was thoroughly established in its own religion, and we didn't think that to try to change the religion was so important. It was the western medical development that was the greatest thing we could do for the Chinese people.

This was a preliminary scouting trip to go all over China, learn their needs, and make recommendations of what could be done with the backing of quite a few millions of dollars. Father probably weighed about 215 pounds when we started, and when he got back from China he was probably down to 180. In his illness he dropped down to 157, later on. His eyes were failing then. Before we went he told me of this for the first time, and one of the reasons for taking me along was because I could see a great many things he couldn't see, and I could be his eyes, so to speak, better than anybody else. It was quite remarkable that a man at the age of 65 would have been eager to face the hardships of such a strenuous undertaking.

Father was thinking incessantly about the Chinese problem. On the steamers and on the road he was constantly planning. He planned a whole railroad system for China while on one of the steamers, working it out in very considerable detail.

Both my father and Dr. Burton worked very harmoniously all the way through.

I should say that the meeting with Tang Shao Yi at the dinner in Washington, when T. C. C. had the encounter with Bryce, was several months before we left. Tang Shao Yi was the right hand man of Yuan Shih Kai, and he gave us letter, including letters to Yuan Shik Kai. As I have explained, Yuan had fallen into disgrace before we reached China and so we could not use our letter to him.

钱伯林
近代中国考察档案文献汇编

The Compilation of Oriental Educational Investigation
Commission's Archives by Chamberlin,1909

下册

张 雷 主编

学苑出版社

目 录

华东地区　上海　江苏　安徽　江西 /1

华南地区　香港　广东　广西 /15

华中地区　湖北　河南 /51

西南地区　重庆　四川 /105

华北地区　河北　山西　北京 /219

东北地区　辽宁　黑龙江 /305

后记 /325

钱伯林近代中国考察档案文献汇编
下册

华东地区
上海　江苏　安徽　江西

　　钱伯林拍摄的华东地区主要包括今日上海、江苏以及安徽等地。1909年2月,钱伯林父子抵达上海,随后前往南京拜访两江总督端方。本篇照片主要在上海和南京所拍摄,包括上海的租界、运河、庙宇以及南京的城墙等。

老城寺庙（上海）

老城生活（上海）

运河景色（上海）

国际问题研究所（上海）

中西结合的租界街景（上海）

租界内的私人院落（上海）

镇江火车站的旅人（江苏）

南京城(江苏)

南京城墙(江苏)

船队在长江上(江苏)

长江薄暮（江苏）

安庆小孤山（安徽）

九江街景（江西）

舟中看九江城墙（江西）

九江码头（江西）

钱伯林近代中国考察档案文献汇编
下册

华南地区
香港　广东　广西

钱伯林拍摄的华南地区主要指今日的香港、广东和广西。1909年2月，钱伯林父子前往两广考察，先至香港，随后沿西江而上至广西梧州，又折返至广州。本篇照片主要包括香港城市景观、西江流域的帆船与古塔、广州的墓地等。

灌园农夫（香港）

花市（香港）

华南地区
香港 广东 广西

维多利亚山山顶（香港）

街景（香港）

街景（香港）

云咸街（香港）

园林一景（香港）

热带植被（香港）

大教堂(香港)

大教堂塔影(香港)

街边榕树(香港)

华南地区
香港 广东 广西

港口风光（香港）

远眺港口（香港）

华南地区
香港　广东　广西

植物园（香港）

植物园（香港）

山坡住宅（香港）

华南地区
香港 广东 广西

香港岛顶部(香港)

香港城景(香港)

印度巡捕操练（香港）

华南地区
香港　广东　广西

九龙砾石（香港）

九龙砾石（香港）

九龙脉石中的砾石(香港)

九龙东的砂石沙丘(香港)

西江岸边的房舍（广东）

三水魁岗文塔（广东）

华南地区
香港 广东 广西

东江、西江交汇处的房屋（广东）

西江三水段的帆船（广东）

西江三水段的船只（广东）

华南地区
香港　广东　广西

江边一角（广东）

三水香火庙（广东）

三水香火庙（广东）

三水香火庙的装饰细部（广东）

三水江畔（广东）

三水街道（广东）

三水魁岗文塔（广东）

梧州山峦(广西)

梧州白云山顶峰俯瞰西江(广西)

梧州顶峰俯瞰西江（广西）

华南地区
香港　广东　广西

西江（广西）

梧州城墙（广西）

从英国领事馆看梧州(广西)

华南地区
香港　广东　广西

广州田中劳作（广东）

广州污水处理（广东）

广州白云山墓地(广东)

广州白云山墓地（广东）

广州白云山墓地（广东）

广州白云山（广东）

广州白云山（广东）

钱伯林中国考察档案文献汇编
下册

华中地区
湖北　河南

　　钱伯林拍摄的华中地区主要指今日的湖北和河南。1909年3月，钱伯林父子返回上海，溯长江至湖北考察。随后前往四川，之后又顺长江返回武汉。1909年5月，再沿京汉铁路北上考察河南。本篇为了编写方便，将湖北和河南所拍摄图像合为一篇，其照片主要包括长江风景、武汉三镇、宜昌峡谷、河南铁路以及乡村。

长江汉口段帆船（湖北）

汉口英国领事馆（湖北）

汉口俄国租界（湖北）

汉口江边的俄国领事馆（湖北）

汉口外国租界（湖北）

汉口民居（湖北）

华中地区
湖北　河南

汉口（湖北）

汉口洼地（湖北）

汉口新水厂（湖北）

汉口的菜园（湖北）

汉口伦敦会后院（湖北）

汉口郊区（湖北）

华中地区
湖北　河南

汉口郊区民居（湖北）

汉阳铁厂（湖北）

汉阳龙山寺庙（湖北）

华中地区
湖北　河南

放汽艇勘探长江（湖北）

沙市附近乡村（湖北）

华中地区
湖北 河南

宜昌货船（湖北）

宜昌墓地（湖北）

宜昌墓地与稻田（湖北）

华中地区
湖北　河南

水田插秧（湖北）

水牛耕田（湖北）

宜昌长江岸边风景（湖北）

宜昌长江岸边风景（湖北）

宜昌附近（湖北）

宜昌对岸的江畔(湖北)

船接近宜昌峡(湖北)

宜昌峡入口的渔船（湖北）

宜昌峡（湖北）

华中地区
湖北　河南

宜昌峡（湖北）

长江上的帆船（湖北）

华中地区
湖北 河南

峡谷风光（湖北）

江村庙宇（湖北）

华中地区
湖北　河南

激流之舟（湖北）

抛锚船只（湖北）

巫山女神峰（湖北）

进入巫山峡（湖北）

巫山峡（湖北）

巫山峡（湖北）

峡谷货船（湖北）

华中地区
湖北 河南

穿越山谷的桥（湖北－四川）

湖北－河南南北交界处（湖北）

向考察团火车致敬的士兵（湖北）

华中地区
湖北　河南

京汉铁路站台（湖北）

南部的稻田（河南）

火车上拍摄的平原景象(河南)

火车上拍摄的平原景象（河南）

新蔡乡村（河南）

新蔡乡村(河南)

茶摊（河南）

荥阳黄土壁立村景（河南）

黄土坡（河南）

黄土乡村（河南）

华中地区
湖北 河南

黄土地（河南）

黄土乡村（河南）

黄土深壑（河南）

华中地区
湖北 河南

黄土峡谷（河南）

一排黄土窑洞（河南）

黄土窑洞（河南）

河南府（今开封）里的旗杆（河南）

城墙与护城河（河南）

河南府（今开封）城墙（河南）

华中地区
湖北 河南

河南府（今开封）附近下沉的道路（河南）

河南府（今洛阳）外的牌坊与黄河堤岸（河南）

黄河边车站（河南）

黄河上的帆船（河南）

在沙暴中渡过黄河（河南）

卫辉府（今卫辉）西部下沉道路（河南）

华中地区
湖北　河南

卫辉府（今卫辉）西部山前（河南）

卫辉府（今卫辉）附近的村民（河南）

卫辉府（今卫辉）道观（河南）

卫辉府（今卫辉）的乡村（河南）

华中地区
湖北　河南

农田与压水井上的喜鹊（河南）

彰德府（今安阳）的塔（河南）

彰德府（今安阳）的塔（河南）

站在彰德府（今安阳）西门俯视东西主干道（河南）

谷仓与打谷场（河南）

西南地区
重庆　四川

钱伯林拍摄的西南地区主要指今日的重庆和四川。1909年3月至4月，钱伯林父子穿越三峡入川，之后在万县（今万州）登陆，徒步横穿成都平原，随后顺岷江而下至宜宾，再顺江而下至武汉，前后共月余。本篇的照片主要包括四川与重庆的稻田、河流、盐井、水车、牌坊、石桥、古塔、庙宇、旅店等，所涉城市有成都、宜宾以及重庆等。

夔州府（今奉节）街道（重庆）

夔州府（今奉节）的庙（重庆）

夔州府（今奉节）百姓早餐（重庆）

夔州府（今奉节）庙内（重庆）

夔州府（今奉节）江岸草席晾麦（重庆）

考察团的船（重庆）

船家（重庆）

西南地区
重庆 四川

考察团的纤夫（重庆）

低水位的云阳（重庆）

云阳张飞庙（重庆）

瞿塘峡（重庆）

考察团在万县（今万州）登陆（重庆）

万县（今万州）躲避洪灾的高脚楼（重庆）

万县（今万州）戏台（重庆）

万县（今万州）乡村（重庆）

考察团的随行在理发（重庆）

万县（今万州）河流阶地与寺庙（重庆）

万县（今万州）浣妇（重庆）

穿越陆路的第一个下午（重庆）

西南地区
重庆 四川

村舍（四川）

道上的石桥和贞洁牌坊（四川）

分水梯田（四川）

西南地区
重庆 四川

溪桥（四川）

大竹西部的稻田（四川）

大竹西部山区的煤矿（四川）

大竹新旧石桥（四川）

李渡河东部的稻田(四川)

李渡河东部的牌坊与桥（四川）

李渡河东的庙中神像（四川）

李渡河桥（四川）

李渡河西风景(四川)

山丘前的稻田(四川)

清晨小景（四川）

渠县吴家场的贞洁牌坊与坟墓（四川）

渠江和嘉陵江的分水岭（四川）

罗家场附近的庙（四川）

西南地区
重庆 四川

草垛（四川）

雪松与稻田（四川）

西南地区
重庆 四川

水牛（四川）

顺庆对面的河流风景（四川）

顺庆岸边的塔（四川）

顺庆乡村石桥（四川）

路边的风景（四川）

猪市（四川）

打草为燃料（四川）

民众围观考察团（四川）

村中石桥（四川）

蓬溪县东部的梯田（四川）

蓬溪县山中小憩（四川）

西南地区
重庆 四川

蓬溪县西部的孤丘（四川）

蓬溪县西部的盐井(四川)

废庙兴学（四川）

路旁学校的男童（四川）

乡村石桥（四川）

西南地区
重庆 四川

山道（四川）

稻田（四川）

水车（四川）

太和镇的灌溉水车（四川）

太和镇庄园（四川）

观音庙（四川）

村外围观者（四川）

西南地区
重庆 四川

太和镇牌坊（四川）

稻田与梯田(四川)

快运挑夫(四川)

西南地区
重庆 四川

村民围观（四川）

庐与墓（四川）

山中溪流小桥（四川）

西南地区
重庆 四川

乡村铸造（四川）

兴隆场(四川)

兴隆场的路上牌坊(四川)

兴隆镇乡村美景(四川)

被相机惊吓的采花女孩(四川)

灌县城门（四川）

灌县道上（四川）

西南地区
重庆 四川

灌县道上的行人（四川）

灌县二王庙道上（四川）

灌县渠首（四川）

灌县山前（四川）

灌县水工（四川）

灌县平原（四川）

灌县的油菜田（四川）

灌县二王庙（四川）

灌县二王庙（四川）

灌县二王庙（四川）

灌县二王庙大殿（四川）

灌县以上的岷江（四川）

灌县以上的岷江（四川）

成都平原稻草堆（四川）

成都平原的农舍与稻田（四川）

成都平原农舍（四川）

西南地区
重庆 四川

成都平原的乡村景色(四川)

成都平原的乡村景色（四川）

西南地区
重庆 四川

成都郊区景色（四川）

华西大学棒球队(四川)

考察团车队接近成都（四川）

成都污水处理（四川）

成都街道（四川）

西南地区
重庆 四川

成都牌楼（四川）

成都私人院落(四川)

成都老皇城街景(四川)

西南地区
重庆 四川

成都鸟瞰（四川）

城墙上俯视成都（四川）

成都南关（四川）

成都城内人口稀少区（四川）

成都美以美教会大院（四川）

成都街道（四川）

西南地区
重庆 四川

成都汉城一角（四川）

成都满城（四川）

西南地区
重庆 四川

成都满城（四川）

运送收成入城（四川）

农家（四川）

郫县田中的塔（四川）

郫县路旁坟地（四川）

高山（四川）

运货的人（四川）

山坡小屋(四川)

山区景观(四川)

轿子(四川)

河流与塔(四川)

乡村（四川）

站在山顶遥望西藏（四川）

竹索桥（四川）

竹索桥与河流阶地（四川）

集市露天戏台（四川）

中国式后院（四川）

村妇（四川）

王翻译拍摄一群围观者(四川)

大帽小脚妇女(四川)

当地人出行（四川）

乡村独轮车和行人（四川）

路上的牌坊(四川)

街上吸烟老妇(四川)

西南地区
重庆 四川

村民（四川）

路旁灌溉渠道（四川）

江口罂粟田（四川）

运木（四川）

西南地区
重庆 四川

嘉定古塔(四川)

运甘蔗的农人(四川)

考察团的车队（四川）

考察团的随从（四川）

西南地区
重庆 四川

考察团的卫队（中间为妇女，四川）

江口对面的溪流（四川）

江口以下的水车（四川）

嘉定（今乐山）古塔（四川）

江上鱼鹰捕鱼（四川）

岷江鸬鹚捕鱼（四川）

嘉定（今乐山）江岸（四川）

西南地区
重庆 四川

嘉定（今乐山）劳工的冲突（四川）

嘉定（今乐山）劳工的冲突（四川）

叙府（今宜宾）庙山上的人群（四川）

叙府（今宜宾）河边寺庙（四川）

叙府（今宜宾）童子在山顶庙宇求雨（四川）

叙府（今宜宾）进香队伍（四川）

西南地区
重庆 四川

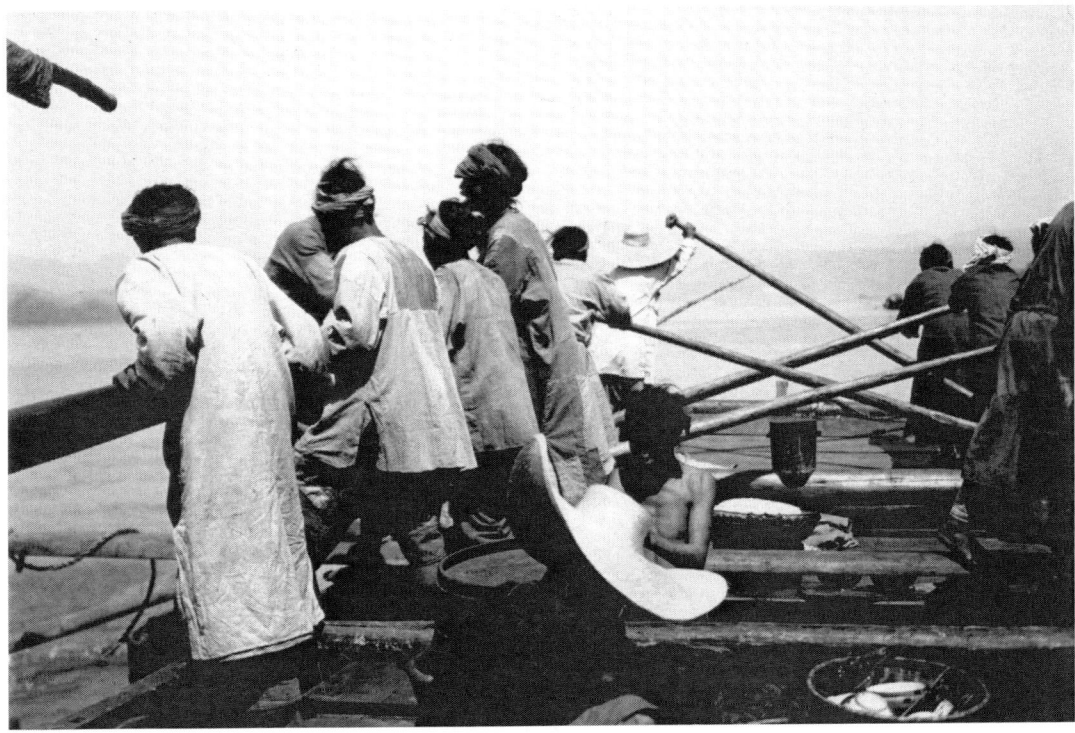

船上的划手（四川）

考察团船只的围观者（四川）

考察团船只重返长江（四川）

四川煤矿与石窑（四川）

长江上游的石灰崖（重庆）

长江上游的石灰崖（重庆）

江岸的海关（重庆）

城内的塔（重庆）

古城与城墙（重庆）

山顶寺庙（重庆）

长江江岸(重庆)

低水位的长江(重庆)

江岸的德国军舰（重庆）

日暮江畔（重庆）

石山耕作（重庆）

划船比赛（重庆）

在江中举行划船比赛（重庆）

顺江而下去万县（今万州）（重庆）

考察团的船长及其表弟（重庆）

烟雨清晨（重庆）

忠州（今忠县）石宝寨飞来石（重庆）

有九层庙的石宝寨（重庆）

西南地区
重庆 四川

忠州（今忠县）郊区（重庆）

忠州（今忠县）外的乡村小桥（重庆）

风箱峡与夔州府（今奉节）屋顶（重庆）

夔州府（今奉节）城墙远眺（重庆）

夔州（今奉节）段以上长江的午后天空（重庆）

华北地区
河北　山西　北京

　　钱伯林拍摄的华北地区主要是指今日的河北、山西和北京。1909 年 5 月，钱伯林父子沿京汉铁路北上，穿越河南至石家庄，然后从石家庄乘坐石太线至太原。之后，原路返回石家庄，前往北京。在北京稍事休整之后，乘坐京张线至张家口。本篇的照片主要包括太原、北京、张家口以及内蒙古高原边境风景。

石家庄街景（河北）

石家庄客栈（河北）

石家庄附近景色（河北）

华北地区
河北　山西　北京

石家庄西部的乡村（河北）

太行山前的平原（河北）

石家庄附近的大片麦田（河北）

石家庄西部山区的午后阳光（河北）

华北地区
河北　山西　北京

村民打水（河北）

乡村景色，远山因为干旱几为荒漠（河北）

铁路沿线即景（山西）

华北地区
河北　山西　北京

村舍与羊群（山西）

东部乡村即景（山西）

土墙村巷(山西)

远眺太原府(今太原)双塔(山西)

华北地区
河北　山西　北京

半干旱地区的典型景观（山西）

守护太原府（今太原）的双塔（山西）

太原府（今太原）（山西）

太原府（今太原）砖院（山西）

华北地区
河北 山西 北京

路边的房舍（山西）

太原府（今太原）（山西）

太原府（今太原）客栈外院（山西）

华北地区
河北 山西 北京

太原府（今太原）内的客栈（山西）

太原府（今太原）城内的菜园（山西）

马、牛和驴混合拉车（山西）

华北地区
河北　山西　北京

太原府（今太原）南门（山西）

当地人休息（山西）

门前村民（山西）

华北地区
河北 山西 北京

法师街头施法（山西）

太原府（今太原）城南大街（山西）

太原府（今太原）街道（山西）

华北地区
河北　山西　北京

太原府（今太原）街道（山西）

路行妇女（山西）

太原府(今太原)城中商贩(山西)

太原府(今太原)城内小女孩特写(山西)

华北地区
河北　山西　北京

太原府（今太原）西门沙尘（山西）

太原府（今太原）内破败的庙宇（山西）

干旱的乡村（山西）

山村即景（山西）

华北地区
河北 山西 北京

路边小镇(山西)

铁路旁小镇即景(山西)

回民聚落（山西）

铁路站台（山西）

铁路警察（山西）

保定府（今保定）满族妇女和女佣（河北）

观象台（北京）

观象台（北京）

城中街道（北京）

旧贡院（北京）

旗人妇女（北京）

考察团抵达京城南门（北京）

华北地区
河北　山西　北京

鼓楼（北京）

鼓楼俯视京城（北京）

城中的"满城"（北京）

钟楼（北京）

"满城"和紫禁城（北京）

紫禁城的城门（北京）

华北地区
河北　山西　北京

紫禁城的城门（北京）

紫禁城的护城河（北京）

紫禁城煤山(北京)

华北地区
河北　山西　北京

北京的婚礼队伍（北京）

北京的婚礼队伍（北京）

华北地区
河北 山西 北京

天坛（北京）

天坛大理石桥(北京)

天坛附近空地(北京)

葬礼撒纸钱（北京）

为皇帝驾临搭设行宫（北京）

京张铁路西直门车站（北京）

怀来车站（河北）

华北地区
河北　山西　北京

怀来观看火车的妇孺（河北）

怀来北山（河北）

怀来北山（河北）

宣化黄羊山北坡之一（河北）

华北地区
河北 山西 北京

宣化黄羊山北坡（河北）

宣化下花园晨景（河北）

宣化下花园东部村景（河北）

华北地区
河北　山西　北京

宣化下花园和火山岩山丘（河北）

道旁房屋（河北）

宣化城外（河北）

宣化一带的京式马车（河北）

宣化街景（河北）

宣化市场（河北）

城中村童（河北）

宣化城中店铺前的妇孺（河北）

华北地区
河北　山西　北京

宣化西门外（河北）

宣化的城门与道路（河北）

骑驴的女孩(河北)

半干旱乡村的沙路(河北)

华北地区
河北　山西　北京

驼队（河北）

考察团前往张家口的大车（河北）

去往张家口途中所见的黄土谷地（河北）

张家口道上所见的纪念塔（河北）

华北地区
河北　山西　北京

张家口的驼队（河北）

张家口街道(河北)

华北地区
河北　山西　北京

张家口街景（河北）

张家口客栈的蒙古马贩（河北）

华北地区
河北　山西　北京

张家口露天市场（河北）

张家口店铺外的骆驼(河北)

张家口关口(河北)

张家口郊区

前往蒙古的张家口大道

来自蒙古高原的驼队(河北)

华北地区
河北　山西　北京

途遇来自蒙古高原的骑士（河北）

途中遇到蒙古运碱大车（河北）

途遇蒙古农民（河北）

华北地区
河北　山西　北京

蒙古将军及其卫队（河北）

途遇骑驴的蒙古人（河北）

蒙古高原的景观（河北）

华北地区
河北 山西 北京

蒙古高原边缘（河北）

张家口头台子附近俯视高原边缘(河北)

张家口头台子附近蒙古高原的侵蚀地形(河北)

华北地区
河北　山西　北京

张家口头台子后山风景（河北）

张家口头台子客栈的大车（河北）

华北地区
河北　山西　北京

穿越沙漠（河北）

山景（河北）

头台子乡村（河北）

华北地区
河北　山西　北京

张家口的长城（河北）

张家口以北的高原上村落（河北）

青龙桥附近长城(北京)

青龙桥附近长城（北京）

半干旱地区的乡村民居(北京)

南口车站山区即景(北京)

南口长城（北京）

南口山岭（北京）

南城商贩小巷（北京）

华北地区
河北　山西　北京

人力车夫中午食粥（北京）

街头小贩（北京）

城里妇孺（北京）

城里妇女（北京）

华北地区
河北　山西　北京

典型的中式后街（北京）

砖窑（北京）

华北地区
河北 山西 北京

山海关长城（河北）

山海关长城终（河北）

钱伯林近代中国考察档案文献汇编
下册

东北地区
辽宁　黑龙江

　　钱伯林拍摄的东北地区主要是指今日的辽宁和黑龙江。1909年6月，钱伯林父子从北京穿越东北，以便从黑龙江搭乘西伯利亚铁路返回美国。本篇的照片主要包括沈阳街景、清陵以及东北平原等。

满洲南部景色之一（辽宁）

满洲南部景色之二（辽宁）

沈阳车站一景（辽宁）

沈阳满族人的后院（辽宁）

沈阳东门残破的塔楼（辽宁）

连接寺庙装饰塔（辽宁）

沈阳北关的塔（辽宁）

沈阳街道(辽宁)

沈阳的茶摊（辽宁）

沈阳城里商店的招牌（辽宁）

沈阳城里商店的招牌（辽宁）

沈阳日俄战争的日本纪念碑（辽宁）

沈阳东郊（辽宁）

沈阳东关寺庙（辽宁）

沈阳福陵（辽宁）

沈阳福陵（辽宁）

沈阳福陵（辽宁）

沈阳福陵（辽宁）

沈阳福陵的松道（辽宁）

沈阳福陵（辽宁）

哈尔滨南部的俄国火车（黑龙江）

满洲平原（黑龙江）

西伯利亚铁路满洲西部即景（黑龙江）

后 记

2013年春天，一次偶然的机会在网上发现钱伯林档案，当时惊叹于其文字记录之详细，照片拍摄之广泛而清晰，如同大清帝国的晚照。同时又感叹中美学术之隔阂，使得如此与中国息息相关之资料，藏诸深山无人知，遂决心出版之。

彼时，钱伯林日记和照片均可在比洛特学院档案馆的网站上阅读。而笔记则深藏于芝加哥大学档案馆。是年暑假，驱车千里至芝加哥大学，得以拜读钱伯林的中国考察笔记。此后两年，忙中偷闲，整理文稿和照片。

2015年3月，有幸受比洛特学院邀请，前往学院做关于钱伯林中国考察的报告。时值春假，雪后的校园寂寥，担心无人来听。结果来者四五十余人，济济一堂。随后获学院档案馆的书面授权，遂得以正式出版此书。返回纽约途中，路经芝加哥大学，又得以补充查阅档案，终于在2015年5月完成此编。

在编著过程中，特别致谢美国比洛特学院档案馆的Lisa Viezbicke女士，Fred Burwell以及Josh Hickman先生，比洛特学院语言与文学系教授Dr.Daniel Youd，美国芝加哥大学档案馆，以及北京的学苑出版社杨雷师姐所提供的帮助与支持。

张 雷
2015年7月于美国雪城